L.G. Mietzner

THE
MARRIAGE
AFFAIR

THE MARRIAGE AFFAIR

The Family Counselor

Edited by J. Allan Petersen

TYNDALE HOUSE PUBLISHERS
Wheaton, Illinois

Fourteenth printing, June 1981

Library of Congress Catalog Card Number 72-152119
ISBN 8423-4171-4, paper
Copyright © 1971 by Tyndale House Publishers,
Wheaton, Illinois 60187.
All rights reserved.
Over 160,000 copies in print.
Printed in the United States of America.

To Mr. and Mrs. D. J. Witherspoon,
whose unselfish family concern
has reached beyond their own home circle
of David, Michael, Patrick, and Lisa
— and whose greathearted encouragement
has made this book possible.

CONCORDIA UNIVERSITY LIBRARY
PORTLAND. OR 97211

CONTENTS

FOREWORD

DR. BILLY GRAHAM

I take special delight in saying a word about a book that is needed for our times. In a day when the divorce rate is climbing and marital unfaithfulness is so common, there is great need for a word to be said from the Christian point of view. The Reverend J. Allan Petersen has done just that.

It is a book to which many capable persons have made their contribution. They are saying the things that need to be said to young men and young women, to families that are on the verge of breaking up, and also to those couples who are happily married and interested in knowing the basis upon which their happiness can continue.

I commend this book to all people because romance and marriage are a part of our being. The missing ingredient in our present age is the spiritual one which permits the commitment of two people to Christ as the foundation and basis for a stable, successful marriage. J. Allan Petersen, with his host of contributors, has said this in a convincing and refreshing way.

It is my prayer that this book will go far to answer questions, solve problems, and bring new joy and happiness into family circles everywhere.

PREFACE

The Bible is a book of life and relationships. Its truths are of universal significance and will work successfully in any society or era. Regardless of who discovers or develops these life principles, they have a basis and illustration in the Scriptures even though the person involved may not realize it.

Hence the diverse nature of this book. Here is a smorgasbord of information and inspiration from many sources — organized, practical, and dealing with every phase of marriage and the family. Some authors have a strong scriptural approach, and others tell what they have learned in the arena of life through trial and success. Some stress the biblical precepts, while others emphasize the practical outworking. Both are necessary, so there is balance.

The authors represent a broad spectrum of background. Some are clergymen, others laymen; some are highly trained professionals, others ingenious housewives. Some are comparatively unknown, others are household names; all have something important to say.

The articles are of various styles, scope, and aim. The genius of this anthology is in its comprehensiveness, balance, and practical value. It will serve as an encyclopedia of marriage and family success secrets that the reader will refer to often when specific questions or problems arise. To glean this material from our extensive library has been a most rewarding and at times exciting experience. I am sure you will sense this also as you read and find that "something good is going to happen to you."

The extensive preparation necessary for this volume has forcefully reminded me of a fact I have long known — no accomplishment is the result of one person's effort. No one succeeds alone. Including all of the authors, publishers, and my stimulating friends, hundreds are involved.

Special thanks to Ron Jackson, congenial coordinator of our Family Life Series, who did much of the research. My loyal and dedicated secretaries, Bernice Grove and Phyllis Watson, gave important supervision to the whole project, while Genevieve Frew and Ruth Cozette condensed and prepared the manuscript.

Several wonderful couples from widely scattered areas were especially helpful and each made a unique and important contribution: Mike and Jewel Nothum, Joe and Marianne Nothum, Harvey and Carrie Schmucker.

The greatest contribution has been made by my wife, Evelyn, whose happiness and vivacity have been so enjoyable; who has willingly sacrificed during my years of travel, doing a commendable job in rearing our three boys; and who has greatly encouraged me in everything I have ever undertaken.

All of these wonderful people share my desire to help our generation where the need is the greatest — at home.

— J. Allan Petersen
Omaha, Nebraska

ACKNOWLEDGMENTS

"Everybody's Business," by Louis H. Evans, is reprinted by permission from *Your Marriage — Duel or Duet?* (Old Tappan, N.J.: Fleming H. Revell Company). Copyright © 1962.

"Mature Enough to Marry," by Evelyn Duvall, is reprinted by permission from Chapter 4 of *The Church Looks at Family Life* (Nashville, Tenn.: Broadman Press). Copyright © 1964.

"God's Masterpiece," by Stephen Olford, is reprinted by permission from *The Sanctity of Sex* by Stephen Olford and Frank A. Lawes (Old Tappan, N.J.: Fleming H. Revell Company). Copyright © 1963.

"Male and Female," by Julius Fritze, is reprinted by permission from *The Essence of Marriage* (Grand Rapids, Mich.: Zondervan Publishing House). Copyright © 1969.

"Listen to Understand," by Paul Tournier and translated by John S. Gilmour, is abridged and reprinted by permission from *To Understand Each Other* (Richmond, Va.: John Knox Press). Copyright © 1967 M. E Bratcher.

"Don't Blame Your Parents," by Dr. Jacob H. Conn and Edith M. Stern, is reprinted by permission from the October 1952 *Reader's Digest.* Copyright © 1952 The Reader's Digest Assn., Inc.

"Why You Are You," by Tim LaHaye, is reprinted by permission from *How to Be Happy Though Married* (Wheaton, Ill.: Tyndale House Publishers). Copyright © 1968.

"Love Yourself," by R. Lofton Hudson, is reprinted by permission from *Growing a Christian Personality* (Nashville, Tenn.: Broadman Press). Copyright © 1955.

"You Are Somebody," by Maxwell Maltz, is reprinted by permission from *Psycho-Cybernetics: The New Way to a Successful Life* (New York: Prentice-Hall, Inc.). Copyright © 1960.

"Measuring Your Emotions," by William C. Menninger, is reprinted by permission of Hawthorn Books, Inc., from *A Treasury of Success Unlimited,* copyright © 1966 Combined Registry Co.

"Exactly Where Are You Going?" by Mack R. Douglas, is reprinted by permission from *How to Make a Habit of Succeeding* (Grand Rapids, Mich.: Zondervan Publishing House). Copyright © 1966.

"Masculine Men," by Wallace Denton, is reprinted by permission from *What's Happening to Our Families?* (Philadelphia: Westminster Press). Copyright © 1963 W. L. Jenkins.

"The Head of the House," by William E. Hulme, is reprinted by permission from *Building a Christian Marriage* (New York: Prentice-Hall, Inc.). Copyright © 1965.

"Stumbling Blocks or Stepping Stones," by Paul Popenoe, is reprinted by permission from Publication No. 138, American Family Institute of Family Relations, Los Angeles, Cal.

"Man, the Initiator," by Raymond C. Stedman, is reprinted by permission from *Eternity* magazine, copyright © 1969 Evangelical Foundation.

"The Lover," by Dwight Hervey Small, is reprinted by permission from *Design for Christian Marriage* (Old Tappan, N.J., Fleming H. Revell Company). Copyright © 1959.

"Put Him in His Place, Wife," by Alice Patricia Hershey, is reprinted by permission from *Christian Life* magazine. Copyright © 1967 Christian Life Publications, Inc.

"She Has No Equal," by Gladys Hunt, is reprinted by permission from *Sunday School Times,* copyright © 1962 Union Gospel Press, Cleveland, Ohio.

"When the Honeymoon Is Over," by Cecil Osborne, is reprinted by permission from *The Art of Understanding Your Mate* (Grand Rapids, Mich.: Zondervan Publishing House). Copyright © 1970.

"You Incredible Homemaker!" by Ann Landers, is reprinted from *Omaha World Herald,* by permission of Publishers-Hall Syndicate. Copyright © 1968.

"Obeying Two Masters," by Shirley Rice, is reprinted by permission from *The Christian Home* (Norfolk, Va.: Tabernacle Church of Norfolk). Copyright © 1962.

"Let's Talk about Beauty," by Dale Evans Rogers, is reprinted by permission from *Time Out, Ladies!* (Old Tappan, N.J.: Fleming H. Revell Company). Copyright © 1966.

"The Unforgettable Woman," by Ardis Whitman, is reprinted by permission from *Woman's Day,* October 1962. Copyright © 1962, Fawcett Publications, Inc. Copyright © 1963 The Reader's Digest Assn., Inc.

"Hike the Price, Husband," by Earl Nightingale, is reprinted from *This Is Earl Nightingale* by permission of Doubleday & Company, Inc. Copyright © 1966, 1967, 1969 Nightingale-Conant Corp.

"Why God Gave Children Parents," by W. Robert Smith, appeared in *Command* magazine, and is reprinted by permission of the author.

"It Makes the Home Go 'Round," by Lars Granberg, is reprinted with permission from *Church Herald.* Copyright © 1964.

"The Difficult Art of Parenthood," is an essay reprinted by permission from *Time,* The Weekly Newsmagazine. Copyright © 1967 Time, Inc.

"Is Jesus at Home?" by Paul Jongeward, is reprinted by permission from *Eternity* magazine, copyright © 1969 Evangelical Foundation.

"The Crime against Children," by Oswald Hoffmann, is used by permission of the Lutheran Laymen's League, from a broadcast on The Lutheran Hour.

"Understanding Age Growth" chart is reprinted by permission from *Sex Education* (Minneapolis: Sacred Design Associates, Inc.). Copyright © 1968.

"Wise Parental Love," by Hazen G. Werner, is reprinted by permission from *Christian Family Living* (Nashville, Tenn.: Abingdon Press). Copyright © 1958 The Graded Press.

"When to Say No," by W. Taliaferro Thompson, is abridged and reprinted by permission from *Adventures in Parenthood* (Richmond, Va.: John Knox Press). Copyright © 1959 C. D. Deans.

"Pleasurable Discipline," by Henry Brandt, is reprinted by permission from *Build a Happy Home with Discipline* (Wheaton, Ill.: Scripture Press). Copyright © 1966 by the author.

"Demand Their Best," by Arthur Gordon, is reprinted by permission of the author. Copyright © 1961 Fawcett Publications, Inc., Greenwich, Connecticut.

"Angry Children," by Stanley E. Lindquist, is reprinted by permission from *Christian Life* magazine, copyright © 1962 Christian Life Publications, Inc.

"Worship, Family Style," by Howard Hendricks, is reprinted by permission from *The Navigators Log,* copyright © 1966.

"Kazoku," by J. Roland Conlon, is reprinted by permission from *Christian Life* magazine, copyright © 1970 Christian Life Publications, Inc.

"The Family That Plays Together," by Ken Anderson, appeared in *NSSA Link,* and is reprinted by permission of the author.

"Character Building Blocks," by John R. Rice, is reprinted by permission from *The Home: Courtship, Marriage and Children* (Murfreesboro, Tenn.: Sword of the Lord Foundation). Copyright © 1946.

"Christian Training, When?" by Theodore H. Epp, is reprinted by permission from *Good News Broadcaster,* copyright © 1966.

"Needed, Growing Parents," by Anna Mow, is reprinted by permission from *Your Teenager and You* (Grand Rapids, Mich.: Zondervan Publishing House). Copyright © 1967.

"Coping with Rebellion," by Warren Wiersbe, is reprinted by permission from *Moody Monthly* magazine, copyright © 1968 Moody Bible Institute of Chicago.

"Keep Talking!" by Leslie E. and Ruth Small Moser, is reprinted by permission from *Guiding Your Son or Daughter toward Successful Marriage* (Grand Rapids, Mich.: Baker Book House). Copyright © 1967.

"I Trust You," by Bill McKee, is reprinted by permission from *Shut Your Generation Gap* (Wheaton, Ill.: Tyndale House Publishers). Copyright © 1970.

"Changing Homes, Changing Nation," by Lacey Hall, is reprinted by permission from *Moody Monthly* magazine, copyright © 1967 Moody Bible Institute of Chicago.

"The New Morality," by Letha Scanzoni, is reprinted by permission from *Sex and the Single Eye* (Grand Rapids, Mich.: Zondervan Publishing House). Copyright © 1968.

"Sex Education — Whose Responsibility?" by John Drescher, is reprinted by permission from *Good News Broadcaster.* Copyright © Back to the Bible, Lincoln, Nebraska.

"The Turned-on Generation," by Gordon McLean, is reprinted by permission from *High on the Campus,* by Gordon McLean and Haskell Bowen (Wheaton, Ill.: Tyndale House Publishers). Copyright © 1970.

"Homosexuality Begins at Home," by David Wilkerson, is reprinted by permission from *Parents on Trial* (New York: Hawthorn Books, Inc.). Copyright © 1967.

"Social Drinker to Alcoholic," by Jerry G. Dunn, is reprinted by permission from *God Is for the Alcoholic* (Chicago: Moody Press). Copyright © 1965 Moody Bible Institute.

"Wives on the Time Clock," by Martha Nelson, is reprinted by permission from *The Christian Woman in the Working World* (Nashville, Tenn.: Broadman Press). Copyright © 1970.

"Profit from Your Mistakes," by Douglas Lurton, is reprinted from *A Treasury of Success Unlimited* (New York: Hawthorn Books, Inc.), copyright © 1966, and is used by permission of Margaret Lurton Kahle.

"Seven Rules for a Good Fight," by Charlie Shedd, is reprinted by permission from *Letters to Philip* (New York: Doubleday and Company, Inc.). Copyright © 1968 Charlie W. Shedd and copyright © 1968 The Abundance Foundation.

"Should I Confess?" by David Augsburger, is reprinted by permission from *70 x 7* (Chicago: Moody Press). Copyright © 1970 Moody Bible Institute of Chicago.

"Your Reactions Are Showing," by J. Allan Petersen, is reprinted by permission from *Who Runs Your Life?* (Lincoln, Neb.: Good News Broadcasting Association). Copyright © 1967.

"Ins and Outs of In-Laws," by Gordon and Dorothea Jaeck, is reprinted by permission from *I Take Thee* (Grand Rapids, Mich.: Zondervan Publishing House). Copyright © 1967.

"See the Marriage Doctor," by Clyde M. Narramore, is reprinted by permission from *Happiness in Marriage* (Grand Rapids, Mich.: Zondervan Publishing House). Copyright © 1961 Clyde M. Narramore.

"Before the Divorce," by Norman Vincent Peale, is reprinted by permission of the author, from September 1964 *Reader's Digest*, copyright © 1964 The Reader's Digest Assn., Inc. Condensed from *Guideposts*.

"Talking with the Heart," by James H. Jauncey, is reprinted by permission from *Magic in Marriage* (Grand Rapids, Mich.: Zondervan Publishing House). Copyright © 1965.

"Busy Signal at Home," by Milo Arnold, is reprinted by permission from *The Sunday School Times and Gospel Herald,* copyright © 1968 Union Gospel Press.

"Words Can't Say It," by Howard J. Clinebell, Jr. and Charlotte H. Clinebell, is reprinted by permission from *The Intimate Marriage* (New York: Harper & Row). Copyright © 1970.

"Crossing Barriers and Bridges," by Elof G. Nelson, is abridged and reprinted by permission from *Your Life Together* (Richmond, Va.: John Knox Press). Copyright © 1967 M. E. Bratcher.

"Diplomacy at Home" is reprinted by permission from the *Royal Bank of Canada Monthly Letter,* December 1969.

"Giving Is Living," by A. T. Pierson, is reprinted by permission from *The Alliance Witness.*

"Money, Marriage, and Romance," by W. Clark Ellzey, is reprinted by permission from *How to Keep Romance in Your Marriage* (New York: Association Press). Copyright © 1965.

"Keep Your Money Alive," by D. G. Kehl, is reprinted from *Today's*

Living by permission of Baptist Publications, Denver, Colorado.

"The '10-70-20' Formula for Wealth," by George M. Bowman, is reprinted by permission from *Here's How to Succeed with Your Money* (Chicago: Moody Press). Copyright © 1960 Moody Bible Institute of Chicago.

"Teach Your Kids to Manage Money," by William Bard, is reprinted by permission of the author from *Precis.*

"William's Partner," by Philip Jerome Cleveland, appeared in *Christian Economics* and is reprinted by permission of the author.

"What the Bible Says about Sex," by Billy Graham, is reprinted with permission from the May 1970 *Reader's Digest,* copyright © 1970 Reader's Digest Assn., Inc.

"The Art of Married Love," by David Mace, is used by permission of the author.

"The Superlatives of Sex," by S. I. McMillen, M.D., is reprinted by permission from *None of These Diseases* (Old Tappan, N.J.: Fleming H. Revell Company). Copyright © 1963.

"Understanding Sex in Marriage," by Herbert J. Miles, is reprinted by permission from *Sexual Happiness in Marriage* (Grand Rapids, Mich.: Zondervan Publishing House). Copyright © 1967.

"The Best Is Yet to Be," by Wayne Dehoney, is reprinted by permission from *Homemade Happiness* (Nashville, Tenn.: Broadman Press). Copyright © 1963.

"Prepare Your Wife for Widowhood," by Donald I. Rogers, is reprinted with the author's permission from *Teach Your Wife to Be a Widow* (New York: Holt, Rinehart & Winston, Inc.). Copyright © 1964 Donald I. Rogers.

"How I Conquered Grief," by Catherine Marshall, is reprinted by permission of Atlanta Newspapers, Inc., Atlanta, Ga. Copyright © 1953.

"The Later Years," by A. Donald Bell, is reprinted by permission from *Family in Dialogue* (Grand Rapids, Mich.: Zondervan Publishing House). Copyright © 1968.

THE FOLLOWING SHORT FEATURES are printed with the kind permission of the copyright owners. "In a solemn . . . ," by Gordon and Dorothea Jaeck, from *I Take Thee,* © 1967 Zondervan. "What are some . . . ," by Frank Waldorf, from *Eternity* magazine, © 1967 Evangelical Foundation, Philadelphia. "You shall love . . . ," by E. Stanley Jones, from *Christian Maturity,* © 1957 Abingdon. "There is still . . . ," by Nathan C. Brooks, and "The most influential . . . ," by Ruth Hampton, both from *Home Life* magazine, © 1967, 1968 respectively, Sunday School Board of Southern Baptist Convention. "Blessed is the . . . ," by Alice Kay Rogers, from *Christian Mother* magazine, © 1968 Standard Pub. Co. "Read this affirmation . . . ," by Robert H. Schuller, from *Move Ahead with Possibility Thinking,* © 1967 Doubleday & Co. "So you've got . . . ," by W. Clement Stone, from *Success Through a Positive Mental Attitude,* © 1960 Prentice-Hall, Inc. "Money management is . . . ," by Robert J. Hastings, from *How to Manage Your Money,* © 1965 Broadman. "The man and . . . ," by Joseph B. Henry, from *Fulfillment in Marriage,* © 1966 Revell.

1

THE BLISSFUL VENTURE

Opportunity Unlimited!

by J. Allan Petersen
Founder and President, Family Concern, Inc.

I am a concerned man. Not pessimistic, negative, or hopeless — but much concerned. Concerned because we're not hearing the right voices in our day. If we listen only to the voices behind the headlines, some modern educators, psychologists, and movie stars, we would have to conclude that marriage and the family have had it. They talk as if they have considered the whole subject in depth and found that the traditional one man-one woman relationship is now passé — doomed. And who is to deny that there is an increasing public acceptance of broken marriages and a decreasing sense of its stigma?

British psychologist James Heming, in *Marriage Guidance,* official organ of Britain's Marriage Guidance Council, predicts, "Engagement rings are doomed; weddings will be rituals of the past; couples will wed, if at all, only *after* they have 'lived together.' " The Associated Press comments, "If Dr. Heming is right, the word 'marriage' itself could become obsolete." Many now advocate trial marriages — non-structured relationships. Dr. Albert Ellis, well-known psychologist, says an adulterous relationship can be beneficial to some marriages, and talks about "healthy adultery." A professor in behavioral science asks, "Should we try to enforce a 50-

year contract on a 20-year-old girl or man? . . . a healthy divorce, no matter what the age of the partners, may well have the same kind of social value as a healthy marriage."

These voices begin and end at the same place — with man. Looking only from a human standpoint, they can do little more than reflect man's deepest frustrations and most recent experiments — not change them. These "now" experts do not have a proper sense of history. Do they know what happened in Greece in 300 B.C., in Rome in A.D. 300? Have they read the lesson of history that no nation has ever survived the disintegration of its home life?

When the Family Service Association of America warns that "family breakdown is fast reaching epidemic proportions and now ranks as America's No. 1 social problem," that concerns me.

When Dr. George Macer of U. S. C. Medical School says, "The decline of modern marriage has reached a point where a happily married couple seems to be an oddity," that concerns me. He continues, "Despite the rise of higher education, education certainly has not taught the way toward marital maturity; it seems that the higher the education the more conflicts and tensions are present. It seems more marriages are unhappy and in jeopardy than ever before."

When Dr. Margaret Mead, the anthropologist, said years ago, "In every known society we find some form of the family," but now says, "We must find a substitute for the family," that concerns me. Frederick Engels, the apostle of Communism, said the same thing one hundred years ago.

I am concerned about the increasing acceptance of homosexuality as a wholesome way of life.

I am concerned that more than 20 million U. S. couples live in desperate unhappiness and unfulfillment. Their sweet dreams have gone sour.

I am concerned that our children are not getting their sex education in the right places. Home and church are negligent. Our young people are being given a definition of love by those who have not experienced it. They know much about sex, little about love. Our teens rush into marriage when they are still utterly unready. About half of these end in divorce and begin adult life with two strikes against them. We have come to tolerate flagrant sexual irresponsibility and use people as things instead of loving them as persons. When I realize our generation now has more "education" against marriage and family life than for it — that bothers me.   ·

While this marriage and family deterioration is taking place and politicians, educators, sociologists, and judges are speaking with alarm about it, what is the church doing? Why are the ministers silent? Have we become merely thermometers registering the moral temperature of our times instead of thermostats calling for a change in climate and triggering the spiritual mechanisms to do it? The church seeks to be "relevant" and hold on to its dwindling membership while Ann Landers becomes the voice of authority and concern that our generation craves in its pitiful struggle with guilt, meaninglessness, and lack of direction. This greatly concerns me.

I am also an optimistic man — the opportunities are unlimited. Never has there been more help for marriage and rearing a family. Sometimes our basic questions reveal our "impossibility complex"; "Will marriage survive? Is there any hope for the family? Is it wise to have children in our day?"

Abraham Lincoln said, "The occasion is piled high with difficulty, but we must arise to the occasion." How men respond to great challenges decides whether or not a culture endures. Our personal reaction determines the destiny of our own lives and influences our country and our world. We can respond negatively. That is so easy, almost automatic. We say, "There is really nothing that I can do. After all, I am just one little person in a fast moving, impersonal world; what can I do?" Every one of us has felt this way at one time or another. But no individual is so insignificant as to be without influence. If you were ever prone to doubt what you can do as an individual, think of Karl Marx writing *Das Kapital* by candlelight. Then think of two unknown disciples, Lenin and Trotsky, who in less than forty years won a third of the world to Communism.

Ultimately, everything depends on the individual! Every choice in society is really personal and every change can be traced to an individual who had an influence. Each one of us has a unique and important contribution to make. Therefore, the big question is not: Will the institution of marriage survive? but, Will my marriage survive? If so, how? If your marriage survives happily, it will have a direct bearing on the success of others — the embryo marriages of your own children, and the marriages of couples you contact.

General Motors discovered in a study that the average person has a strong influence on at least 162 people in his lifetime. Since for most of your adult years you are married, the depth and breadth of your influence will be related to the quality of your marriage.

I counseled a woman whose marriage was disintegrating. She felt it was hopeless, and wept in despair. But she discovered God's resources to be enough to change her life and attitude, and as a result her husband was changed too. Their whole family is now happily united in Christ, and they have had a direct influence on sixteen other couples in only one year's time. If we could maintain this ratio (1:16) we could reverse the trend and change the world!

A single person said to me recently, "I am thirty-six years old, and have met only one happily married couple in my life." This woman did not need logical arguments to convince her of happy marriage possibilities. She needed some examples in living color, flesh and blood people who live in harmony and radiate marital sunshine and optimism. Your marriage can be this: more than just an influence — an inspiration! And since happy marriages are scarce these days, you might even create a sensation! Your very presence could be a life-line to struggling couples around you. We change the world by changing our world; we must begin at home.

Consider the family in our times. No one questions that young people face constant temptation today, a compelling conformity and a competition that wears on them relentlessly. But these facts alone do not justify a couple's remaining childless or limiting their offspring.

When has child rearing been easy? At what time in history have the negative forces been dormant or subjugated by overwhelming righteousness? Without minimizing the pressures of our time, we must recall that each age has its own peculiar hazards and anxieties. It has always been tough to rear unselfish, responsible, and godly children. We should realize, as someone has said, that "it probably takes more endurance, more patience, more intelligence, more healthy emotion to raise a happy human being than to be an atomic physicist, politician, or psychiatrist."

There have to be sufficient spiritual resources in Jesus Christ to enable parents and children to succeed in this day — or else Christianity is a hoax. It is an impractical philosophy — something for the hothouse instead of the open road — that thrives only under ideal conditions which never really exist.

I believe parents can be optimistic in these days if we do three things: maintain a positive outlook; assume our God-given responsibilities; and major in children's training during their first few years.

If you really believe, as David Livingstone said, that God's promise is the word of a Gentleman of the most strict and sacred honor, then your overall perspective has to be positive. He enables for what he asks. His promises are enough for the problems. His building of the house assures us that our labor will not be in vain (Psalm 127:1). A. B. Simpson declared: "When God calls us to a work far beyond our natural strength or endowments, the emergency only throws us upon him, and we will always find him equal to the need which his wisdom and providence have brought our way."

Beyond our realization must be a decision to be responsible in rearing children. The principles of the Bible work, but somebody has to work them. Marriage roles are clearly set forth, but they must be personally assumed. Just reading or memorizing them does not make them operative. Parents must deliberately and determinedly initiate the right action. Many refuse responsibility, remain passive, and then blame others for children's waywardness.

Over one-half of the intelligence and personality development of a child is completed by the age of five. Therefore, the most important period of a child's life is before he enters school. The kind of problems you face in your teenager is influenced strongly by what you do with them when they are small. We must focus on these formative years and give our best attention in this period when the child first learns the meaning of love and the rewards of responsibility.

I am optimistic about the possibilities of marriage because we know what we need to do. Though we probe the problems of communication, money, and sex, we know these are symptoms, not causes, of divided families. "There are no unhappy marriages, only marriage partners who are immature," says Dr. David Mace. The problem is not the marriage, but the people in it. If the partners can develop more mature attitudes, all areas of their relationship will improve. The journey toward a happy marriage is the journey from childishness to maturity, from egocentricity to the commitment of love. Maturity, then, is the secret of a well-adjusted marriage in any society.

Maturity delivers a person from a childish preoccupation with himself and the use of his partner to satisfy his own desires and needs. Maturity gives a person the ability and willingness to act. The mature one accepts responsibility and the consequences of his own decisions. Such a person is able to take the long look and patiently persevere while looking for a way through his present difficulties — not a way out of them.

The successful marriage partner has learned the positive value of problems, that they are important teachers and their "notebook" is filled with lessons learned in no other school. He knows problems are meant to be solved, not shelved or skirted. They are not to be feared but to be faced — with faith. The life of the mature person reveals a willingness to change; he is not content with mediocrity, and he believes "good enough" is not enough. The key to maturity is desire; in the final analysis we have the kind of marriage we really desire — what we are willing to work and pray for.

The Christian is in a unique position with regard to his home and his society. He alone has the spiritual resources necessary to give him an enviable marriage. And God has given him a privilege and responsibility no one else bears: a happy family that is an example to the world of the power of God's love. In terms of ministry, perhaps never has this successful Christian marriage been more needed than today. And never have the opportunities to achieve it been greater.

Twenty-five years ago premarital counseling was hardly known and pastors generally gave scant attention to it. Those who preached on family subjects did it only spasmodically, the majority not at all. "Sex" was almost considered a bad word, and the beautiful biblical picture of sexuality was not recognized. Books on Christian marriage were scarce and skimpy, and hardly anything comprehensive was available to give to a couple contemplating marriage. This is all changed.

Many ministers hold several counseling sessions before they marry a couple. The pastor's study has become a counseling chamber, as 42 percent seek their minister first when they have a problem. Pastors get their largest crowds when they announce a series of messages on the home and family. The sordid sex scene of our society offers a contrasting background for display of the real jewel given us by God. Books, numerous, practical, and godly, give personal and wise counsel.

Truly, there is no necessity for marriage failure. God has given us the responsibility and the spiritual resources to carry it out. The world has given us the challenge and the opportunity. We must respond, work, learn, build, love. It is a wonderful day for marriage — opportunity unlimited. Congratulations to the happy couple!

•-•••-•-••-•-••-•-••-•-••-•-••-•-••-•-••-•-•••

God has set the type of marriage everywhere throughout the creation. Every creature seeks its perfection in another. The very heavens and earth picture it to us.

— MARTIN LUTHER

Everybody's Business

by Louis H. Evans

Author, Your Marriage: Duel or Duet, *and Minister-at-large, Presbyterian Church in the U.S.*

A young couple came to my office in Hollywood some years ago and said, "Well, Dr. Evans, we think our marriage might go on the rocks, but after all, that is definitely our business."

I said, "Don't talk like that! Your marriage is everybody's business!" And it is.

Marriage is a nation's business. When a pier juts out into the ocean, it is utterly at the mercy of the individual pilings on which it stands. Strike out a piling from beneath it and the whole structure suffers a shock and the pier is weakened. Every nation juts out into the social sea, resting upon the pilings of its individual homes. Every time a home is destroyed, the whole nation suffers a severe thundershock. No nation can stand for long with one-quarter of its pilings gone or damaged.

It may be that Edward Gibbon's 1788 analysis of the collapse of the Roman Empire is strikingly contemporary. We see evident parallels between that society and ours: the rapid increase in divorce, undermining the dignity and sanctity of the home; the increase in taxes (and in the case of the Romans, the expenditure for free bread and circuses for the benefit of the populace); the present mad craze for pleasure; the building of gigantic armaments to the neglect of the real enemy within — the decadence of the people; the decay of religion with faith fading into mere form, losing

———

Copyright 1962 Fleming H. Revell Co.

touch with life and becoming impotent to warn and guide the people.

Your marriage is very much the nation's business. The decay of the American home as the national unit is one of the most perilous characteristics of our age.

Marriage is definitely the child's business. The child is like a seismograph. It registers every domestic earthquake and every marital shock. Sociologists tell us that they very seldom see a case of disintegration in the personality of a child but that can be traced back to either a broken or an unhappy home. The home can make a child fall in love with love or else it can scar it with antisocial instincts and fixations. Too many children are scarred today in the battles that are raging between parents. Somehow they always stand in the way of the blows and can seldom be shielded from them. Marriage is very much a child's business.

Marriage is very much God's business. God finds himself in the difficult situation of endeavoring to explain his infinite character to our finite minds. When a boy builds a house of blocks, he can only build as large a house as he has blocks with which to build. When he runs out of blocks he stops building. If you and I build up the inherent, infinite character and nature of God, we must do it by means of blocks of our experiences: syllogisms and parallelisms that we understand. When we run out of blocks we stop defining God in a definite way. Most of these blocks by which God explains himself are domestic blocks.

"As a father pities his children, so the Lord pities those who fear him" (Psalm 103:13). Here, through a father's pity and understanding, God is able to explain himself to the child. But if a father is not pitying, nor understanding, then God loses that means of explanation.

"As one whom his mother comforts, so I will comfort you . . ." (Isaiah 66:13). If a mother is not comforting, then that block of experience is gone.

"There is a friend who sticks closer than a brother" (Proverbs 18:24). But if a brother does not stand by, then that syllogism, too, is gone.

"Husbands, love your wives, as Christ loved the church and gave himself for her" (Ephesians 5:25). This is an instruction some people object to strongly, because their marriage has failed to function properly; their marriage does not portray this deep, high, close relationship that Christ has with his church. Thus, when a home is destroyed, God loses one of the greatest theological seminaries in the world, one of his chief ways of explaining himself. Marriage is very much God's business.

It is difficult to build the home today for various reasons. They used to reinforce the old cathedrals with "flying buttresses." The cathedral was thus held together by outside pressure. Now most churches are built with cantilever construction, with inner ties hidden away in the masonry. The home of yesterday was kept together largely by outside pressure, in much the same way "flying buttresses" were used. You simply could not afford to be divorced. If you were, you were often isolated and people drew their skirts aside; you were passed by on the city street. Not so, today. Only a relatively small number of persons frown upon divorce today, or consider this sort of domestic breakage a sincere tragedy.

The outside pressures that once held the home together have changed their nature, and social pressures of today are more likely to cause a crash in the home than they are to preserve it. This has made the situation much more difficult than in former years.

There is one factor in marriage which makes us both pessimistic and optimistic — that is the fact that the home is made up of individuals. Individuals being fickle, marriage often proves to be the same. But individuals being changeable gives us the hope that the home and marriage picture may be changed. Of course, you can never change marriage without changing people. Marriage is made up of human equations. It is not primarily an institution. It is two people, human beings, combining together to do something. Whenever human selfishness barges in, difficulties arise. The trouble with defining marriage as merely an "institution" lies in the fact that in this word you have three "I's" and only one "U". And the minute the *you* gives way to the *I* and selfishness pervades, we have the decay and destruction of marriage.

•-•··•··•··•-•··•··•··•··•··•··•··•··•··•··•·

Prayer by a Bride and Groom

Our gracious heavenly Father, who givest the supreme gift of love to thy children, we thank thee for each other. We thank thee for all who love us and who have given so much of themselves to make us happy. We thank thee for the love that has bound our hearts and lives together and made us husband and wife.

As we enter upon the privileges and joys of life's most holy relationship and begin together the great adventure of building a Christian home, we thank thee for all the hopes that make the future bright. Teach us the fine art of living together unselfishly that, loving and being loved, blessing and being blessed, we may find our love ever filled with a deeper harmony as we learn more perfectly to share it through the years.

Help us to keep the candles of faith and prayer always burning in our home. Be thou our Guest at every meal, our Guide in every plan, our Guardian in every temptation.

None can know what the future holds. We ask only that we may love, honor, and cherish each other always, and so live together in faithfulness and patience that our lives will be filled with joy and the home which we have this day established become a haven of blessing and a place of peace.

— WESLEY H. HAGER

Mature Enough to Marry

by Evelyn M. Duvall
Author, The Church Looks at Family Life *and other books in this field*

The United States Bureau of the Census tells us that marriages today are taking place in larger numbers and at younger ages than ever before. Why the increase in young marriages?

The first, and very possibly the most important, social reason is the relative affluence of present-day America. Both bride and groom not only expect to work but usually do work until their family is established.

During economic slowdown, the marriage age tends to be higher. As soon as times are good again, the number of marriages goes up. There's a very close relationship between economic prosperity and young age at marriage.

A second point of very real importance that is not widely recognized is that parents today are more able and more willing to help the young couple in many substantial ways. We make generous gifts under the counter so the neighbors won't know, and do all kinds of things that older generations always have done, but we do it in a less obvious and more generous way today.

In the third place, in times of wartime economy and of general "floating anxiety," as the psychiatrists put it, marrage rates and young marriages increase.

Fourth is the increased amount of early dating, going steady at earlier ages. Courtship proceeds at a faster pace and at earlier ages than was the case a few generations ago.

Copyright 1964 Broadman Press

Fifth, many of our young marriages are being forced by pregnancy. There has been a very obvious increase in the number of these premarital pregnancies. The percentages not only vary by the area but also by the religious orientation, by the way.

Sixth is the idealization of marriage as a desirable adult status. Marriage is a kind of instant status for a youngster who is discouraged in other areas. One of the reasons why some of these very young marriages work out so badly is that the very people who are least prepared for marriage are those who plunge into marriage most precipitately.

Seventh, the increase in young marriages is very definitely related to the increase in the number of unhappy homes, schools, and communities. Children from unhappy homes marry at younger ages than those from happier home situations.

Eighth is the chain-reaction effect of young marriages encouraging more young marriages within a given community. In some schools the vast majority of senior girls are already either engaged or married. In many communities, getting married at young ages has attained almost epidemic proportions.

Early marrying youngsters tend to be those boys and girls who feel discouraged about themselves and as a rule have low aspiration levels. The girl who marries young tends to marry the boy who is already established at some low-paying job with little future in it. He got it because it is all he can get after dropping out of school.

Why be concerned about young marriage? First of all, because of its human development hazards.

There seems to be little question but that early intimacy and early domesticity among teen-agers curtails the development of full personality potential. The individual becomes preoccupied in the creative and procreative aspects of life which all of us know have such terrific drive and central force. Therefore, that individual does not get the time or the chance to dream, to travel, to explore and to find out what the world is made of and know the kinds of people and the forces and attitudes and points of view that are present. He or she does not get the opportunity to develop as a full-fledged individual to the place of developing the very complex, intricate, marvelous capacity to love in its fullest sense.

This is the reason why young marriages should not be recommended in our society. But there is another reason too. This is that young marriages do break up in large numbers. All studies to date conclude that young marriages are not as stable as those of more mature persons.

Why are young marriages so unstable? Because marriage is not child's play. It requires a very complex ability to carry responsibility and to settle down as a mature enough person to found a family. Young marriage is very frequently a lunge toward independence and freedom from control. Therefore, it tends to take place most frequently among the most rebellious, the most anarchistic, the least well-adjusted young people. "You can't push me around; I'll get married and show you I can run my own life" kind of attitude is adolescent rebellion at its most immature form.

The young married are often emotionally immature even though they may be sexually sophisticated. Less emotional maturity is related significantly, clinically, and statistically, to sexual irresponsibility, promiscuity, and general sophistication sexually.

Why are young marriages unsuccessful in terms of both permanence and happiness? Because young people have less opportunity to prepare themselves specifically for marriage and family, less opportunity to find out what marriage is all about, less opportunity to understand themselves and what it means to become a husband or wife, a mother or father, less opportunity to learn anything at all about what it is going to mean to become parents.

These youngsters oftentimes recognize all too late that the

problems of marriage are 'way beyond their anticipations. What are the pressures and problems of young marriages? First of all are the economic problems and pressures. They have less money, more unemployment, less of an educational base, and the wife is poorly prepared to help. About all she can do is get a job as a waitress, or pounding somebody's typewriter, or other more or less dead-end jobs.

A second pressure on these young marriages is that of housing. A large number of these young couples live with their folks even though our culture says "no roof is big enough for two families." This is a very real problem, and it may be a real disappointment.

Young marriages have in-law problems. They have three times as many in-law problems as we find among more mature couples. Why? Because parents more frequently disapprove of the young marriage and, therefore, are on the lookout for trouble. Annoyance and disappointment on the part of parents increase the concern from the parents' point of view which the young people, in turn, interpret as interference.

Another hazard is the social pressures. Young husbands run around much more than do more mature men. "He is out bowling with the boys." "He is still chasing around" is the kind of complaint that very frequently comes from the young wife.

The young mother oftentimes finds that the constant care of a baby ties her down. Here the girl is stuck twenty-four hours a day, seven days a week, with an irresponsible husband who is off goodness knows where; so she parks the baby any place she can and tears off whenever possible. Irresponsible, sure, because she is not ready for this kind of responsibility.

What do we mean — mature enough to marry?

First of all, mature enough to have established a sense of personal identity, to have discovered one's self and to have developed a direction for one's life that offers promise for the future.

Second, mature enough to be ready to settle down with one person exclusively, with responsibility.

Third, grown up enough to have outgrown childish dependence upon parents or adolescent independence thrusts to the place where one is ready for interdependence with husband or wife.

Fourth, a person is mature enough to marry when he or she is ready to love and to be loved deeply and fully as a whole person. The kind of love that takes time to mature does not blossom overnight, even in relationships between mature persons.

Fifth, education sufficient for a full life as a man or woman both in and outside the home. There should have been enough education before marriage to kindle the love of learning in both of the pair so they will both keep on with their education afterwards.

It is this love of growth that probably more than anything else is a measure of maturity. Education is important for a full life. So we advise youth — prepare for what marriage involves. Become ready to assume the roles and even enjoy the privileges of marriage. Know what it means to become a husband, what it means to become a wife. Learn what will be expected and enough of the skills to carry on with some competence as a married partner, as a parent, as a householder, as a homemaker.

Those of us who have anything to do with children in the full twenty years of the first two decades of life need to constantly recognize that more important than preaching, more important than scolding, more important than reminding is encouraging young people to develop those facets of themselves that have promise. As we can show a youngster from the very earliest days our pleasure, our pride, our admiration for something that he is or does or is capable of, we inspire him to continue growing. When we whittle down or nag too loudly, too frequently — all we do is increase the sense of guilt and shame and disappointment and self-abasement that is not in the line of growth.

I have been accused of being an optimist. I'm not. I'm concerned, because I see mankind around the world investing literally billions in implements of destruction, and I see even our most concerned persons giving but a very small fraction of their time, their energy, and their money to trying to tap the precious power in the human spirit. That is the only antidote I know to the rampant anxiety and hate that are abroad today. It is only as we can call concerned persons like you to take a new look at what we might be doing in developing people, and the homes of tomorrow, that our future can be secure.

·•··•··•··•··•··•··•··•··•··•··•··•··•··•··•··•·

In a solemn moment each of us who are married once affirmed that lovely vow, "I take thee. . . ." Only as marriage begins and continues as one shared experience after another, can the significance of such an encompassing commitment be discovered. Then we begin to learn that in marriage we are constantly "taking" each other — in every revelation of ourselves as we really are, in each new experience, "till death do us part."

— GORDON and DOROTHEA JAECK

God's Masterpiece

by Stephen F. Olford

Co-author, The Sanctity of Sex, *and Pastor, Calvary Baptist Church,
New York City*

In the God-planned life, after courtship and engagement comes the long looked-for wedding day, with its attendant rapture of joy and promise of happy years to follow. This union of two lives constitutes what the Scriptures describe as marriage.

The Lord Jesus spoke the final word on this institution of marriage when he answered the critics of his day, and declared: "Have ye not read, that he which made them at the beginning made them male and female, and said, For this cause shall a man leave father and mother, and shall cleave to his wife: and they twain shall be one flesh? Wherefore they are no more twain, but one flesh. What therefore God hath joined together, let not man put asunder."

If we would be instructed aright, we must obey our Lord's words and turn to the early chapters of the Bible and discover in Genesis the divine pattern of marriage. From these remarkable statements we learn that:

1. Marriage is desired by God. "And the Lord God said, It is not good that the man should be alone; I will make him an help meet for him" (2:18).

Notice, it was God who took the initiative in reading Adam's heart. It was God who approached Adam concerning his life partner, and it is still God who is concerned about the need in your life. Will you not trust him com-

Copyright 1963 Fleming H. Revell Co.

pletely to know what is best for your life, notwithstanding the pressures and temptations to direct your own affairs?

From these opening verses of the Old Testament, we learn that marriage is desired by God for the purpose of human pleasure: "The Lord God said, It is not good that the man should be alone." There was obviously something missing in Adam's life so that he could not enjoy the fulfillment of pleasure which God had designed for him.

This is not to suggest that there is not a divine compensation for a life of singleness, or celibacy. As a matter of fact, God sometimes calls certain people to a life of singleness in order that they might better fulfill the purpose of the gospel. In either case, however, it is the plan of God for our lives that we must seek after, and not merely the preferences or desires of our own hearts. However, it is evident that a life of singleness is the exception to the rule; for the majority, the plan of God is the marriage state. For such, God's desire is that this union of life and love should be supremely happy and pleasurable.

Marriage is desired by God, not only for human pleasure but also for human partnership. The whole idea behind this expression is that of partnership, or a partner of help.

What a thing it is to know partnership in life, in love, and in service! Think, for instance, of the joy and effectiveness of partnership in prayer. "Did not our Lord refer to such fellowship," asks F. B. Meyer, "when he spoke of being specially with *two* who met in his Name, agreed in the symphony of perfect musical accord? Nothing will more quickly detect any division of feeling, or bring together two souls in mutual confession, forgiveness, and agreement."

There is yet another reason why God desires marriage, and that is for the purpose of human parenthood. To the primeval couple, he said, "Be fruitful, and multiply, and replenish the earth, and subdue it" (1:28).

One of the most precious and sacred ministries of married life is that of bringing little children into the world. Here is a privilege that is denied angelic beings, but is committed to men and women in general, and to believers in Jesus Christ in particular. Oh, to catch the wonder and glory of this holy conception of God's intention and man's fulfillment in marriage!

2. Marriage is determined by God. "And the Lord God caused a deep sleep to fall upon Adam, and he slept: and he took one of his ribs, and closed up the flesh instead thereof; and the rib, which the Lord God had taken from man, made he a woman, and brought her unto the man" (2:21-22).

Here we see love's preparation. "And the Lord God caused a deep sleep to fall upon Adam, and he . . . made . . . a woman. . . ." So in quiet submissiveness, the first man ever to be created slept in the will of God, while a beneficent Creator prepared a partner for him.

Adam's action should teach us to trust God implicitly for what is best for us, and to wait for God's timing and never lose patience. Young person, will you grasp this truth? If you do, it will save you a life of frustration, heartbreak, and even tragedy.

If we are prepared to fulfill love's preparation, there comes the moment of love's revelation. "And . . . the Lord . . . made . . . a woman, and brought her unto the man" (2:22). What a moment that must have been to Adam in all the purity and sweetness of that Edenic setting!

There are various ways in which God reveals to us who is the partner of his choice. Suffice it to say that when love's revelation comes to us, it is unmistakable. It may be "love at first sight," or a growing affection which eventually becomes a conviction of love in the presence of God.

St. Augustine beautifully summarized this affinity when he said, "If God meant woman to rule over man, he would have taken her out of Adam's head. Had he designed her to be his slave, he would have taken her from his feet, but God took woman out of man's side, for he made her to be a help meet and an equal to him." Happy are the pair who come to love's revelation with this glorious sense of affinity and certainty!

The wedding day holds more for us than love's preparation and revelation. It is, in fact, love's consummation. "Therefore shall a man leave his father and his mother, and shall cleave unto his wife: and they shall be one flesh" (2:24). This is a high and holy concept, and we dare not enter upon it "thoughtlessly or lightly, but reverently, seriously, with true affection, and in dependence on God."

We strongly urge young couples to spend much time in prayer and preparation before this great moment in their lives. The high standards of the God-ordained marriage should be pondered seriously and solemnly. Remember that the Bible teaches that marriage involves monogamy, fidelity, and indissolubility. This love can only be strong, sweet, and unfailing, if it is perfected through the reading of God's Word, sanctified by prayer, and released by the power of the indwelling Spirit.

3. Marriage is defended by God. "Therefore shall a man leave his father and his mother, and shall cleave unto his wife: and they shall be one flesh" (2:24). There is nothing good which the devil does not attack, and marriage is no exception.

Among the many devices he uses to spoil the harmony and happiness of married life is that of personal incompatibility. The wedding day has come and gone, the honeymoon has passed, and married life in earnest has begun. Little differences emerge and become worse and worse until the two lives become estranged and the man and woman begin to doubt what they might call "the compatibility of their personalities."

The glory of the Christian gospel is that we can triumph over these human failures by the power of the indwelling

Christ. Every one of the potential threats to marital bliss can be defeated. Indeed, one of the romances of married love in Christ is what has been called "mutual adjustment in love." See to it that you never allow so-called personal incompatibilities to threaten your home.

These are sobering truths, and to submit to their cleansing effect is to know lives that are pure, noble, strong, and steadfast. To build your married life on this teaching is to know a oneness which is unshakable, and a future which is as bright as the promises of God. Only as the Church returns to this kind of teaching will her people become strong in their lives, pure in their homes, effective in their witness, and the world will feel the impact, and civilization will return to something like sanity.

So we see that the ideal marriage is desired by God, determined by God, and defended by God. If this be true, then "What . . . God hath joined together, let not man put asunder."

.•··•··•··•··•··•··•··•··•··•··•··•··•··•·

The sanctity of marriage and the family relation make the cornerstone of our American society and civilization.

— JAMES A. GARFIELD

Male and Female

by Julius A. Fritze
Author, The Essence of Marriage, *and Clinical Counselor*

If a marriage counselor were invited to tell what topic he would consider of paramount importance to human welfare, perhaps he would take as the basic theme a part of the 28th verse of the first chapter of Genesis: "Male and female created he them."

A man and a woman are basically different psychologically. The thread of these different traits runs through every society in history as well as at the present time. An attempt to change men and women, or a desire to rationalize the differences and act accordingly, would violate all creation and its basic design. This is the basic reason why marriages in our society, as well as in others, are breaking up.

A man is basically a logical, rational creature; a female is basically an emotional creature. A man is more active and more aggressive. He is more emotionally stable and well controlled about big things than is a woman. However, he is more irritable, excitable, and impatient about small things. He is a vain, boastful exhibitionist. He is more optimistic than a woman and more businesslike. He is more ready to admit that he is mistaken — his logic demands it. He is more objective and consistent, which is another evidence of logic. He is more able to concentrate on a consistent basis without his emotions getting in the way.

Man is more of a nomadic creature. This can be observed in our mobile society. It does not disturb a man as much

Copyright 1969 Zondervan Publishing House

as it does a woman when he is transferred from one city to another. This emotionally frustrates her because her security is threatened by a lack of roots.

A man is slower to mature, both physically and emotionally. However, a man, all things being equal, grows to a greater depth of maturity. A woman, being an emotional creature, is hindered in reaching this depth.

The average man is likely to be more direct, truthful, sportsmanlike, and businesslike in communication with his fellowman. He is more likely to be sincere in his friendship to another man than a woman is to another woman. Such a friendship is deeper and more secure.

A man is more democratic in his dealings and is able to keep separate his business and personal relationships. A man in speaking to his next-door neighbor inquires where he purchased his lawnmower, the type of motor, the type of blade, the type of action, and the construction of the frame. The answers will be direct and to the point. This same man can sit down at the table and start cutting a piece of meat that his wife has served him and ask one simple question: "Where did you get this meat?" She will answer: "What's the matter, isn't it any good?" The emotional woman always thinks in relationship to herself. This is a subjective, emotional type of individual. It is feminine.

A man ordinarily is less religious than a woman. There is much in Christianity, as well as in any religion, that defies logic. It is this logic that gets in a man's way and keeps him from being as religious as a woman. The woman's emotional dependency finds a solidarity in religious concepts.

A man in relationship to a woman is and must be, because of his structure, a dominant individual. He is the aggressive person in the relationship. He is the hunter, fighter, provider, defender, protector, and lover of his mate. This dominance and aggressiveness has its biblical correlation in the words, "The male is the head."

The female is the submissive creature. She is the one to be hunted for, fought for, provided for, defended, protected, and loved. The female is the dependent creature. She is dependent upon her male for her emotional security. She is his helper — he is her leader. Being a dependent creature, she places, and wants her male to take, responsibility for many things in the relationship.

A man was made to love, a woman was made to be loved. A man does not need love, he needs respect. This he must earn. He will receive it if he is a dependable man. This is what a woman wants and needs. She expresses it in the words, "I want a man."

The little things count with a woman. It is a little bunch of violets on a cold day without any reason at all, just because the husband loves her. It is that wink during a commercial while watching a television program. It is an unexpected "I love you" during a telephone call or even during the evening meal. These little gestures, genuinely and continuously flowing give the security the woman needs.

A woman is a sensitive creature because she is an emotional being. Her sensitivity is necessary, not only to complement her husband, but also to be sensitive to her motherhood.

A wife is a husband's greatest asset, his greatest possession. She belongs to him and is above his wealth, his money, his job, his status, his position, and, in a sense, himself. She is his purpose for life. Without her contribution all his traits and forces would be frustrated for lack of fulfillment. The Lord validated this when he said of the man, "He that findeth a wife, findeth a good thing."

On the basis of the above premises, conclusions can be drawn in relation to the marital state. Nowhere in psychological literature will you find the statement that directs a woman to love her husband. You can search the Bible from Genesis to Revelation and you will find no statement where God has commanded or demanded that a woman love her husband with an agapé love. It's always turned around — "Husbands, love your wives." A woman is like a pump that must be primed. If the water of love is put into her she will automatically respond with love; she does not have to be commanded to do so. This is innate in the feminine character.

Therefore, since marriage in its essence is an emotional relationship between a male and a female, and this emotion is love, the responsibility for the success or failure of a marriage weighs far heavier upon the man than it does upon the woman. This is the design of creation; it cannot be changed.

The most successful marriages operate on an equalitarian or democratic basis which gives both an opportunity to exercise their identity in their interrelationship. However, we must remember that every democracy must have its head — which is natural to the male. To this the mature woman wants to submit ("obey").

Take another look at your spouse. Learn to understand each other within the basic structure which you really are. Learn to know yourself so you can fulfill the role for which you were intended. Do not confuse yourself with your spouse nor expect from your spouse what you are. Marriage is not competition, rather it is complementation. With this constantly kept in mind, your marriage definitely will be improved because "male and female created he them."

.•--•--•--•--•--•--•--•--•--•--•--•--•--•-

A happy marriage is a new beginning of life, a new starting point for happiness and usefulness.
— A. P. STANLEY

Listen to Understand

by Paul Tournier, M.D.

Author, To Understand Each Other *and other books on psychological-spiritual problems*

The first condition for the achievement of understanding is the will to understand. The second condition is expressing oneself. Every human being needs to express himself. There are men who complain of the poor health of their wives without realizing that the latter are sick simply because their husbands never listen to them. In order to express oneself, there must be a feeling of warm and kind receptivity and of attentive listening.

Each of us easily finds cause for avoiding real encounter. One wife told me, "When I start to speak to my husband about important matters, he puts on his hat and goes out; he heads off to his lodge." Another wife, however, may interrupt an important conversation in order to go take care of useful matters, but matters which could well be looked after when her husband is at the office. A deep encounter rarely takes place in a few moments. It must be prepared for by hours of careful drawing together.

A complete unveiling of one's inner thoughts, an absolute necessity for real and deep understanding, demands a great deal of courage. I was listening for some time to a woman who was telling me about her husband; speaking about him, in fact, much more than about herself. "Really," I said to her, "you are afraid of your husband." Our contact was strong enough for her to answer me honestly, "Yes, I am afraid of my husband."

Let us not suppose for a moment that wives are alone in

Copyright 1967 M. E. Bratcher

being afraid. Husbands too are afraid of their wives. A man will hide his fears by means of his authoritarian manner. By one word, harsh and cutting, he stops his wife's talking and puts an end to the conversation which he fears. Or else he gives grandiose intellectual and scientific explanations which save him from any personal commitment. He wants to have the last word always, and veils through his overtalking his fear of being contradicted. Perhaps the same end is achieved through a display of anger or, again, through obstinate silence.

What is this fear? I believe there are two parts to it. First, there is the fear of being judged, the fear of criticism. This is a universal fear, and far greater than we generally suppose. Moreover, it is from our wife, or our best friend, from the very people that we admire and love the most, that we fear critical judgment the most. This is precisely because their admiration and love mean so much to us.

It is true that many couples are quick in judging one another. One judgment responds to another in a sort of vicious and diabolical circle. Each, in order to protect his failings from the other, denounces the other's shortcomings, either inwardly or out loud. Few people really accept the fact that their marital partner behaves in a profoundly different way from themselves. How often you hear them say, "I cannot understand my husband" or "I cannot understand my wife."

"I cannot understand my wife," a husband says; "she complains of fatigue and yet in the evening she can never decide to go to bed. She runs around doing a thousand useless things. It's useless for me to tell her to go to bed. Nothing doing. It is both stupid and irritating." It would be important to know what makes her so nervously active in the evening.

Here is a wife who complains, "I cannot understand why my husband finds it so hard to get up in the morning. I have to call him again and again. Then, when he does arise, he has no time for breakfast and he arrives late at his office. He will end up by losing his job. It is senseless." What would be most interesting to know is why this man finds getting up so difficult. He probably doesn't know the reason himself. What he does know is that his mother scolded him for the same thing years ago, and that all his resolutions to improve have remained unfulfilled.

The "I cannot understand" really means, "I cannot understand that my husband is different from me, that he thinks, feels, and acts in a quite different manner than I." So the husband feels judged, condemned, criticized. All of us fear this, for no one is satisfied with himself. We are specially sensitive to blame for shortcomings which we ourselves find stupid, and which we have never been able to correct in spite of our sincerest efforts.

There is a second fear, that of receiving advice. Let us take the example of a husband who is having trouble at the office. At first he mentions this to his wife, but she, carried away by a zeal to come to his aid, replies too readily, "You absolutely must get rid of that ineffective associate. Stand up for yourself, or he'll walk right over you! How many times have I told you already you're too weak! Go and report this to the management . . ." In other words, she gives a shower of inapplicable counsels. This woman does not realize the complexity of the problems which her husband must face up to. And he feels that she holds him responsible for all his problems, and treats him like a little boy.

The husband began by unveiling his anxieties, but in the face of such ready-made answers, he withdraws. He is crushed in his hope before being able to show his wife all the aspects of a delicate problem. The wife's intention was excellent, but she ruined everything by replying too quickly. She should have listened longer and tried to understand.

It is tragic because the wife tried to help her husband. One of the highest functions of a wife is to console her husband for all the blows he receives in life. Yet, in order to console, there is no need to say very much. It is enough to listen, to understand, to love.

People are always much more sensitive than we believe them to be. Often men are just as easily hurt as women, even though they hide it. They are afraid of being hurt by advice just as much as by criticism. They resent it every bit as much. A woman for whom everything seems clear-cut, who confidently tells her husband how he must act in order to do the right things, no matter what the problem may be — such a woman gives her husband the impression that she thinks him incompetent. No husband can put up with this.

Naturally, the reverse is just as true of the husband who replies too readily to the problems his wife confides to him, and who wants to give her good advice. She may be in conflict with a neighbor who gives hurting looks or utters cutting words. "Don't take it seriously," he quickly replies. "Of what importance is all that? You are too sensitive!" The wife then feels misunderstood by her husband. She even feels that he sides with the neighbor — instead of sticking up for her. Thus she becomes in fact ever more sensitive to daily affronts. Nor can she any longer feel free to unburden herself by talking about it to her husband.

In order really to understand, we need to listen, not to reply. We need to listen long and attentively. In order to help anybody to open his heart, we have to give him time, asking only a few questions, as carefully as possible, in order to help him better explain his experience. Above all we must not give the impression that we know better than he does what he must do. Otherwise we force him to withdraw. Too much criticism will also achieve the same result, so fragile are his inner sensitivities.

There are also husbands who say, "I do not want to bur-

den my wife with worry; I keep my problems to myself."
A woman can bear any anxiety when she feels supported
by her husband, and meets every blow head-on, along
with him. The worst worry for a woman is perhaps that of
feeling that her husband is weighed down with problems
which he does not share with her.

There are many misunderstood people in this world.
But when we look at them close up, we realize that they
are always at least partly responsible themselves. If they
are not understood, it is because they have not opened
up.

Why, then, is it that so many people in my office say to
me, "With you I can open up, because you understand"?
The truth is rather the reverse; I understand them because
they open up. Sometimes I understand them much better
than their partners, because they tell me everything they
hold back from them.

Those near to him have already their preconceived image
of the person speaking, and this image is always to some
extent false, and to some extent falsifies the meaning of what
he has to say.

The same is true between man and wife. Each has a certain image of the other, partially right, but just as surely
partially wrong. In any case it is too rigid, an imaginary
view, an idea more or less forced by the other, a sort of
diagnosis superimposed upon him.

As soon as a husband feels that his wife has superimposed her moral diagnosis upon him, from which nothing
can budge her, all true openness, all deep expression of
himself, dries up. It may then happen that this husband
will begin to speak with some girl whom he meets at the
office or the sports club. He will open up easily to her
about many things which he no longer dares to tell his wife.
He will rediscover then the wonderful feeling for which
every human being hungers, that of being understood. He
will perhaps even speak to her of his marital problems.

Men easily soften a woman's heart by means of their marriage disappointments. In my office this husband will possibly say, "I cannot live without that young woman. She understands me, while my wife does not." Tragedy is fast approaching!

.•..•..•..•..•..•..•..•..•..•..•..•..•..•..•.

How Jews Look at Marriage
What are some of the principles of Judaism with regard to marriage?
Judaism takes its text from the patriarch Isaac. Genesis 24 says of Isaac that he took Rebekah, a strange girl that had been chosen by his father's servant as a worthy wife. Isaac took Rebekah, she became his wife, and he loved her.

Young people today need to learn the lesson that love comes after marriage. Too many people today expect marriage to be like courtship. They find little satisfaction in the warm and lasting love that comes after marriage. Their expectation condemns them to unhappiness in marriage even with the most ideal mate.

There is another lesson that Judaism derives from the story of Isaac's marriage: marriages should be contracted on objective factors, such as similarity in background, interest, education, and values.

Still another lesson taught by Isaac and Rebekah is that the couple entered marriage with a commitment to make it work. Many marriages fail today because spouses do not see that in marriage we have as strong an obligation to our partner as we do to ourselves.

What Judaism teaches about marriage is not very startling or unusual. You might call it just common sense.
— Rabbi FRANK M. WALDORF

2

SEEING YOURSELF

Don't Blame Your Parents

by Jacob H. Conn, M.D., as told to Edith M. Stern

Assistant Professor of Psychiatry, Johns Hopkins University Medical School

The unsuccessful, the unhappy at various periods in history have blamed their plight on various things — fate, the gods, demons, innate cussedness, or heredity. Today it is the fashion to hold one's parents accountable for every flaw, from plain laziness to mental illness: "I can't save money because my parents never taught me economy." "I'm a hypochondriac because my mother fussed so much about my health when I was little." "In childhood I wasn't permitted to think for myself."

A woman I know actually blamed her parents for her unattractive appearance. Asked why she didn't wave her hair, powder her nose, or occasionally get a new hat, she answered plaintively, "When I was a child Mother always told me I wasn't good looking." It did not occur to her that as an adult it was up to her, and nobody else, to make the most of her looks.

The current notion is that little children are emotionally fragile, that you can wreck a child's whole future by loving him too little or too much, by teaching him the facts of life too late or too soon, by being too strict or too indulgent.

Copyright 1952 The Reader's Digest Assn., Inc.

Such half-baked misinterpretations of the importance of the formative years ignore the fact that most human beings are blessed with an inner strength. Actually the average child is as tough psychologically as he is physically. Just as the body repels germs and viruses, so has the mind similar immunities and resistances to the unwise or unkind doings of parents.

History is full of examples of men and women who had unhappy childhoods and yet made a success of their lives. John Stuart Mill became a great philosopher and led a harmonious married life despite a father who never praised him, never allowed him to associate with other children, and relentlessly forced him to study night after night. Beethoven's ne'er-do-well father drove and exploited him shamelessly. Florence Nightingale's parents hemmed her in by all the restrictions that went with Victorian gentility, and bitterly opposed her going into nursing.

Ordinary mortals likewise have the capacity to build worthwhile lives despite a past full of psychological handicaps. I do not deny that "parental rejection" or "overdomination" may genuinely handicap some individuals. But a human being is not a machine that once set rolling in the wrong direction is unable to change its course. The essence of maturity or "adjustment" is to make the most of yourself with whatever you have, which includes your physique, your mental endowments, your social opportunities, and your parents.

Almost daily in my practice I see patients who blame their failure to meet life on their parents instead of on themselves. A fearful, immature spinster wept that she "couldn't leave Mother." Yet her mother told me: "Doctor, I wish to goodness you'd help her, so that she'd go and get married." Nothing tied this woman to her mother's apron strings but knots of her own making.

"No wonder I'm the way I am," a seriously depressed man said to me. "Look!" He pulled from his pocket a yellowed newspaper clipping that told of his parents' double suicide twenty years before. He admitted that he had carried the clipping all those years. The heart of his problem was not the shocking memory but his compulsion to dwell on it.

Contrary to popular notion, mental illness or neuroticism is not caused by an event but by the way a person reacts to it. A disturbing incident is only the match which sets off the firecracker; it's the gunpowder within the cracker which actually causes the explosion. It is good old-fashioned character — a compound of inherited tendencies and our ability to tolerate disappointments — that determines whether we withstand childhood tragedies or whether they down us all our lives.

If it were true that what happens during childhood fixes us once and for all, everybody would be neurotic. Certain events in childhood are genuinely upsetting, among them weaning, and a new baby in the family. But the normal individual outgrows the unhappy experiences of his childhood just as he outgrows his baby shoes.

The great majority of normal, healthy-minded youngsters manage, without special help, to cope matter-of-factly with their parents' antics. Just try to spoil a child who has such innate common sense that he doesn't need or want to be spoiled! Or try to dominate the average three-year-old. Children who do not have the neurotic need to be dependent will not be dominated. Maybe they react with tantrums. Maybe they argue. Maybe they are sullenly silent. But whatever the technique for maintaining their integrity, "Momism" won't and can't wreck them.

The psychiatrist's job does not consist — as many of my patients think — of breaking apart a person's past so that he can lay his failings, weaknesses, and peculiarities right at his parents' door. All that a psychiatrist can do is to lead the patient to face the truth about his own wish to be dominated or sheltered or what not, and help him take a stand by himself. Once that point is reached, his past life matters very little. As Dr. Franz Alexander, distinguished Chicago psychoanalyst, put it, "The patient is suffering not so much from memories as from the incapacity to deal with the actual problems of the moment."

A single experience in adult life can so change human beings that it is sheer nonsense to maintain that their natures were immutably determined years before by what their parents said or did to them. A short illness turned St. Francis of Assisi from a frivolous, extravagant young man into a devout ascetic. Gay young blades marry and become serious and responsible husbands; gadabout young wives turn into settled stay-at-homes after the birth of a baby. The human organism is a going, changing concern, with the motives of the present its propelling force.

Too many of us with shortcomings are interested in asking, "How did it start?" Too few ask themselves, "Why do I keep it up?" Anyone who really wants to be grown-up emotionally must first make the frank self-admission, "I am worrisome — or thriftless, or hypochondriac, or irresponsible — because it suits some purpose of my own to be that way."

The cliché "There are no problem children, only problem parents" is as extreme and fallacious a swing of the pendulum as the idea that all children were imps of Satan. Even a little child can be responsible for his own bad upbringing, for it takes two to make an emotional bargain. When a father is too authoritarian it may well be that he is so because the child craves being bossed. When a mother prolongs treating Junior like a baby it may be because she responds to his own need for protection. Children are not mere lumps of clay which adults mold. In the parent-child relationship, as in marriage, one personality modifies and plays upon another.

Parents can set the stage for the drama of their children's lives. They can supply inspiring or uninspiring examples of conduct which will influence basic mental, physical, and spiritual growth. But acceptance or rejection of the background they give is a matter of the child's individual character.

·•··•··•··•··•··•··•··•··•··•··•··•··•··•·

Understanding Yourself

"You shall love your neighbor as yourself."
You must accept yourself. But the snag is this: you cannot accept yourself as you now are. If you did you would accept a self you could not respect. This would mean that you would be adjusted to a half-self.

When psychiatry urges you to accept yourself, both truth and fallacy are involved. It is true that you must not be rejecting and hating yourself. To live in a state of self-rejection and self-hate is as bad as living in other-rejection and other-hate. But there is a sense in which you cannot accept yourself — cannot accept yourself as you are. If you did you would settle down to accepting a half-self instead of a whole self. You would be adjusted on a very low level. And to be adjusted on a very low level is a very high tragedy. The end in view must not be adjustment, but adjustment to the highest — and that highest is Christ.

Then the Christian position, as I see it, is this: accept yourself in God. In yourself you do not accept yourself, for that would mean the acceptance of a low type of self. It would mean a moral and spiritual stalemate. But when you surrender yourself to God then you can accept yourself there. First of all, because God accepts you, and if he accepts you then you must accept when he accepts. And, second, because you accept a self that is in the process of being made.

— E. STANLEY JONES

Why You Are You

by Tim LaHaye

Author, How to Be Happy Though Married, *and Pastor, Scott Memorial Baptist Church, San Diego, California*

"What makes people like us marry in the first place?" asked a Christian woman after thirteen years of marriage. "We have a hopeless personality conflict! We seem to bring out the worst in each other." Although this example is more extreme than most of the Christian couples I have counseled, it has been apparent to me for years that opposite personalities attract each other.

What makes people different? There are four basic inborn temperaments of people, each with their strengths and weaknesses, and the Holy Spirit working in the life of a Christian is able to help him overcome his weaknesses. Usually one temperament type predominates in an individual, but strains of one or two of the others will always be found.

A person with the *Sanguine* temperament is warm, buoyant, and lively. He is naturally receptive and his emotions rather than reflective thoughts are the basis of most of his decisions. He enjoys people and is often "the life of the party."

He is likely to speak before thinking, but his open sincerity has a disarming effect on many of his listeners, causing them to respond to his mood.

Mr. Sanguine is usually voted "The Man Most Likely to Succeed," but he often falls short of this prediction. His weakness of will may make him ineffective and undepend-

Copyright 1968 Tyndale House Publishers

able. He tends to be restless, undisciplined, egotistical, and emotionally explosive.

The *Choleric* temperament is found in the hot, quick, active, practical, and strong-willed person. He tends to be self-sufficient, independent, decisive, and opinionated. He has a practical, keen mind that is capable of making instant decisions and planning worthwhile, long-range projects. He takes a definite stand on issues and can often be found crusading for some great social cause. He possesses dogged determination and is still pushing ahead after others have become discouraged and quit.

Mr. Choleric's emotional nature is the least developed part of his temperament. He does not sympathize easily with others. Indeed, he is often embarrassed or disgusted by the tears of others. He is not given to analysis, therefore he tends to look at the goal for which he is working without seeing the potential pitfalls and obstacles in the path. Once he has started toward his goal, he will run roughshod over individuals who stand in his way.

His weaknesses usually make him a difficult person to live with, for he may be hot-tempered, cruel, impetuous, and self-sufficient. The person with this temperament is often more appreciated by friends and associates than by members of his family.

The *Melancholy* person is an analytical, self-sacrificing, gifted perfectionist with a very sensitive emotional nature. He is usually dominated by his emotions. Sometimes his moods will lift him to heights of ecstasy and at other times he will become gloomy and depressed, and quite antagonistic.

Mr. Melancholy is a faithful friend, but he does not make friends easily. He will not push himself forward to meet people, but rather waits for people to come to him. He is perhaps the most dependable of all the temperaments, for his perfectionist tendencies do not permit him to be a shirker or let others down when they are depending on him.

He has a strong desire to be loved, but disappointing experiences make him reluctant to take people at their face value, and thus he is suspicious when others seek him out or shower him with attention.

His exceptional analytical ability causes him to diagnose accurately the obstacles and dangers of any project. This characteristic often finds the Melancholy either hesitant to initiate some new project or in conflict with those who wish to.

Mr. Melancholy usually finds his greatest meaning in life through personal sacrifice. He seems to have a desire to make himself suffer and will often choose a difficult vocation involving great personal sacrifice. He has much natural potential when energized by the Holy Spirit.

The weaknesses of the Melancholy are numerous. He tends to be self-centered, sensitive, pessimistic, critical, moody, and vengeful. He often has more problems making emotional adjustments to life than others, and when overwhelmed by weaknesses he is consumed by persecution complexes, excessive guilt complexes, depression, hypochrondria, groundless fears, and hostility.

The *Phlegmatic* temperament is calm, cool, slow, easy going, and well balanced. He is the one temperament type that is steadily consistent. He feels much more emotion than appears on the surface and has a good capacity to appreciate the fine arts and the better things of life.

He tends to be a spectator in life and tries not to get too involved with the activities of others. He and Mr. Choleric may see the same social injustice, but their responses will be entirely different. The crusading spirit of the choleric will cause him to say, "Let's get a committee organized and campaign to do something about this!" Mr. Phlegmatic would be more likely to respond by saying, "These conditions are terrible! Why doesn't someone do something about them?"

Mr. Phlegmatic is usually kindhearted and sympathetic, and is a natural peacemaker.

The Phlegmatic's chief weakness, and the one that often keeps him from fulfilling his potential, is lack of motivation — or laziness.

He is usually easy to live with, but his careless, low-pressure way of life can be a source of irritation to an aggressive partner. Phlegmatics usually make good companions to their children; it is easier for them to stop what they are doing and play with the children than for the activist temperaments. Many a hard-driving husband will say of his Phlegmatic wife, "She is a wonderful wife and mother but a lousy housekeeper." Conversely, the flawless housewife may be a "poor" mother. She would like to stop and play with the children, but the floor needs scrubbing, the clothes need washing, etc. These subconscious reactions to life-situations are a part of our temperaments.

Temperament is important to this study in marital happiness because it helps explain why people are so different. It also offers a key as to why opposites attract each other.

The subconscious mind has far more influence on us than most people realize. This is graphically seen in the way we usually select our friends — and particularly by our choice of a life partner. The loud, gregarious, extroverted Sanguine subconsciously wishes he could control himself better. When he returns from a party, he is often secretly embarrassed by his endless chatter and domination of conversations. The sweet, quiet Phlegmatic or Melancholic person subconsciously thinks, "I wish I could be more outgoing and expressive." It is very easy to see why these contrasting types will be interested in each other when they meet. He is everything she wishes to be, and she is just what he would secretly like to be; thus, they seem naturally to complement each other. The important thing to note is that people are attracted to each other on the basis of strengths, but each natural strength has a corresponding weakness.

Most couples are so much in love they see only the strengths of the other person before marriage. After the novelty of marriage is over, however, each partner's weaknesses (and every human being has them) begin to appear. These weaknesses call for adjustment — that is, learning to live with the partner's weaknesses. It is important for a married couple to have the Holy Spirit's help so that they might be "gentle, patient, kind, and self-controlled" while adjusting to these weaknesses. Also, the Holy Spirit helps turn weaknesses into positive attributes. Galatians 5:22-23 points out nine characteristics available to the Spirit-filled Christian: a strength for every natural weakness. A Spirit-filled Christian attains more enjoyment in his marriage because he uses the Holy Spirit's help to overcome his weaknesses; and thus, he becomes less objectionable to his partner. In addition, the Holy Spirit gives him grace to overlook and joyously live with his partner's weaknesses.

Personality conflicts are in reality conflicting weaknesses and could be called temperament conflicts. They are weaknesses in one partner that irritate the weaknesses in the other. Here are some examples I have encountered in counseling.

Mr. Sanguine's carelessness and unfinished projects create a great conflict for his Melancholy wife's perfectionist and faithful tendencies. When he comes home late from a sales meeting and his wife has had supper waiting for two hours, she has a hard time "forgiving and forgetting" his thoughtlessness.

Mr. Choleric gives his active mind to the business of making a living and his wife feels neglected. She doesn't realize that before marriage she was his project and that he had given himself 100 percent, as he usually does, to reaching his goal of marrying her. Now that the "marriage project" is accomplished, he is off on the next step in his plan, to support her. If she is careless, he may get very irritated at her disorganization and lash her with cruel, sarcastic words. He now sees her gracious, calm manner — as he thought of her before marriage — as "laziness and lack of motivation."

Mrs. Melancholy often falls into a black mood shortly after marriage. The natural letdown after the tense, exciting anticipation of her wedding can lead to a period of depression. If her husband is impatient and frustrated, she may lapse into silence, hypochondria, or weeping. Her supersensitivity can make her suspicious that "he doesn't love me any more." Her perfectionism when motivated into housekeeping can create a flawlessly kept house in which her husband can seldom feel relaxed and at home. She can get upset if he puts his feet on the coffee table or doesn't pick up his socks. One of her biggest temptations is to keep all of her frustrations bottled up inside her, where they ultimately "explode" or produce nervousness, ulcers, or other maladies.

Mr. Phlegmatic's lack of motivation becomes a drain on his partner. A natural "stay at home" type, he can become boring unless he learns to push himself for his partner's sake. However, he can begin an activity "just for the wife's sake" and, before he realizes it, have a good time himself. He does a good job of house repairs — if she can ever get him going. One Choleric mother I know gave her Choleric daughter, married to a Phlegmatic husband, this sage advice: "Shirley, when you get him up, keep him moving." A Phlegmatic partner is less inclined to be generous than a Sanguine, and this factor added to quiet stubbornness can create great resentment and frustration.

Differences between partners need not be fatal! No disagreement is a threat to a marriage; it's what a couple does about disagreements that determines the success or failure of a marriage. Many a good marriage today once experienced vigorous temperament conflicts.

The following suggestions are given to help you make the right kind of adjustments.

When you feel frustration, resentment, or some other form of hostility, stop and take an objective look at what causes it.

Pray about it. First, confess your sin of grieving the Holy Spirit (Ephesians 4:30-32). Your peace of mind does not depend on your partner's behavior. After facing your inner hostility and anger as sin and confessing it (1 John 1:9), ask God to fill you with his Spirit (Luke 11:13) then walk in the Spirit (Galatians 5:16). Second, pray about your partner's actions, asking God to help him see his shortcomings and to lead you in discussing the matter with him.

Communicate with your partner about his fault. This should always be done "in love" (Ephesians 4:15). Pick a relaxed time when you can objectively share your feelings without getting overly emotional. Never speak in anger, and always allow time for him to think about what you've said. Then leave the matter up to the Holy Spirit.

Ask God, the giver of love, to fill you with love for him and for your partner so that you can genuinely love him in spite of his weaknesses. Look at his strengths and thank God for them (1 Thessalonians 5:18).

Forget past mistakes and sins! Follow Paul's example: "Forgetting those things which are behind, and reaching forth unto those things which are before, I press toward the mark for the prize of the high calling of God in Christ Jesus" (Philippians 3:13b-14).

If you repeatedly follow this procedure, you will find that your reaction to your partner's actions will be led by the Holy Spirit and your love will increase so that, like paint, it will cover a multitude of weaknesses.

Love Yourself

by R. Lofton Hudson

Author, Growing a Christian Personality, *and Director, Midwest Christian Counseling Center, Kansas City, Missouri*

"Thou shalt love thy neighbor as thyself," Jesus said. "He that loveth his wife loveth himself. For no man ever yet hated his own flesh," wrote the Apostle Paul (Eph. 5:28-29). He meant that it is normal to love self and that it is abnormal to hate self.

One of the most significant findings of modern psychology is that people cannot love others unless they have a healthy self-love. A person who is always striking out at other people in criticism, snobbishness, foul words, bitterness, or gossip is a person who does not feel right toward himself.

This is at the very heart of most of our moral and spiritual problems. If a person does not have a healthy self-love, his religion will not work right; he cannot love his neighbors, and he cannot believe that either they or God loves him. This is one of the most important insights for our spiritual living.

All of us have met religious people who were obsessed with doubt, who felt that they were lost and could not be saved, who seldom felt close to God, and who never felt at home with people. These are people who have contempt for themselves. The depressed person is angry at himself. This is a kind of hate also. Each year between 15,000 and 20,000 people in the United States commit suicide. Self-destruction is the climax of a long period of self-hate.

The facts are, as any experienced and well-trained counselor can tell you, that the ability to love others or to receive

Copyright 1955 Broadman Press

love from others is in direct proportion to a personal self-love. We judge others exactly as we judge ourselves. If we cannot love ourselves, we cannot love our neighbors. If we do not feel secure and worthwhile at the very core of our beings, we will not respect other people as they really are.

After all, I myself am one of the people whom I have a moral obligation to respect. I must accept myself in the very shape and form in which God has made me. Of course, there are some things about ourselves which we do not like, try as we may. And we need a kind of "divine discontent" with our present attainments. But this is quite different from self-hate.

The person who hates himself will pretend to be different from what he is; the hypocrite belongs to this group. Or he will place an abnormal emphasis on money or culture or personal attainments; the superficial belong here. Or he will demand for himself attention, special consideration, and the right to strike out at others if things do not go to suit him. Selfish people are starving for love because they do not love themselves.

There is a kind of self-love which is childish and sinful. The psychologists call it narcissism after the young man in Greek mythology who looked into the water and fell in love with his own image. This kind of person is very much like the child from three to five years of age. He is the "I-me-mine" sort of being. Paul refers to these people in his description of evil men who will inhabit the earth in the last days, "Men shall be lovers of their own selves" (2 Tim. 3:2). Such people can love themselves only or those who are images of themselves. It is a sad state of infantilism.

But the healthy self-love grows out of being loved. If someone loves us, warmly accepts us with all of our individuality and weakness, we learn to give love to others. If this does not occur to us in childhood, we feel inadequate, unworthy, empty, inferior, and worthless.

If we are ever to be comfortable, valuable, self-reliant, and self-directing — under God — individuals, we must make peace with ourselves. This is where the love of God becomes effective. Salvation consists of God's coming to us in love and teaching us that in his sight we are valuable. Then we can love others and enjoy their love.

·•··•··•··•··•··•··•··•··•··•··•··•··•··•·

Love must be learned, and learned again and again; there is no end to it. Hate needs no instruction, but waits only to be provoked.

— KATHERINE ANNE PORTER

You Are Somebody

by Maxwell Maltz, M.D.

Author, Psycho-Cybernetics: The New Way to a Successful Life

At least 95 percent of the people have their lives blighted by feelings of inferiority to some extent, and to millions this same feeling of inferiority is a serious handicap to success and happiness.

In one sense of the word, every person on the face of the earth is inferior to some other persons or person. I know that I cannot lift as much weight as Paul Anderson, throw a 16-pound shot as far as Parry O'Brien, or dance as well as Arthur Murray. I know this, but it does not induce feelings of inferiority within me and blight my life — simply because I do not compare myself unfavorably with them and feel that I am no good merely because I cannot do certain things as skillfully or as well as they. I also know that in certain areas, every person I meet, from the newsboy on the corner to the president of the bank, is superior to me in certain respects. But neither can any of these people repair a scarred face, or do any number of other things as well as I. And I am sure they do not feel inferior because of it.

Feelings of inferiority originate not so much from "facts" or experiences, but from our conclusions regarding facts, and our evaluation of experiences. For example, the fact is that I am an inferior weight lifter and an inferior dancer. This does not, however, make me an "inferior person." Paul Anderson's and Arthur Murray's inability to perform surgery makes them "inferior surgeons," but not "inferior

Copyright 1960 Prentice-Hall, Inc.

persons." It all depends upon "what" and "whose" norms we measure ourselves by.

It is not knowledge of actual inferiority in skill or knowledge which gives us an inferiority complex and interferes with our living. It is the feeling of inferiority that does this. And this feeling of inferiority comes about for just one reason: we judge ourselves and measure ourselves not against our own norm or par but against some other individual's norm. When we do this, we always, without exception, come out second best. But because we think and believe and assume that we should measure up to some other person's norm, we feel miserable and second-rate, and conclude that there is something wrong with us. The next logical conclusion in this cockeyed reasoning process is to conclude that we are not "worthy," that we do not deserve success and happiness, and that it would be out of place for us to fully express our own abilities and talents, whatever they might be, without apology or without feeling guilty about it.

All this comes about because we have allowed ourselves to be hypnotized by the entirely erroneous idea that "I should be like so-and-so" or "I should be like everybody else." The fallacy of the second idea can be readily seen through, if analyzed, for in truth there are no fixed standards common to "everybody else." "Everybody else" is composed of individuals, no two of whom are alike.

The person with an inferiority complex invariably compounds the error by striving for superiority. His feelings spring from the false premise that he is inferior. From this false premise, a whole structure of "logical thought" and feeling is built. If he feels bad because he is inferior, the cure is to make himself as good as everybody else, and the way to feel really good is to make himself superior. This striving for superiority gets him into more trouble, causes more frustration, and sometimes brings about a neurosis where none existed before. He becomes more miserable than ever, and "the harder he tries" the more miserable he becomes.

Inferiority and superiority are reverse sides of the same coin. The cure lies in realizing that the coin itself is spurious.

The truth about you is this:

You are not "inferior."

You are not "superior."

You are simply "you."

"You" as a personality are not in competition with any other personality, simply because there is not another person on the face of the earth like you, or in your particular class. You are an individual. You are unique. You are not "like" any other person and can never become like any other person. You are not "supposed" to be like any other person and no other person is "supposed" to be like you.

God did not create a standard person and in some way label that person by saying, "This is it." He made every human being individual and unique just as he made every snowflake individual and unique.

God created short people and tall people, large people and small people, skinny people and fat people, black, yellow, red, and white people. He has never indicated any preference for any one size, shape, or color. Abraham Lincoln once said, "God must have loved the common people for he made so many of them." He was wrong. There is no "common man" — no standardized common pattern. He would have been nearer the truth had he said, "God must have loved uncommon people for he made so many of them."

An "inferiority complex," and its accompanying deterioration in performance, can be made to order in the psychological laboratory. All you need to do is to set up a "norm" or "average," then convince your subject he does not measure up. A psychologist wanted to find how feelings of inferiority affected ability to solve problems. He gave his students a set of routine tests. "Then he solemnly announced that the average person could complete the test in about one-fifth the time it would really take. When in the course of the test a bell would ring, indicating that the 'average man's' time was up, some of the brightest subjects became very jittery and incompetent indeed, thinking themselves to be morons." ("What's On Your Mind?" *Science Digest,* Feb. 1952.)

Stop measuring yourself against "their" standards. You are not "them" and can never measure up. Neither can "they" measure up to yours — nor should they. Once you see this simple, rather self-evident truth, accept it, and believe it, your inferior feelings will vanish.

Dr. Norton L. Williams, a psychiatrist addressing a medical convention, said recently that modern man's anxiety and insecurity stemmed from a lack of "self-realization," and that inner security can only be found "in finding in oneself an individuality, uniqueness, and distinctiveness that is akin to the idea of being created in the image of God." He also said that self-realization is gained by "a simple belief in one's own uniqueness as a human being, a sense of deep and wide awareness of all people and all things, and a feeling of constructive influencing of others through one's own personality."

There is no use straining to "be somebody." You are what you are — now. You are somebody, not because you've made a million dollars or drive the biggest car in your block — but because God created you in his own image.

Measuring Your Emotions

by William C. Menninger, M.D.

Contributor, A Treasury of Success Unlimited, *and President, Menninger Foundation*

The need to grow up emotionally is vital for each of us, because emotional maturity is related directly to good mental health.

In your total psychological life there are many facets such as the intellectual aspect, the social, and others that we can measure as to their degree of effectiveness and maturity, and any of these aspects can mature alongside of another aspect that doesn't mature.

For example, the intellectual genius who actually is a social blacksmith can't get along with people even though he is so brilliant that he makes the rest of us a little uncomfortable because of his brilliance. There is the successful businessman who is a flop as a father. There is the meticulous housewife who keeps her home so spick-and-span that it's a little uncomfortable to be in and yet, unfortunately, she doesn't know how to make love.

I have selected seven potential yardsticks for measuring your emotional maturity, although there are more. As you read, be honest with yourself, and perhaps you will form ideas that will help you change your personality — and your life.

1. *Deal constructively with reality.* There is much selfishness, suspicion, hostility, lack of understanding, dishonesty, and violence in the world we live in. That's reality. Now it's quite normal for small children and very seriously

Copyright 1966 Combined Registry Co.

ill mental patients to ignore reality, and, although we all try to run from it now and then, most of the time we must stand and face it . . . and sometimes it gets rough.

There are many who cannot accept frustration, and yet reality is such that one cannot live without often being frustrated.

When the going gets rough, how does one maintain his own sense of personal security? There is an internal kind of security that is essential for each of us. In many this is conspicuously absent.

I believe emotional maturity implies that you do not run when the going gets rough nor do you react by destructive fighting. Develop an attitude that is concerned with your aspirations, hopes, and determination for the future, rather than the past. Tell yourself, "I'm making the most of my situation. I can complain about it, but I am a mature person and I will meet the situation with what I have and what I can do." Learn to live without being overwhelmed by the anxieties that surround us all the time.

2. *Have the capacity to change.* Parents, especially, must learn to accept challenges and changes. They cannot expect to run their children as they themselves were brought up. It's a different world. We have a monster that sits over in the corner of the living room, you know, and that, in most cases, pretty nearly destroys family life. There have been many changes in the past twenty-five years, and yet I still see parents who refuse to change or to grow with their children. There are still too many people who go through life by hammering on the desk and wanting what they want, when they want it, because they won't change and they won't grow up.

They fail to learn from experience and so they don't grow. They keep using old techniques and they keep failing.

3. *Be free of tension and anxiety symptoms.* All of us are at times unreasonable, irrational, and often quite illogical.

These are what we call neurotic evasions. Some individuals are too aggressive, many are too passive, too fearful, too lonesome. It is a device that they utilize to get along and we should recognize it.

Our emotions can give us any kind of physical symptom in the book, from a peptic ulcer to high blood pressure to the "tension headache."

Another neurotic evasion that many of us use is to blame someone else. It's the other partner's fault when you're late or when the buttons don't get sewed on. Some good evidence of our maturity is being able to recognize this fault in ourselves.

I believe we all need a little tension and anxiety. I hope we all have a little bit of restlessness, whether you choose to call it "noble discontent," "righteous indignation," or the anxiety to do things when we see they ought to be done. We all need some motivation, but when your anxiety climbs to the point where a tension headache results then there is a maladjustment.

4. *Find more satisfaction from giving than getting.* We all started as infants on the receiving end of the line, but we truly become an emotionally mature adult when our satisfaction is in giving without reflection on "What's in it for me?" Good mental health for the most mature person is finding a "cause" . . . the earlier in life the better . . . and the bigger the better. Try to find a cause so big that you can work at it enthusiastically and hard all your life. "If you really want to save your life . . . lose it." If you don't have some mission in life, it's later than you think. Find the mission and you will find happiness.

5. *Relate to people.* There is much evidence around us of failures in human relationships. How do you treat your children? Do you reject them one time and accept them another? Are you too busy to spend time with them? From

the individual family to the world in general, we just aren't getting along with each other very well.

How do we acquire that combination of honesty and fairness, dependability and willingness to assume responsibility so that people can count on us? Usually you can sense these qualities in others. You can feel it. Hopefully we can also try to assess these in ourselves . . . with honesty.

6. *Control your hostile impulses.* All of us were born with hostile feelings and impulses. When we recognize them, we have a much better chance to handle them before we turn these hostile expressions on ourselves. Whenever we get a guilt feeling it's because we've been forgetful, thoughtless, nasty, or hostile toward someone. We then turn this feeling on ourselves in various types of self-defeatism. Often we refuse to let ourselves succeed, but we do not understand the reasons for our failure.

Frequently we turn our hate on our family without even being aware of it. There are many disguises for hostility toward the spouse or the children, such as shunning responsibilities, running out, neglect, thoughtlessness, rejection, unfaithfulness, and forgetfulness. There is a wonderful command, "Love thy neighbor as thyself." It's an ideal that any of us, in terms of maturity, should be aiming for every day of our lives.

7. *Love.* The most important measurement of your emotional maturity is how much you can love.

We began in infancy completely dependent upon our parents. If we were fortunate, the Almighty gave us parents that really cared about us. They loved us and we learned to love in return. As we grow we form relations with other people, our playmates, our schoolmates, and our college companions. Eventually we find somebody we truly care about and we extend our capacity to care for someone of the opposite sex. Ultimately we become a family which is the richest reward any of us can have.

Gradually we extend our interests and our capacity to care to the neighborhood, the community, the state, the nation, and the shrinking world which should be the concern of every mature person. Now our love has reached its fullest potential.

Hate can only flourish where love is absent. The only neutralization for hate is love. Therefore, it seems to me, the most important goal for any of us to aim at, regardless of our age, is an increase in our capacity to be interested in others, to be concerned with others, to give to others, to care for others, to love others. Love is the preeminent characteristic of the emotionally mature person.

·•··•··•··•··•··•··•··•··•··•··•··•··•·

Every man has a train of thought on which he rides when he is alone. The dignity and nobility of his life, as well as his happiness, depend upon the direction in which that train is going, the baggage it carries, and the scenery through which it travels.

— JOSEPH FORT NEWTON

Exactly Where Are You Going?

by Mack R. Douglas
Author, How to Make a Habit of Succeeding, *and President, Master Mind, Inc.*

Dr. Maxwell Maltz in his book *Psycho-Cybernetics* says: "We are engineered as goal-seeking mechanisms. We are built that way. When we have no personal goal which we are interested in and which means something to us, we have to go around in circles, feel lost, and find life itself aimless and purposeless. We are built to conquer environment, solve problems, achieve goals, and we find no real satisfaction or happiness in life without obstacles to conquer and goals to achieve. People who say that life is not worthwhile are really saying that they themselves have no personal goals which are worthwhile."

The establishment of goals. Your key for personal success is to establish a goal. Distinguish between goals and purpose. Purpose is the long range — the pot of gold at the end of the rainbow. Goals are more clearly defined, and are concrete, measurable, and related to a definite period. Thomas A. Edison said, "The most important factors of invention can be described in a few words. They consist first of definite knowledge as to what one wishes to achieve. One must fix his mind on that purpose with persistence, and begin searching for that which he seeks. When a man makes up his mind to solve any problem, he may at first meet with dogged opposition, but if he holds on and keeps on searching, he will be sure to find some sort of solution. The trouble with most people is that they quit before they start."

Copyright 1966 Zondervan Publishing House

Find out what you really want to do in life above everything else. Determine your goal. Visualize it in your mind. Picture what you want to be, the kind of person you want to become. Then get all the facts about it. Analyze, discuss, and test these facts. Put them in logical order. Determine how you are going to accomplish your goal.

The next thing to do is to set a time schedule. Don't let anything divert you to chasing rabbits. Stay on the path. Finally, don't just talk about it, get at it. Start out this very moment. Remember that a journey of a thousand miles begins with one step. So start in. And of course the best way to begin a work is to have faith that inevitably it will be successfully completed. Remember the words of Paul J. Meyer, "What you ardently desire, sincerely believe in, vividly imagine, enthusiastically act on must inevitably come to pass."

An excellent example of the dynamics of setting goals is the intensity of purpose, the strength of discipline that's involved in an athletic team, particularly a high school group. The hardest work I ever did in my life was getting in shape for football, both in high school and college. While tearing around the field at the end of practice as darkness was spreading across the stadium, I used to say to myself, "This is the hardest work you have ever done. Why do you continue to do it?" Why? I did it to make the team. I did it to help win the game. I did it for the recognition of the school. I did it for my teammates. The goal was there and the dynamics resulted.

The discipline of goals. Napoleon Hill in *Think and Grow Rich* has listed ten causes for failure in leadership. They are: (1) inability to organize details; (2) unwillingness to render humble service; (3) expectation of pay for what they know instead of what they do with that which they know; (4) fear of competition from followers; (5) lack of imagination; (6) selfishness; (7) intemperance; (8)

disloyalty; (9) emphasis on the authority of leadership; (10) emphasis on title. Each of these qualities of failure is the result of a lack of goals. For goals intensely established, regularly checked on, ardently desired, bring wonderful discipline of action.

Harry Emerson Fosdick once wrote, "No horse gets anywhere till he's harnessed, no steam or gas drives anything until it's confined, no Niagara ever turned anything into light or power until it's tunneled, no life ever grows great until focused, dedicated, and disciplined."

The Apostle Paul became the greatest follower of his Master the world has ever known by the impact of his life and by the dedication of his efforts. He had a goal. It is recorded in Philippians 3:13: "This one thing I do, forgetting those things which are behind and reaching forth unto those things which are before, I press toward the mark. . . ."

Be a one-eyed man. That's what Jesus was saying when he said, "When thine eye is single, thy whole body also is full of light." That's what Andrew Carnegie was recommending when he said, "Put all your eggs in one basket and watch that basket." Concentrate on one purpose and then you will be successful.

Dale Carnegie advised: "A shockingly large number of our worries and our hidden tensions stem from the fact that millions of people have never found themselves, and never discovered the kind of work they could love and do well. Instead they seethe with inner rebellion because they spend their lives doing work they despise." Remember that the definition of success is the persistent achievement of a challenging, worthy goal. I dare you to be different. I dare you to be personally, dynamically successful. You can be. Establish your goal and you will. It is inevitable.

In Albert's book *You Are Better Than You Think*, Dr. Charlotte Buhler of the Psychological Institute in Vienna reports the study of lives of 200 famous men and women. They discovered that in every case there was a self-selected goal that directed all the energies of the individual. "Write down what you want to achieve, then frame the paper on which you have written it and hang it on the wall," said Johnson O'Conner.

Lawrence Gould, the psychologist, commented, "Many a man has been puzzled at the lack of results from his grim determination to succeed when his real unconscious desire was to have a good time and to take life easy. A picture that often comes in my mind is the scene in the old-fashioned melodrama when the heroine pretends to yield to the villain's embraces, but behind his back waves a white handkerchief to call the hero to the rescue."

To achieve any goal there must be the conscious and the unconscious commitment of all that you are to the dedication of the effort of that goal! There must be harmony. There must be energy. There must be oneness in purpose if you are to reach your goal.

Five suggestions for success are:

1. Pay the price. Results are directly proportionate to the effort we put forth. We must understand emotionally that as we sow we reap.

2. Practice imagination. Can you see yourself achieving every bit of the goal you've attempted?

3. Practice courage. Talk positively of your goal. Refuse to believe that there is any circumstance sufficient to its defeat.

4. Save 10 percent of what you earn. Make your dollars your slaves to work for you.

5. Act. The achievement of this program of success demands immediate, dynamic action.

The benefit of goals. One of the outstanding benefits of goals is personal happiness. Life is too short to be unhappy. But you will never be happy until you are achieving a worthy, challenging goal. And remember it cannot be selfish nor can it be evil. A worthy goal will benefit your family. It will benefit your community. It will benefit your church. It will benefit your society, yea, even the nation. You see, your abilities are very closely related to your desires. If you desire little you will exercise little of your capacity.

Augustine said, "Happiness comes in the attainment of our desires and in our having only right desires." As Dale Carnegie has so well put it, "If you want to be happy, set yourself a goal that demands your thoughts, liberates your energy, and inspires your hopes. Happiness is within you. It comes from doing some certain thing to which you can put all of your thought and energy. If you want to be happy, get enthusiastic about something outside yourself."

Act now on setting a long-range goal. You can be successful, but there is no easy way to dynamic success.

Henry Ward Beecher said, "Victories that are cheap are cheap. Those only are worth having which come as the result of hard fighting." Never forget those words, "What the mind can conceive and believe, the mind can achieve."

Goethe, the German philosopher, said, "Before you can do something, you must first be something." In other words, you must act the part.

1. Set one goal at a time — the goal that is most meaningful for you at this particular time.

2. Think about it all the time. Build mind-pictures of your achieving it. Use the five senses to bring your total personality to bear upon it.

3. Drive it into your subconscious mind. Remember your subconscious mind takes orders. It is fantastically creative. It never rests. Make your subconscious mind your willing servant by bringing to fruition the goal that you have set for it.

4. Write out this goal in simple, clear language.

You may wish to write a ten-year goal, then break it down into five-year segments. Certainly divide it into one-year periods and have monthly check-ups and weekly planning and a program of daily improvement.

Yes, you can be successful. You can accomplish great things through the persistent achievement of a challenging, worthy goal. Your key for personal success is through goals, but you must act now.

•-•--•--•--•--•--•--•--•--•--•--•--•--•--•--•--•--•

If anyone would tell you the shortest, surest way to happiness and all perfection, he must tell you to make it a rule to yourself to thank and praise God for everything that happens to you. For it is certain that whatever seeming calamity happens to you, if you thank and praise God for it, you turn it into a blessing.

— WILLIAM LAW

3

UNIQUELY A MAN

Masculine Men

by Wallace Denton
Author, What's Happening to Our Families?

"The only thoroughly masculine domain not yet invaded by women," said one bitter male, "is growing a mustache!" Perhaps this accounts for the fact that more and more men are sporting mustaches or beards. In fact, it could be that the practice may spread if men find it increasingly difficult to determine ways of being distinctively masculine.

One of the commonest problems confronted by persons who do marriage counseling is dealing with men who secretly harbor fears that they are not men. Males are born, but men are made. A husband may be sure he is a male, but highly uncertain as to whether he has acquired those attributes which he considers masculine. This uncertainty opens Pandora's box to a whole host of problems in husband-wife relationships. Demasculinized husbands who are attempting to maintain, regain, or prove their masculinity may find themselves, in addition to being resistant to requests from the wife, involved in what they perceive of as masculine activities such as drinking, gambling, extramarital affairs, and making unilateral family decisions.

Copyright 1963 W. L. Jenkins

The basic pattern of family relationships in most civilizations has been patriarchal. This, of course, simply means, "Father is boss!"

Except for a few pockets of isolated cultures, the patriarchal family in the United States is as about as up-to-date as buttonhooks. A new family is emerging in its place, characterized by democratic ideals of equality for men and women, husbands and wives.

But in this new family, men and women are having to rediscover what it means to be a man or woman in a new setting. As a result of the ensuing confusion, many men have become threatened and defensive, which in turn leads to marital discord and unhappiness. Perhaps it might be of help to examine some expressions of this masculine confusion.

1. *Domineering behavior* characterizes the first of these. The domineering male is almost always preoccupied with being "henpecked," will have little or nothing to do with household responsibilities, nor does he feel comfortable with his wife working outside the home.

Mistaking physical strength for strength of character is also a mark of the domineering husband. He cannot tolerate having his decisions questioned.

Men who are men, and know they are men, have no need to remind their families and themselves continually that they are head of the family.

2. *Sexual problems* may also be an expression of the uncertainty and confusion over masculinity; complete or partial impotence can be one expression. Even slight disinterest in intercourse on the part of a wife is enough to discourage some men from trying. In other cases, men can perform successfully only if the wife takes the initiative in sex.

Male homosexuals are another expression of this uncertainty. At least one of the basic aspects of the problem is that the boy in the formative years of his childhood failed to find in his father a person with whom he could identify. The reasons could be that the father was too threatening and punitive. But the father could also be perceived as a weak, mousy, spineless person whom the boy was unable to accept as a desirable model of masculinity.

3. *Passive dependency* can also be an expression of masculine uncertainty. This dependency may be too threatening to admit. At heart he is a shy or perhaps demanding little boy who is still clinging to his mother. His wife has now taken the place of his mother. Beneath the facade of such "masculine" behavior as getting drunk is a man who has trouble standing alone. And the alcoholic frequently marries a woman who is a competent, controlling person, for he needs the kind of security she can offer. He himself has trouble enacting the role of a man and emotionally has fixated at the level of a little boy.

In some instances there is no facade covering the passive dependency. The passive-dependent husband may express the feeling that he outmarried himself when he got his wife. He continues to wonder why she married him, since he is sure she could have had any man she wanted; but he is particularly sure that he has nothing to offer to the marriage that she needs. The balance of power is shifted to that mate who is contributing the most in meeting the needs of the other mate.

4. *Pseudomasculinity* is the final type to be dealt with here. This man may be a big, double-jointed football player, a weight lifter, a paratrooper, a ranger, or go into underwater demolition work. Masculine reassurance is derived from each dangerous mission undertaken. (Of course, this is not to say that every man who engages in sports or dangerous activities is proving his masculinity.)

Many types of extremist behavior are a defense against hidden fears.

Sources of difficulties are sometimes about as elusive as
the pot of gold at the end of the rainbow. There are
three possible factors contributing to the masculine uncertainty that is afflicting multitudes of American males and
in one way or another affecting their marriages and limiting their own ability to achieve a sense of fulfillment.

The first of these is that standards of measuring masculinity and femininity have changed. Women now compete
in the business world, are educated, and are as competent
as men in most fields in which they engage. If women engage in work formerly ascribed to men, what is a man?
This is part of the reason why some men want the women
to "go home where they belong."

The second cause lies in the whole process of their learning to think of themselves as men. The boy's first attachment is to his mother because she is the one who cares for
him. But quite early he begins to get the idea that he is
different from his mother. He is to grow up and become, not
a person like her, the one to whom he is so close, but a
man. If the boy has a father with whom he can learn to
identify, whom he can emulate, he can make the transition.
But if there is no father or father-substitute in the boy's life,
if the father is too harsh and punitive, or if he is a weak,
ineffective type of man, the boy, lacking a model of masculinity, will find himself to some degree pushed in the direction of his mother. The degree to which he fails to find
a masculine model is the measure of the conflict and uncertainty of himself as a man that he is likely to experience
in later life.

A third possible source of masculine uncertainty lies in
certain biological differences. Margaret Mead notes that:
"The girl's history as a female will be punctuated and authen-
ticated by a series of definite, natural, and irreversible bodily occurrences: first menstruation, defloration, childbirth,
menopause. Each of them is concrete, unmistakable proof
of her femaleness. The boy's history will provide no such

dramatic, once-for-all physical signals of his masculinity."
The truth of the matter is that all men and women must
find ways of validating their masculinity or femininity. The
demasculinized male is one who has not yet found adequate ways of reinforcing his sense of masculine identity.
The emerging new man has upon him additional responsibilities not experienced by men of previous ages. As a man,
he is expected to possess certain manipulative skills which
were once reserved for women. It is no longer enough to
impress people with his industry and honesty. He must also
seem to be warm and sincere. As a lover, he is responsible
for his wife's sexual satisfaction as well as his own. As a
father, he continues to bear most of the legal responsibility
for his children, though his authority over them is diluted
by his regular absence from home during the day and particularly by extended absence if his business demands that
he travel. Finally, the modern father has to succeed as the
breadwinner if he is to feel manly, though his success is
threatened by competent women in the business world.
This is one of the most significant means by which a man
validates his masculinity.

The crux of the whole problem for men is not, "Am I in
charge of my family?" but rather, "Am I in charge of myself?" When a man feels in charge or in control of himself,
and is sure of this, the question as to who is in charge of
the family is resolved. His wife can ask that man to mow
the yard and he will see this as no challenge to his authority. He is in charge, in charge of himself. Albert Ellis has
well noted that the husband who complains that his wife is
making less of a man of him was already demasculinized,
and his wife is only aggravating his problem. The solution
to his problem is not to get another wife, but to readjust
and grow up in his own self-concept.

The Head of the House

by William Hulme

Author, Building a Christian Marriage, *and Professor, Pastoral Counseling, Luther Theological Seminary, St. Paul, Minnesota*

"Husbands, love your wives as Christ loved the Church . . . wives, submit yourselves to your husbands" (Ephesians 5:22, 25).

Those who see an unjust demand on the woman in submitting to her husband's headship should contemplate what it means for the husband to love his wife as Christ loved the Church. How did Christ love the Church? He drew her to himself by giving himself up for her. This is love that provides its own stimulus to give of itself. The Greeks called it agape.

The self-giving love of Christ is exemplified in his cross. It is this sacrificial gesture that draws the Church to Christ. She responds. So in a limited way it is the self-giving love of the husband that draws the wife to him. She responds.

The golden-tongued orator of the ancient church — Chrysostom — in a sermon on this, said, " 'But what,' one may say, 'if my wife reverence me not?' Never mind, thou art to love — fulfill thine own duty."

The apostle's point is that the husband should love his wife as his own body. This is in keeping with the analogy of the Church as the body of Christ. The agape love which brings healing to the Church brings its same positive potential to the marital union.

The husband's leadership role in the marriage invests him with responsibility before God for the direction of family living, which his wife in her response helps him to ac-

Copyright 1965 Prentice-Hall, Inc.

cept. This means she is not to sabotage his leadership or usurp it. The wife's role is to encourage and strengthen rather than eliminate it. Marital partners bear one another's burdens — not by one spouse's acceptance of the double load, but by mutual support as each carries his own burdens.

Brutality. Where there is masculine ineffectiveness in the home, we hear occasionally of brutal attempts to assert this leadership. If a man's confidence in his masculinity is low, he may attempt to elevate it by bullying those who seem weaker than he. He is only manifesting how inadequate he is to be a head.

The husband's leadership is not domination of his wife, but rather is a partnerlike leadership based upon the respect inherent in agape love. We have in the headship of the husband a needed structure to family life, and modern resistance to it has already proved costly. The abusive tyrant who dominated his family is no longer with us.

Instead, "You heard what your mother said," he says as he backs up the regime. "Do what your mother tells you!" When the children come to him, however, the hoped-for strength in the shouting is gone. "Ask your mother," he says.

Children often agonize over their father's default in the leadership role.

"There is no use talking to my father," said one youngster. "He won't or can't do anything in opposition to mother. But if my dad would only be a person with a mind of his own — yes, if he would only be a man, things would be a lot better for us kids, and I think even for Mom."

Columnist Sydney Harris would agree. "It seems to me," he says, "that when a woman nags her husband, it is not because she wants to dominate him, but because he has been unable to dominate her — nagging is usually an expression of a woman's unsatisfied need to be dependent."

Domination. The woman's desire for masculine leadership is an expression of her femininity.

Yet, while the woman may wish that the man would assume more of his responsibility in the family, she may unconsciously resist making room for him to do this. She may even criticize his faltering or bumbling attempt to exert his masculine leadership. The noted criminal judge, Samuel Liebowitz, says, "If mothers would understand that much of their importance lies in building up the father-image for the child, they would achieve the deep satisfaction of children who turn out well." Perhaps then, he suggests, she would not have to stand before him in juvenile court with tears in her eyes to say those words he hears so often: "What did I do that was wrong, Judge — what did I do that was wrong?" On the basis of his long experience, the judge offers a nine-word principle for reducing juvenile delinquency — "Put father back at the head of the family."

Because they were made to feel inferior to men by discriminatory practices, some women have sought their equality by being manlike. In so doing, they are denying the equality of their own sex.

Discrimination. The male attitude seems to be that women are wonderful so long as they stay in their place. This is the familiar acceptance pattern of the prejudiced. Those who "know their place" are those who know their inferior position, and as a reward are even admired by their superior. Women, says the male discriminator, exist primarily to please men. That means that they have no independent worth.

When it comes to intelligence, women are good competitors. Girls more often than not excel boys in grades. Fathers perpetuate the myth of male superiority by saying that girls have less need for education than boys, since all they do is get married, anyhow. The implication is that education has little value for a homemaker.

When a woman begins to use her intelligence in a serious way, men become uneasy. They do not wish to take women seriously because they do not wish to disturb their illusion of male superiority.

Since men have traditionally maintained their dominance in the rivalry of the sexes, women may reverse the process with a vengeance when they have the opportunity.

Usually, it is in her family role that woman has her opportunity to dominate the man. Under the guise of justified resentment, but with a betraying obsessiveness, she may repeatedly cause her husband to feel small. His maleness is already under attack in his competition in the socioeconomic world, and he may have little resistance left when his wife continues the attack from her own vantage point in the home.

Genuine equality for woman is the equality of woman as a woman. The healing of the wounds takes place in the woman's acceptance of her own unique, indispensable function as a woman. Only then can she be satisfied with equality with men, rather than domination over them.

Her conviction of equality as a woman enables the wife to accept her difference in function from her husband in marriage. Our present male ineffectiveness might indicate that the woman has not yet arrived at this conviction. Describing the result of this confusion of roles in family living, Gibson Winter says, "Our tendency today is to assume that we can eliminate the authority of husband over wife and yet retain the authority of husband-wife over the children. The Bible is more realistic about marriage than modern man, for the truth is that in dissolving the one hierarchy we destroy the other."

Leadership. Is this not the trend of which we are all aware? First father was eliminated from family leadership and replaced by mother. Now mother is being eliminated and the children are replacing her. The growing revolt of parents toward permissive child care is a revolt against children who are dominating the family.

But husband and wife may have to settle their own feud before they as parents can reassert parental leadership over the children. The head is not alone. Can you imagine a head without a body? Even Christ is inseparable from his body, the Church. If man's function in marriage is comparable in its leadership quality to the function of the head in the body, the organ most analogous to the feminine function represented by the Church would be the heart.

In the Bible the heart is used symbolically as the location of the deep feelings and passions of the human spirit. "I will praise thee with my whole heart" (Psalm 138:1). In this biblical connection, the heart describes the nature of femininity as a complement to masculinity. No one would argue over whether the head or the heart is the more important for the life of the body. As with masculinity and femininity, the only issue regarding these organs is one of difference in equally important functions.

·•··•··•··•··•··•··•··•··•··•··•··•··•··•··•·

There is still a place for the father as an authoritarian figure — something to offset the spineless democracy in which the wisdom and dedication of God-fearing parents are no more meaningful than the inexperienced opinion of groping youth.

Needed is an intelligent democracy that values the authority rooted in dynamic experience. When a father can express this kind of authority, he affords a rock to stand on amid shifting sands. The presence and power of the Holy Spirit in a father's life give him the right kind of authority.

— NATHAN C. BROOKS, JR.

Stumbling Blocks or Stepping Stones

by Paul Popenoe
Founder and President Emeritus, American Institute of Family Relations

Seven barriers there are to the attainment of a good marriage, seven rocks on which a husband may stumble, and often does, if we may trust his wife's account. If the husband can avoid these seven difficulties, his wife will think herself fortunate above all others.

That is the report of Belgian wives who were queried by an agency in Brussels. These seven obstacles are also reported by wives in every civilized country and some of the uncivilized ones. They are such standard hazards that every husband ought to know them by this time.

1. Lack of tenderness was put at the head of the list by most of the women. "A man full of energy and ability is certainly able to show tenderness to his wife, but a false diffidence or false modesty often prevents it," one wife complained. "If he could only be a little less self-centered. If he could only whisper 'I love you' once in a while. He is able to complain when things go wrong. Why can't he show a little appreciation when things go well, as they do most of the time?"

2. Closely allied to this is courtesy, common politeness. It is often remarked that any marriage would be successful if husband and wife were as polite to each other as they are to total strangers. The husband is impatient, but sees no reason why his wife ever should be. He is tired, but can't understand that his wife might be tired, too. After all, what has she been doing all day? She was at home where she could rest any time she wanted to. He forgets to

show her a little consideration, which he expects in large measure from her.

3. Sociability in the family came next on the list of qualities desired. "My husband is the most entertaining kind of person when he is out in company. Why can't he be entertaining at home once in a while? Instead he slumps into a grouchy silence as soon as he crosses his own threshold." Of course, the wife would like him not merely to be good company at home but to take her out once in a while into good company outside of the home. This need for companionship was emphasized over and over, just as it is by wives in the rest of the world.

4. Husbands should understand their wives' temperaments and peculiarities and be more patient. A husband knows in theory that his wife goes through a cycle, or perhaps several cycles, of fluctuations of mood in the course of a month. Why can't he have enough self-control to bear this in mind and act on it? Why must he always assume that he has a right to give way to every feeling without the slightest attempt at self-control, but that she must exercise complete self-control regardless of her feelings?

5. Fairness in financial matters came next. "My husband doles out a little money for housekeeping expenses and seems to think that somehow I possess the magic of multiplying it by three," said one wife. Another husband was continually commenting on how well their friends and neighbors lived and assuming that it cost them nothing to live. Good business management in the home, just as in handling the family finances, were two requirements that almost every wife felt were needed.

6. No more snide remarks and sneers at the wife in company or before the children — that is a demand on which there was no compromise. "I know my husband loves me, and when we are alone he tells me I am wonderful; but when we are out with others he is continually

poking fun at me, ridiculing me. That doesn't make sense, and it doesn't make a good marriage."

7. Finally, plain honesty, truthfulness, straightforwardness. When a wife can no longer trust him, she finds it hard to love him.

If he wants to be a satisfactory husband and have a satisfactory marriage, a man should take account of these seven faults and avoid them.

.●••●••●••●••●••●••●••●••●••●••●••●••●•

Whenever you hear of a man doing a great thing, you may be sure that behind it somewhere is a great background. It may be a mother's training, a father's example, a teacher's influence, or an intense experience of his own, but it has to be there or else the great achievement does not come, no matter how favorable the opportunity.
— CATHERINE MILES

Man, the Initiator

by Raymond C. Stedman
Pastor, Peninsula Bible Church, Palo Alto, California

Marriage involves a husband and a wife, and each partner must play his part in making that marriage go. The Scriptures, in their great wisdom and practicality, do not leave us adrift in this area. They deal with this subject forthrightly and plainly. In 1 Peter 3:7 Peter gives a brief and cogent summary of a husband's duties in marriage.

"Likewise, you husbands, live considerately with your wives, bestowing honor on the woman as the weaker sex, since you are joint heirs of the grace of life, in order that your prayers may not be hindered" (RSV).

Here Peter puts his finger squarely on the prime role of man in marriage, that of intelligent leadership. As the King James Version puts it: "Likewise, you husbands, dwell with your wives according to knowledge."

Every husband is ultimately responsible to God for what his home becomes. In writing to the Corinthians the Apostle Paul says, "The head of every man is Christ, and the head of the woman is the man, and the head of Christ is God." Thus within the framework of total leadership in the universe he puts the responsibility on the husband to exercise leadership within the home.

This is a role for which woman was not made, one which essentially and basically she does not want. I know it is popular to make jokes about bossy wives and henpecked husbands but, having observed the marriage scene for considerable time and having personal involvement in it, I

Copyright 1969 Evangelical Foundation

would say the problem is not so much due to the demand of wives to assert leadership as it is the refusal of husbands to assume their responsibilities. Men often give themselves to careful, responsible leadership in business, but when they get home they expect everything to rock along all right without any thought, direction, or leadership on their part.

We call women the homemakers, but it is the man who is to choose the values that go into a home. It is the father who ought to decide the emphases that are to be expressed within a home. True, it is often the mother who implements these choices but, by and large, it is the man who makes the choice of what the home shall be, whether he does it consciously or unconsciously.

Some men give only lopsided leadership. They feel that their major concern is to make a living and it is the wife's job to run the home. They give their whole attention to the business of making money so they can provide the comforts of modern life for their family. They take this responsibility (properly part of the responsibility of marriage) very seriously, but they leave the rest of it to their wives. The moral values of the home are left for the woman to incorporate. But this is a denial of what Peter suggests as man's first responsibility. Men must act in knowledge, he says, and choose intelligently what comes into their homes.

Then Peter moves to a second matter. He says that man must also exercise deliberate love toward his wife — "bestowing honor on the woman as the weaker sex." When Peter says that men should dwell with their wives according to knowledge, he strongly suggests that it is possible for men to understand women, regardless of the common view in that respect. And one of the first and most important things they must understand about women is that a woman needs to feel secure in her husband's affection. His love is the horizon of her whole life and, therefore, it is his job to make her feel highly regarded, to honor her. Or, as Paul puts it in Ephesians 5, to love her as his own body, to show honor to her under all conditions, to honor and love her as Christ loved the Church.

This is man's second responsibility. He is to show courtesy to her, thoughtful consideration under every conceivable circumstance. This means that one of the most devastating things that can occur in marriage is for the husband to become critical toward his wife, to treat her with scorn, or to be sarcastic toward her. This is one of the important causes of disintegration in marriage, for such an attitude threatens the basic nature of woman. As Lord Byron put it,

> "Man's love is of man's life a thing apart.
> 'Tis woman's whole existence."

It is the man's job, therefore, to make his wife feel important to him and never to let his love decay into taking her for granted.

Interestingly enough, this is the most common complaint of wives to marriage counselors. They say, "My husband simply takes me for granted. I'm only important to him for what I do for him, not for what I am." She no longer feels secure in her husband's affection, and she reacts in one of two ways.

She may react by what men may call "womanly perverseness," seemingly unreasonable reactions. Perhaps a man comes home, makes some commonplace statement and, to his surprise, his wife blows up and flounces out of the room in a huff. The poor man is left there in his bewilderment, saying to himself, "What did I say? What have I done?" If he gets angry in reply and blows up, it only confirms her suspicions and thus deepens the viciousness of the circle. The wise husband learns that in times like this it is necessary to be quiet, loving, and considerate, and he will reestablish her feeling of security in his affection and all will work out.

The second way a threatened wife may react is by self-protection. If her insecurity goes on long enough, a wife will try to build a life for herself apart from her husband. She will try to erect barriers that protect her from getting hurt. Every wise husband must learn to avoid any unconscious threat to her feeling of being loved. When he senses it, he shows love all the more. That is why the word of Scriptures speaks so powerfully and simply: "Husbands, love your wives."

The third area that Peter speaks of is the need for unlimited sharing of the husband's life with his wife. "You are joint heirs," he says, "of the grace of life." This means that a husband must recognize his wife's right to share every part of his thinking, of his whole life. All the barriers must come down between them, all the channels of communication must be open. There should be no off-limit areas that he keeps secret from his wife. They can only be heirs together of the grace of life.

Peter has one more point. It is not a word of exhortation, but one of warning. Failure by the husband to observe these things, he says, means spiritual impoverishment in that home. "Your prayers will be hindered." Prayer here is the symbol of dependence on God, from whom all the richness and glory of life must come. It is only God that can make human life rich. Prayer, that sense of dependence, that expression of faith that makes possible all God's giving to man, is hindered, Peter says, when man fails to fulfill his role and responsibility within the home.

If the husband's failure prevents oneness, the togetherness that marriage is intended to be, then inevitably marriage grows dull and the glow departs. It becomes routine, humdrum, lifeless, boring, because the glory is gone; the flow which the presence of God makes possible is gone. The man learns that he cannot go ahead of his wife in this respect. He cannot advance beyond her spiritually for he discovers that he cannot grow in grace apart from bringing her along. Life can only be full and satisfying when they move together into a deeper, day-by-day contact with an indwelling God. This is what makes for richness in a home.

This is why the Scriptures insist that a man never be given spiritual leadership in the church unless his home is in good order, for he cannot grasp, he cannot assimilate, he cannot appropriate the knowledge and the richness of God to manifest it in the church unless he can do it first in his home. That is why he is forbidden to exercise spiritual leadership if he has not yet learned to rule well in his own home.

•-•-•-•-•-•-•-•-•-•-•-•-•-•-•-•-

If everything else in religion were by some accident blotted out, my soul would go back to those days of reality. For sixty years, my father kept up the practice of family prayer. No hurry for business or market, nor arrival of friends or guests, no trouble or sorrow, no joy or excitement ever prevented us from kneeling 'round the family altar, while our high priest offered himself and his children to God.

— JOHN G. PATON

The Lover

by Dwight Small
Author, Design for Christian Marriage, *and Pastor, Peninsula Covenant Church, Redwood City, California*

Paul sets forth a mandate in Ephesians 5, which is a singularly complete word to husbands in New Testament instruction.

The husband is to take the initiative in love; he is made responsible for married love. He is the lover. The command is: "Husbands, love your wives." One will seek in vain to find such a command for wives! It never says: "Wives, love your husbands." Some would suppose that this is unnecessary because husbands are such lovable fellows anyway! But hardly!

Rather, the whole mystery of creative and reciprocal love is embodied in this principle. It is the logical counterpart in marriage to the love relation between Christ and the believer. It is love creating its own response. In loving his wife, the husband causes her to love him in return.

This design of God is not meant to be reversed. Whenever the wife must be the one who initiates love and the husband only reciprocates, there is a deep fault in the relationship, sufficient in fact to bring it to an end.

Paul proceeds to set forth just exactly how husbands are to love their wives. It is "as Christ loved the Church." Amazing! What loftier ideal could ever be put before husbands! The fullness of Christ's love for the Church suggests five major characteristics for husbands to emulate by the power of the indwelling Holy Spirit:

Copyright 1959 Fleming H. Revell Co.

1. Christ loved the Church realistically. He was under no illusions when he sought us in love! It was not a romantic sentiment that moved the Son of God to love us. John does not say: "For God so felt a sentiment of love toward us that he gave his only begotten Son. . . ." No! He knew us just as we were: sinful, unlovable, and unresponding. Our only capacity for love was to direct it to ourselves. But "while we were yet sinners Christ died for us" — in love! His love was not prompted by anything in us at all. And of equal significance, neither was his love for us diminished or withheld by anything in us! Our need and inability only added a quality of depth and utter self-giving to that love.

Husbands, then, must love their wives realistically. None can afford to be so realistic with each other as two redeemed Christian persons who set their love in the pattern of Christ. If this love is going to work in their lives it must be based on fact, not fancy. It must embrace all of the faults and failures, the unlovely and disagreeable elements. For this Christ's love is adequate!

2. Christ loved the church sacrificially. He ". . . gave himself for it" (verse 25). How costly is love! In 1 John 3:16 we read: "Hereby perceive we the love of God, because he laid down his life for us. . . ." The supreme demonstration of the costliness of love is the acceptance by the Lord Jesus Christ of the death of Calvary! He counted the cost of love's new creation, and paid it joyfully. He gave himself up completely to undertake what only sacrifice could accomplish. Thus did love its mighty work!

The very life of love is to spend itself for the sake of another. Yet couples will complain: "The hardest thing to give is in." Is it not because they know so pitifully little of what sacrifice is? Hence how little of what love is?

There are two thoughts on the meaning of love that go together and supplement each other. One is that emphasized by Thomas Aquinas who stressed the element of giving. This is brought out as a characteristic of Christ's love for the Church. It is a willing, desiring, and doing in order to accomplish the good of the beloved. Love takes the lover out of himself and his own needs when he gives; it identifies him with the needs of the beloved. His highest happiness, then, is in the happiness of the one he has loved with such self-giving love.

Husbands must love their wives sacrificially. They must be willing to give up all that is required to fulfill the life of the beloved. This may involve giving up some of their interests, their time, their pleasures, their ambitions, and their friends. It means that nothing shall have priority over their responsibility to fulfill the needs of their wives. There is no substitute for the giving of oneself. How many wives confide to marriage counselors that their husbands give them everything but themselves. A mink coat can never substitute for a husband's love!

The very meaning of the word "sacrifice" is arresting. It originally meant "to make holy." Since it was a costly thing to accomplish redemption, and it is ever a costly thing to strive for holiness, the word has come to mean "costliness in achieving some end." How appropriate is this word, for marriage success is a costly thing and the end is a holy end.

3. Christ loved the Church purposefully. His purpose was "that he might present it to himself a glorious Church . . . holy and without blemish" (verse 27). The purpose of Christ is the eventual perfection of his Church. To this end the Lord Jesus Christ communicates his own life of blessing and power. He leads the Church in all of its growth, directs all its walk. He perfects the Church's joy. He nurtures the Church's life of holiness. He does his greater works through the Church which is his body.

Augustine emphasized the nature of love as chiefly the design of the lover to be one with his beloved. Love creates a void in the heart that can only be filled by the beloved.

Thus the lover is ever seeking a closer union of heart and life with his beloved. In the union of the two the meaning of life and love are realized. In Christian marriage the husband is ever to seek a deepening unity with his beloved in thought, expression, and in the shared life. This he finds possible of accomplishment through the Lord Jesus Christ in whom the union is established and sustained. As another has put it so beautifully: "Husbands, thou shalt love the Lord thy God with all thy heart, with all thy soul, and with all thy mind, and thy beloved as his gift."

So it is not enough for the husband to sing: "Take my wife, and let her be consecrated, Lord, to thee"! He must love her purposefully. This will take time and thought, prayer and work, patience and persistence!

4. Christ loved the church wilfully. With no motivating cause outside of himself, God willed to love us. Agape love is not an affair of the emotion only, but is an activity of the whole personality, including the will. The mind, the heart, and the will must cooperate in loving. And it is blessedly true that where there is the will to love, there will arise feelings of love as well. Very few young people seriously consider to what a large extent love is dependent upon the action of the will. Besides the emotion there must be a degree of faith, and there must be the determination of the will.

5. Finally, Christ loved the Church absolutely. His love for us was without limit, without condition, and without reserve! Ephesians 5:28 reads: "So ought men to love their wives as their own bodies. He that loveth his wife loveth himself." Whether or not we are quick to acknowledge it, this is the best illustration of absolute love that can accommodate our experience: our love for ourselves!

The thought here is that a husband should not neglect his wife any more than he would neglect his own body. Actually, the underlying concept of Scripture is that they are "one flesh"; the wife is part of his body! The husband cannot neglect her without neglecting part of himself. On the same principle, all he does for his wife shall return in blessing upon himself.

We summarize by saying that only grace operative in the redeemed heart can make a wife subject to her husband, and only that same grace can fill the husband's heart to rule his wife in love.

The word of Paul to husbands and wives is in perfect harmony with the complementary natures of them both. It recalls a fine word by Norval Geldenhuys: "The husband finds in the wife his complement and corrective, and vice versa. Without the woman the man quite easily becomes callous, licentious, and selfish; without the man the woman's tenderness easily degenerates into weakness, her love into sentimentality. Just as the woman cannot do without the man's independence and strength, so the man requires the dependence and tenderness of the woman. Marriage is therefore founded on the nature of both."

Eros must be transcended and transformed by agape; human love must be infused with divine love. This is possible when two persons bring their love to Christ. Through redemption the love of God comes into human life as mercy and grace, teaching the mystery and power of forgiving love in human relations. In returning love to Christ, husband and wife find their own love purified and strengthened.

.•··•··•··•··•··•··•··•··•··•··•··•··•··•·

The most important thing a father can do for his children is to love their mother.
— THEODORE HESBURGH

Put Him in His Place, Wife

by Alice Patricia Hershey
Homemaker and free-lance writer

I was flipping through a rack of dresses when I became aware of a disagreement going on beside me. A teen-age girl was holding a miniskirt up to her waist. Her mother shook her head halfheartedly.

"Lynn, you know what your father thinks about those short skirts," she said.

"I don't care," the girl replied. "He'll never know if you don't squeal. Look at all the times I've kept secrets for you. Besides, you took Bill's part when he decided to wear his hair long."

My visit of the afternoon before suddenly came into sharp focus by way of comparison. I had gone to the home of Katrine, a new girl in my Sunday school class, whose parents had migrated to the United States only five years before.

The mother was a warm, friendly person. Even her house exuded hospitality. What impressed me most, though, was her constant reference to her husband. Whenever there was a lull in the conversation, a boy about four would ask, "Is it almost time for Papa?"

Later, the children came in from school, greeted me politely and went to their chores.

"I'm going to start some of Papa's favorite muffins for supper," the oldest daughter said, heading toward the kitchen.

As I rose to leave, Katrine asked wistfully: "Can't you wait a small moment and see Papa?"

By this time I was undeniably curious about this remark-

Copyright 1967 Christian Life Publications, Inc.

able man who commanded such love and respect from all his family. I didn't really need the mother's second invitation: "Yes, sit a moment until Lawrence comes."

The shock of meeting Lawrence was almost too much. Instead of a well-dressed man of brilliant speech, a small man, twisting nervously at a mustache and talking brokenly in the accent of his native tongue, greeted "the teacher of his leetle Katrina."

All day I had pondered the mystery of this man's place in his home. Now as I overheard the conversation next to me, the answer came. It's not who or what the father is personally, but the mother's attitude toward him that makes the difference.

Our husbands can take their proper place at the head of the house only as we respect and honor their wishes, thereby giving our children the desire to do likewise.

Wives set the example of attitudes toward submission. And the obedience we demand from our children will be given us in direct proportion to that which we give our husbands.

"Aw, do I have to do it now?" my preschooler grumped when I asked him to leave his play to run an errand for me.

Somehow those words sounded familiar. Then I remembered. The previous night when my husband had asked me to do something for him, I had grumbled: "Does it have to be done now?"

In Proverbs we read, "I have taught thee in the way of wisdom; I have led thee in right paths." I strive to teach my son cheerful obedience, but my teaching and training will be effective only when there is also a leading — a showing of the way. We may say Dad is boss, but deep in our hearts we know that this is not so, for we generally do as we please if there is a conflict of wills. Children are quick to notice the difference between professed attitudes and real attitudes.

The other day when I was at a neighborhood coffee session, the hostess laughingly pointed to a gayly decorated motto above her husband's desk. "See what I bought yesterday," she said. We all stopped to read:

"The sentiments expressed by the man of the house
Are not necessarily those of the management."

"I guess that put Phil in his place," Marian said with a giggle.

Ann countered: "God says, 'Wives, submit yourselves unto your own husbands as unto the Lord. For the husband is the head of the wife.' " Instantly the laughter was gone. The subject changed and I could sense the embarrassment. We felt that those verses in Ephesians were not meant for us in today's changing society!

They were never easy to follow. Back in the seventeenth century, Pastor Byfield said of wives, "Nature makes her a woman; election, a wife; but only grace can make her subject." However, one of the greatest things a woman can do for her family and her country is to give her husband his rightful place as head of their home.

A minister was counseling a young couple about to be married. He asked if they had any questions. "Why isn't the word 'obey' in the vows?" the bride-to-be asked.

"Modern brides prefer that the word be left out," the surprised minister replied.

The girl was adamant. "Sir, all of my life I have observed my mother joyfully obeying my father," she said. "He was a happy, contented man and I was a happy, contented child. I want that kind of a home. And I want the word 'obey' back in my ceremony."

We wonder today at the rebellion of our children. At least part of the answer would appear to lie in our homes where basic Bible truths have been neglected. Discipline and obedience must be instilled in children at an early age. If we disregard the Word of God in this significant principle, all the churchgoing and Bible reading in the world

will not really help. Our children must not only be told —
they must be shown, for the heart of teaching is example.
What an exacting responsibility falls on us mothers!

If my husband is respected and loved by me, my child
will acquire the same feeling for him. If he sees that what
father says and wants counts with me, he cannot fail to be
impressed and influenced. Young children need a hero.
Why not Dad? It is an immeasurable boost to a father's
ego to know that he is the most prominent person in his
child's life. He will do all that is within his power to live
up to what his child believes he is. It is the attitude of
Mother that can make Dad a hero. A child needs experience before he can learn. A child cannot verbally be told
Dad's place in the home; he must be shown the practical outworking of this truth.

Since my own discovery, my son David greatly anticipates
the return of his daddy every evening. This is the climax of
his day — and of mine. Since morning we've been talking
of things we want to tell Daddy. We lay the paper on his
footstool, prepare something for supper that Dad likes, pick
up toys in the living room so that it will look nice for Daddy.
All of these things say to David that his dad is important
and that, because we love him, we spend part of every day
trying to please him.

A man who is privileged to have a wife who is lovingly
submissive and who creates within the home an atmosphere
free from bitterness and unfair criticism will meet the struggles of life without being unduly shaken. He will feel a
peace within. Nervous problems are unlikely to afflict him,
for he has a place where the storms and misunderstandings
of the outside world can be forgotten. His future may be uncertain — but a man who is foremost in his own home is
equipped to face the world.

Many years ago, Shakespeare saw the importance of the
role of the wife to her husband. He wrote:

"Thy husband is thy lord, thy life, thy keeper, thy head,

thy sovereign; one that cares for thee, and for thy maintenance! Commits his body to painful labor, both by sea and
land; to watch the night in storms, the day in cold, while
thou liest warm at home, secure and safe, and craves no
other tribute at thy hands, but love, fair looks, and true
obedience, too little payment for so great a debt. Such duty
as the subject owes the prince, even such a woman owes
her husband. . . ."

Recently a national magazine recognized the trend of today and printed an article entitled:

"A Message To: The American Man —
Urge you return to head of your family soonest."

My husband may not have any outstanding talents that
the world would acclaim. But he is unique in that he is
God's gift to me. A husband needs to be taken and loved
for himself. We need to stop regretting what he isn't and
put more emphasis on what he is. In obedience to God, let
us love, honor, cherish, and obey him. Let us put Father in
his place — as head of his household.

•−•−•−•−•−•−•−•−•−•−•−•−•−•−•−•−•−•

*A man's house is his fortress in a warring world,
where a woman's hand buckles on his armor in the
morning and soothes his fatigue and wounds at
night.*

— FRANK CRANE

4

UNIQUELY A WOMAN

She Has No Equal

by Gladys M. Hunt
Author, Honey for a Child's Heart *and other books*

Women are confused. They are urged to take their rightful place in the world of affairs and, in the next breath, told that they have deserted their calling. They are educated in the same curriculum as men, and then told they have lost their femininity.

Today's woman hears and talks much about her rights. Equal wages, equal opportunities, equal honors. Having won rights and opportunities, has she lost the *honor* of being a woman?

Equality with men is a terrible burden for women to bear. Equality really is not the question. Women are neither inferior to men nor superior to them. We are simply a different creation. Another pulse beats in our veins, another way of thinking, of feeling, of being. God did not make us like men. That is why we are wonderfully good at being women; superior, if you please, at being feminine — but tragically poor in assuming man's role. We need to ask ourselves: What did God create us to be? What are the special gifts inherent in our being? What is our role? We need to discover who we are.

In the beginning, the first thing God said was "not good"

Copyright 1962 Union Gospel Press

was that man should be alone. Adam had no one like himself with whom to fellowship. So God in his love to the man made a helper for him. He could have made another man, but he did not. He made Eve. A "helper fit for him" — someone who met Adam's need, who answered back to the inner cry of his heart.

Did you ever stop to consider how special Eve must have been, so fresh from the hand of God? Adam recognized this when he said, "This is now bone of my bones, and flesh of my flesh: she shall be called Woman, because she was taken out of Man." Therefore, a man leaves his father and his mother (the most basic relationship in life) and cleaves to his wife and they become one flesh.

Eve was the first woman — made with a capacity for sensitivity to another's need, for genuine love, for self-giving, for understanding. Each of her daughters potentially bear her inner likeness. God places human lives in her hands, whether single or married. As a married woman, she may experience God's creative power in her own body as she bears children. Denied this experience, this same creativity expresses itself in her relationships with others.

But while woman was made by God with ability to bring this kind of benediction to life, it is tragically true that she also can work havoc, scarring souls like no other.

It all begins when girls are very young. Parents are concerned with daughter's popularity, about her "fitting" in with her peers, about not making costly mistakes. As they grow older, the statistics of a body become vitally important, and girls are found hating thick legs more than a selfish disposition. Clothes become important — specialized clothes for each occasion, matching clothes — an endless circuit.

So they grow up quickly, becoming the women of tomorrow. There are assorted shapes and sizes with all kinds of personalities. Some are strong and dominating, while others are weak, clinging vines. But whatever their personality type, all have the capacity to mark another's life for good or for evil.

Understandably, we need to discover what we are and what God intended us to be. The discrepancy must jolt us into the realization that we need help. Our personalities need to be controlled by Jesus Christ. We need to let him so live out through us that the beauty of Christian womanhood may do its work in the world.

Women generally want to be needed, wanted, and understood. Basically, there is an emptiness, a loneliness, inside her that needs filling. How many sins have been blamed on this! The happy woman is one who knows the control of the Spirit of God in her life, the one who has found that Jesus does indeed satisfy.

There is no substitute for a life given over to Jesus Christ, for a genuine relationship with God. A Christian woman is one who has gotten off the throne of her own life and let Jesus Christ reign there. There must be an interchange between the Lord and ourselves, a time of daily fellowship together. Meeting God each morning for a time of fellowship in the Bible and in prayer is vital to our Christian lives. We are not collecting facts, but becoming acquainted with our Lord. We are learning to understand righteous principles so that they can be worked out in our lives by the power of the Holy Spirit.

God can not only make us pleasant to be with, but work through us to make a positive contribution to the lives of others. People ought to say about us, "She makes me a better person — just knowing her."

Our sensitivity to life and people should make us exciting to be with because we are letting Christ expand our horizons. There is so much to learn, to be. When is the last time you learned a new poem, explored a new talent, cooked a new dish for the sheer joy of adding to another's life? How long has it been since you did something unexpectedly special for someone else?

We ought to be comfortable to live with, because we are not demanding, but understanding. Controlled by Jesus Christ, we are free from obsession with self, and can listen, love, and pray. *and touch others in a very*

Our basic fulfillment does not come from marriage, from prestige, from position, or possessions. It comes as we are so indwelt by God that his fellowship meets our inner need and we experience the outworking of his love through us.

·•–•–•–•–•–•–•–•–•–•–•–•–•–•·

The most influential position in the nation today is held by a woman. She enforces law, practices medicine, and teaches — without degree, certificate of competence, or required training. She handles the nation's food, administers its drugs, and practices emergency first aid. This for all the spiritual, physical, and mental ills of the American family. A man literally places his life and the lives of his children in the hands of this woman — his wife.

— RUTH HAMPTON

When the Honeymoon Is Over

by Cecil Osborne

Author, The Art of Understanding Your Mate, *and West Coast Director, Yokefellows, Inc.*

When you married, you probably brought to marriage certain preconceived ideas of how life was going to be — perhaps a kind of perpetual romance, a continuation of the honeymoon. Then came grim reality. It wasn't the way you had dreamed it. He changed, didn't he? And without realizing it, you weren't always the same loving, patient, starry-eyed, adoring young woman he married. You both changed. Now let's see how we can go about restoring some of the stardust.

1. *Learn the real meaning of love.* You thought you were in love, and no doubt you were. Since then you may have wondered; maybe it was all a terrible mistake.

Well, love isn't what you thought it was when you were in your teens. It is much, much more, and far more complex. If you want to be loved, you must make yourself lovable — not for a day or a week, but on a permanent basis. This may involve a radical change of attitude on your part. You want your husband to change, of course; undoubtedly there are many areas in which he needs to change. But you will never change him without a mature love. "Love never fails," said the Apostle Paul in his first letter to the Corinthians.

Love is basically love of life, love of God, proper love of oneself, love of others, and the expressing of this love in manifold ways. Almost no one ever receives enough love.

Copyright 1970 Zondervan Publishing House

If you would be loved, learn to give mature love in a form your husband can accept.

Love can be expressed through patience, tolerance for the failings of your husband, meeting his needs, and by avoiding criticism. Love does not demand, it gives. Your own need for love can make you unlovable if it is expressed in a demanding or martyred manner.

2. *Give up your dreams of a "perfect marriage" and work toward a "good marriage."* There are no perfect marriages for the simple reason that there are no perfect people. Teenage expectations of an idealized marriage are unrealistic. There are some more or less ideal marriages, but they are generally the ones which have been worked out through the years.

Marriage is the most difficult and complex of all human relationships, and it requires patience, skill, tact, and emotional and spiritual growth. You can "grow a good marriage" if you are willing to work at it.

3. *Discover your husband's personal, unique needs and try to meet them.* He is not precisely like any other person on earth. He, like you, is unique. He has needs and preferences, failures and weaknesses, virtues and strengths in a combination unlike anyone else.

Abandon any preconceived ideas as to what men are like and discover what your man is like. You will be unable, at first, to meet all of his needs. No one person can meet all the needs of another individual. You need not become a doormat or a household slave. You can seek to meet his needs out of a strong love rather than out of weakness or a need to "buy" his love.

4. *Abandon all dependency upon your parents and all criticism of his relatives.* "I always feel like an eight-year-old girl when I visit my mother," complained one wife of thirty-eight. "She takes over my children, tells me how to treat my husband, and what I ought not to do. I love her, but

she refuses to let me grow up. Even after I get back home my mother writes lengthy letters of advice. I wish she'd let me alone and permit me to make my own mistakes, and learn from them."

A basic rule in marriage is to never, never criticize the relatives of your marriage partner! It's all right for him to express resentment of his parents, but your attitude should be one of tolerance.

5. *Give praise and appreciation instead of seeking it.* One husband said, "My wife is always complaining because I don't appreciate her efforts. She says I don't comment on a new dress or tell her how nice she looks. When she spends a whole day cleaning up the house and has it looking just right, she feels put out because I don't praise her for doing what, to me, is her normal everyday job. Good grief! When I bring home a paycheck, she doesn't squeal with delight and praise me for being a loyal, hardworking, dependable husband. Why should I be expected to go into raptures over an omelet or a good meal or a new hairdo! Isn't that her job, just as it is mine to knock myself out every day at the office?"

Men are sometimes far less aware of their surroundings, what they are eating, or even of what their wives are wearing than a woman would be. They are less given to little expressions of approval.

You, as a wife, cannot command your husband's approval. You cannot make him more thoughtful by complaining. Such tactics may cause him to retreat or become hostile. Your task is to offer him the same sort of recognition and praise which you expect of him. Love and tact can win when petulant demands fail.

Your husband will learn more by "osmosis" — through unconscious absorption of your attitudes — than if you make irritable demands upon him. It takes a wise and patient wife to make a good husband. They seldom come ready made.

6. *Surrender possessiveness and jealousy.* These two traits are close relatives. Everyone has the capacity for jealousy, and some jealousy is normal. It is only when it becomes possessive and all-pervasive that it is destructive. Extreme possessiveness stems from insecurity.

If we are to live creative, happy lives, we must seek out the origin of our insecurities and try to resolve them rather than justify them.

Overpossessiveness will drive a man away or cause him to retreat into the cold, gray castle of his own loneliness or into the arms of another woman. If you are unduly possessive, you are basically very insecure. You probably cannot resolve this deep-seated condition all alone. You will need the help of a professional counselor, and it will take time.

7. *Greet your husband with affection instead of complaints or demands.* You would appreciate some warmth and affection from your husband when he comes home. Your needs are valid. But if they are not being met, you can initiate response yourself. He too has needs. Perhaps he wonders why you don't greet him at the door with a warm hug and a kiss. Instead, you may greet him with the news that Jimmy has been bad, the washer is out of order, and the garbage needs to be taken out. "Oh, yes, and there's a notice from the bank that we're overdrawn." That does it!

Delay the bad news until after dinner! Don't hit him with it the minute he walks into the house. Greet him with some affection whether you feel like it or not. It pays big dividends. "Give and it shall be given unto you. . . ." Give your husband appreciation and affection. "Kill him with kindness," and see what happens. Your marriage will be better.

8. *Abandon all hope of changing your husband through criticism or attack.* Almost everyone is familiar with the basic threefold axiom: We can change no other person by

direct action; we can change only ourselves; and when we change, others tend to change in reaction to us. If you want a better marriage, you must abandon, once and for all, any hope of changing your husband by direct action. This applies not only to husbands, but to all other persons including children. Love changes people. Hostility breeds hostility, but love begets love.

9. *Outgrow the Princess Syndrome.* Not every woman suffers from this, of course, but many do, just as many men grow up with the Prince Syndrome. In essence, the Princess Syndrome is the feeling that you are "special." No one is special; unique, yes; special, no.

A "princess" doesn't give. She asks, demands, becomes petulant when she cannot have her way. She buys luxuries with money that should be saved for necessities. She delivers ultimatums, or if she is subtle she manipulates to achieve her ends. If you see any of these traits in yourself, however small, begin now to abandon them as a holdover from childhood.

10. *Pray for patience.* The urge to be married, establish a home, and have children is so strong in most women that they are often blind to faults which are only dimly perceived before marriage. There is a partly unconscious belief in the minds of most women that "love will surmount all." In most instances the right kind of love can solve any marital problems. The right kind of love involves patience. "Love is patient and kind," we read in the New Testament (1 Corinthians 13:4). A mature love has this quality of patience. An immature love wants results right now. "Lord, give me patience, and give it to me right now," is the unconscious prayer of such persons.

"Love bears all things . . . hopes . . ." (1 Corinthians 13:7). Give up the tendency to complain, criticize, and control. You cannot control another human being even if you are entirely right in what you desire. The more you criticize and condemn, the more likely you are to drive your husband farther from you. If he drinks or golfs or watches television to excess; if he seems to ignore you, forgets anniversaries, and is in other ways thoughtless or inconsiderate, your petulant demands or hurt expression will seldom bring the desired results. It takes a great deal of patience to put up with unacceptable conduct, but good marriages are built on a foundation of patience.

·•··•··•··•··•··•··•··•··•··•··•··•··•··•··•··•·

It is one thing to feel chained to the dishpan, and another to feel that we have an important part in making a house a home. We can't hoax ourselves into feeling jolly about dishwater, but when a morning comes that we find ourselves singing over the sink and stacking the dishes with genuine indifference — or even with a kind of tenderness — then we know that we have stumbled upon the meaning of small tasks in the heavenly economy.

— MARGUERITE HARMON BRO

You Incredible Homemaker!

by Ann Landers
Syndicated columnist

It is high time someone took on the free-swinging feminists who have decided for everyone that the married woman who stays at home is a brass-plate dummy, a lazy three-toed sloth, or a traitor to her Radcliffe graduating class.

In the 1950s, "housewife" suddenly became an insult. And now it appears that "homemaker," too, has fallen into disrepute.

Why has the American woman been made to feel ashamed because she is at home cleaning, washing and ironing, and taking care of her own children? This was once considered noble and gratifying work. We were told that the hand that rocks the cradle rules the world.

What happened?

Today one-third of all employed people in the United States are women, and the percentage is steadily rising. The reasons are fairly obvious. Easy credit, higher taxes, and the built-in economic pressures of twentieth-century living have made it essential for some wives to beef up the family income.

I am not knocking all married women who work. Some married women must work because they truly need the money. Others are compelled to work for emotional reasons. I have no quarrel with them either. The woman to whom I address my remarks is the mother who could stay home if she wanted to but refuses because she is ashamed to be "only a housewife."

The nesting instinct is a normal and lovely thing. Most

Copyright 1968 Publishers-Hall Syndicate

women marry because they want more than anything in the world to be wives, homemakers, and mothers. This is not adolescent hogwash or sloppy sentimentalism. It is real. It's what woman is all about.

Fact No. 2: There is no special magic about a paid job. A great many women who have left jobs — good jobs — insist that the business world is dull and confining compared with running a home and raising a family.

The homemaker has infinitely more freedom than the career woman has. The homemaker can move about at her own speed and use her time as she wishes. She can go back to class and get her high school diploma or her college degree. She can become involved in political-club work and civic affairs. And she should.

Outside activities are highly desirable outlets. A woman must recharge her emotional and mental batteries by doing something not home-connected at least one day a week. She owes it to herself and to her family.

A day away from the house and kids will make her a more interesting person and a better wife and mother. Often women who write to me say, "I'm going loony, stuck in this house from morning till night, but my husband says we can't afford a sitter." I reply: "Tell him a sitter is cheaper than a psychiatrist and, for heaven's sake, get some relief."

The homemaker has an unparalleled opportunity to exercise creative ability. She does it when she selects and arranges furniture, when she chooses wallpaper, paint, and floor coverings; when she hangs art, plans meals, prepares food, and entertains guests. A woman's home is a faithful reflection of her interests and her personality. If a woman loves her home and the people who live in it, it shows. If she doesn't, that, too, shows!

Only a fool would suggest that Mrs. Homemaker U.S.A. has a cinch. Housekeeping and raising kids demand energy — and plenty of it. The notion that the American housewife has been completely emancipated by timesaving appliances and convenience foods is nonsense. Cooking is an art, and no matter how many short cuts are produced in our nation's test kitchens, there are no substitutes for those magic ingredients, love and imagination.

To be a first-rate housewife and mother requires courage, unselfishness, and the judicious budgeting of time as well as money. It can also test a woman's ability to see the humor in a seemingly catastrophic emergency. This gift can spell the difference between survival and cracking up.

A high-priced executive whose wife had an unexpected appendectomy admitted he had no idea of what went into running a house until he tried to take over for two days. "It all looked so effortless when I was a spectator," he wrote me. "I was amazed to discover the things my wife has to put up with — things I had never even heard of." He closed his letter with these words: "Believe me, Ann, I've got a lot more respect for that woman now. She could run General Motors."

So much has been written about the educated woman's obligation to society to "do something" with her education that one gets the impression the college graduate who stays home is copping out. I believe the reverse is closer to the truth. In my opinion life's classic cop-outs are the women who have abdicated their responsibilities to their husbands and children, and to society, because they lack the maturity to stay home and do the job they bargained for.

To be a successful housewife and mother demands infinitely more emotional balance and moral fiber than is required to hold down a job. Chauffeur, maid, cook, referee, philosopher, rescue squad, hostess, tutor, and psychiatrist — put them all together and they spell "Mother."

She must be equal to every crisis imaginable. She must expect the unexpected: the child who falls downstairs and cracks his head open; the flooded basement; the busted oil heater; the minor and major battles among her children.

Coping with these emergencies is the real challenge. How much easier to wriggle into a girdle and beat it out of the house in the morning! That's what millions of American mothers are doing — and their kids show it.

Which brings me to the central theme of my message. The most valuable untapped natural resources, the most priceless assets of any nation are its children.

Ninety-six percent of our kids are *not* out stealing hubcaps, slugging teachers, killing pedestrians, smoking marijuana, and taking LSD. The huge majority of American teens are better-educated, more sophisticated, more serious, more sensitive, and more thoroughly committed than we were at a comparable age. I have unlimited faith in the upcoming generation, and I believe they will do a better job of running the world than we are doing.

To raise an emotionally healthy, morally responsible child is a stellar achievement. And in this day and age, when so many kids have the disadvantage of too many advantages, raising such a child is not easy. Motherhood is the original do-it-yourself project. Hired help is peachy when it comes to washing and ironing (if you can afford it). A strong, dependable day lady can be a godsend when you want to get out and have lunch with someone who is not wearing a bib. But children need day-to-day parental direction. They need consistent discipline. They need the emotional support provided by the physical presence of a mother.

I speak from experience when I say that raising a child can be head-splitting and nerve-shredding. There will be days when you feel you have done everything wrong. There will be moments when you are sure you are going to wind up in Menninger's. Then suddenly you discover that you must have done more things right than wrong because you see before you a lovely human being, a whole person with the qualities you hoped would be there. So take heart, mothers, and stay at home with your kids. They need you. One day they will rise and call you blessed.

Obeying Two Masters

by Shirley Rice
Author, The Christian Home

Marriage is a complete upheaval of the settled routines of two adults. And it goes on and on! There is no going back. Here is where so many marriages break down — the individuals involved keep looking back over their shoulders at the beloved personal freedom they had before and are unwilling to make the permanent adjustments that will be necessary for the two to live in harmony. After all, married or not, they are still individuals.

And I want you to know that God loves you as an individual, and he values your love as an individual. He knows the ins and outs of your individuality and will use them to manifest his life to the world. You are responsible to him for this.

His purpose in marriage is to glorify him — to be an exhibition of the way God loves the individual, to be a picture of the way Jesus Christ loves that one who has put his trust in him, to manifest to a lost world his love and his power. Your marriage is as individual in his scheme as you are. This is the whole idea: the yielding up of your individual will to his will for the carrying out of his purpose in the world, and the giving over of your purposes in your marriage to his purpose.

C. S. Lewis says, "Self exists to be abdicated. In self-giving we touch a rhythm, not only of all creation, but of all being, for the Eternal Word also gives himself in sacrifice."

This is the way the Son obeyed the Father. This is our

Copyright 1962 Tabernacle Church of Norfolk

example for submission to God. I would like you to see that submission is an attitude before it is an act. It is an attitude of will that bends eagerly and willingly under the hand of God, seeking ways to obey: "I delight to do thy will."

This is submission — complete confidence that his will for me is the very best thing that could happen to me.

Now, what is the will of God for the husband-wife relationship? It is that my husband should be the head of my house (Ephesians 5:22-24, Amplified). It is that he should be my teacher (1 Corinthians 14:35). The whole teaching of the Word of God is that the husband should be not only the head of the house in all practical matters, but also the head of the house in all spiritual matters. If you are the strong-willed, independent sort of person I am, this hits you where it hurts.

You say, "I can't lean on my husband. How do you lean on someone who has spaghetti for a backbone?" Yes, you can because underneath are the "everlasting arms." Your dependence is on God, and you can go out on the end of a limb in obedience to his Word, which says, "Obey this man — leave the consequences to me." In a mystical way I can't describe, God will strengthen him as you lean. (Think of how a mother grows and matures as children lean on her.)

With the attitude of submission, it is no longer a question of, "How much must I obey this man?" but, rather, with delight, "How far can I go in obedience to this man without really transgressing some direct command of the Lord?"

When real conflict comes in this matter of obedience to husbands, the line would be drawn on what is morally right according to the Word of God. This is a very subtle and delicate thing and will not always be the same for each wife, even on a given question.

1. Your obedience is always to God; obedience to your husband is the outflow of that.

2. God's Holy Spirit will lead you by God's Word. It will be a lamp to your feet and a light to your pathway. You must feed on his Word. If you turn to it each day, praying for guidance and for wisdom to understand it, he will guide you through it.

3. You must spend time in prayer, consistently. It is through your intercession that the Holy Spirit can minister to your husband.

4. The attitude of your heart must be: Jesus Christ shall rule in my heart. I shall constantly look to him for wisdom. I shall constantly, moment by moment as each need arises, yield over my will to his direction.

Now, let us see if we can sort out the main categories where conflict comes.

Social life. When you become a Christian, it is true that your desires change. But if your husband is not a Christian he does not have your new appetite. He is not interested in your new way of life. He wants you to go here or there, do this or that. How shall you obey him and obey God too?

The line is drawn on revelings, orgies, drunkenness, carousals, sensual lusts, and such like (Galatians 5:19-21). These are forbidden to you now. You have no obligations to follow your husband in obedience to anything of this sort (1 Peter 4:1-5, Amplified). May I warn you about your attitude when you have to refuse to take part in something of this sort.

What about church? You want to go and he doesn't. Well, go if he does not forbid it. Don't condemn him for not going. It is not your duty but the Holy Spirit's (John 16:7-11). When you have to go out the door and leave your husband at home, try to have the same attitude you have when you leave for the grocery store. Kiss him goodbye and leave. You do not make him feel condemned when you go to the store, do you?

Another thing, don't "church" him to death. Don't line up church meetings all through the week and leave him at home.

If he will not permit you to go at all, you can worship the Lord at home and fellowship with believers on television church programs or the radio. Then take the problem to the Lord. "Father, you see that he will not let me go. Help me to be so obedient to him and to thee that you can soften his heart, and I may be permitted to go in thy time." This will certainly drive you to a closer walk with the Lord in your private devotions even if you cannot have the strengthening influence of church services.

Family devotions. If he will not take charge of them, you do it. Invite him to join if the opportunity affords itself: "Dear, don't you want to hear the children say their prayers, after I read their Bible story?" "Would you like to read to them? You read so well, and they enjoy it." If it is not possible to draw him into it, then do it alone with your children.

If you do not have children, there is no need for you to parade your private devotions before your husband. He does not need this evidence of your Christianity if you are living before him with the love of Christ.

If he won't say the blessing at the table, you say it or ask one of the children to do it.

Discipline and handling of children. You have a duty to protect your children morally, physically, emotionally, and spiritually. If he teaches a child there is no God, you teach the child there is. Explain that the reason Daddy says this is because he does not know God. But you know him, and you have his Word which tells us all about him.

If he should give a child liquor, tobacco, or drugs, forbid this. If he should teach a child to lie, tell the child God's Word forbids this. If he mistreats the child physically, you certainly interfere. If he mistreats him morally, you prevent it, forcibly if necessary. You do not permit a man to "beat a child" with mental cruelty. If a father persistently tells a child he is stupid or belittles him in such a way as to break his spirit, you must build the child up and assure him that this is not so. May I point out that so often when a father treats a child in this manner, it is because of a great need in his own life. Could it be that God would use you to fill a great vacuum in this man's life, loving him in such a way that he can have love to give and can have a normal, giving, loving relationship with his child? *Money matters.* Take your hands off and let him manage it. You won't starve! God won't let you when you are doing this in obedience to him.

What are you willing to do to bring this husband to God? How much do you love his soul? Love edifies; it builds up in a mysterious way. Paul said to the Corinthians, "Dearly beloved, we do everything to your edifying." Will you look at your husband right now and make that verse personal, just for him: "Dearly beloved, I do all things for your edifying."

••••••••••••••••••

There can be no higher ambition for a Christian woman than to be a faithful wife and a happy and influential mother. It is the place which God has given woman, and she who fills it well is as honorable and honored as the most illustrious man can be.

— G. A. STODDARD

Let's Talk about Beauty

by Dale Evans Rogers
Author, Time Out, Ladies *and numerous other books*

So many women and girls have asked me what I do to
"look so young," what I do to "keep going"; at my age, they
want to know what the secret is. Well, there's nothing mysterious about it. It's as Stuart Hamblen puts it in his hit
song, "It is no secret, what God can do"! The credit
doesn't belong to me at all; it belongs to God. Since I accepted the Lord Jesus as Savior and Lord of my life, and
asked him to work through me, the responsibility for my
staying young was upon him, for I became the instrument
through which he worked his Way, and his way is the way
of the eternally young in spirit.

Once I had done that, I found that of myself I could accomplish nothing really worthwhile, but that anything was
possible when I gave Jesus the reins. Jesus said that if we
have faith as a grain of mustard seed, then "nothing shall
be impossible unto you" (Matthew 17:20). It is as simple
as that.

I do try, by his grace, to take care of my body and my
mind; I think this is a large part of his plan for me. The
Bible says that our bodies are the temples of his Holy
Spirit. It is, therefore, our responsibility to take care of
those bodies so that he can work better through us. I do
not dissipate with late hours, alcohol, tobacco, overeating,
or intemperance in anything. I watch my weight and I exercise every day. I eat lots of raw vegetables (what I can
eat raw, I rarely cook), lots of fresh and stewed fruits,

Copyright 1966 Fleming H. Revell Co.

skimmed milk and yogurt and buttermilk, eggs and lean meat, and I try to get plenty of sleep. I read a lot — Scripture, devotional books, and the newspapers —to see what is going on in the world. I do lots of praying; I couldn't live without prayer. I pray at home and in the street and in my car.

Of course, I try to look my best. I think a Christian woman is obligated to look her best and to do the best she can with what the Lord gave her. A minister said once, as he passed a woman on the street who wore the ugliest possible clothes and no makeup at all, "We're ugly enough as it is, without adding anything to it!" But let me keep it clear that I believe the chief adornment of the Christian woman is the adornment of the Spirit of God glowing on her face and in her eyes. This is always breath-takingly beautiful to me, and you can never miss it. Whether she wears jewelry or lipstick, or not, any woman looks somehow colorless without that Spirit lighting her countenance; it's what's inside that counts.

The good Lord in his wisdom gave us the songs of the birds; he expected us to enjoy them. He gave us love; he expects us to enjoy it. Don't you think so? I believe that the birds sing his praises, and I believe that a well-dressed woman or girl does the same thing, with the Spirit of Christ in her heart; she is "wondrous to behold." The Bible is severe in its judgment upon overpainted women. Jezebel, looking out from her overdone face, is a repulsive woman. Some of us have outdone Jezebel, and are doing something even she never dared to do: we have invented the topless bathing suit, and the topless cocktail dress. There are two things I want to say about this nudity business, and the first is this: women (especially once they've passed twenty-five) will be smart if they do not unveil their "heavenly" charms. A woman is far more alluring when her curves are covered — and any honest woman knows it, and most men seem to think so.

We're far out, girls. Clean gone. If we really want to "charm," we'd better get back to the old niceties of womanhood that provided a little cushioning for the harsh realities of life. Is this mid-Victorian reasoning? If it is, make the most of it! I like it better than the twentieth-century shock treatment we women are giving out to the poor, outnumbered and helpless men who start laughing once the initial shock has registered. I believe women were happier when they observed the time-honored proprieties. There was a security in that which we do not have now.

All right, call me a square if you want to. I've been called that, and a lot worse, and I don't mind it a bit. As a matter of fact, I like that word "square," and I think it was and still is a very good and worthy word in its original meaning. To be square means to be honest with myself and with others. It has the meaning of the old song we used to sing, "I'd Rather Be Right Than President." I still think it is better to be decently honest than to imitate the girl who is so "show-business-conscious" that she calls in the photographers for her horseless Lady Godiva debut. I think she's a nut — and, if you don't mind the pun, she's riding for a fall.

And I like the old-fashioned biblical approach to the human body. The Bible calls the body "the temple of the Holy Ghost," and I just haven't any respect for any human being who will blaspheme and outrage this or any other temple.

·•··•··•··•··•··•··•··•··•··•··•··•··•·

There is no spectacle on earth more appealing than that of a beautiful woman in the act of cooking dinner for someone she loves.
— THOMAS WOLFE

The Unforgettable Woman

by Ardis Whitman
Free-lance writer

"I did but see her passing by,
And yet I love her till I die."
No one is sure to whom these haunting lines were addressed. But one thing is certain: since the beginning of time there have been women like that, women who seem to have been born with a grace and charm that makes them live on forever in the hearts of those who know them.

What makes them unforgettable? Why does one woman have this magic while others, though they are kind and attractive, pass and are gone? There is no easy answer. Yet if you query men, who should know, certain characteristics are mentioned again and again.

Sex appeal, of course, most unforgettable women have; yet by itself it is not enough. Many of the memorable women of history retained their captivating charm in old age, and kept the devoted attention of the men who had loved them in their youth. Beauty, certainly, does no harm, but some of the most intriguing women have not been beautiful.

Perhaps the most universal answer is that the unforgettable woman is warm, responsive. In my own informal poll three out of four men thought that responsiveness was what endeared a woman to them most of all. "There are people," said the brilliant French essayist, Raoul de Roussey de Sales, "who transmit to others their particular emotional atmosphere; who show you how to love, to suffer, to be happy, to laugh at the humorous things in life."

Copyright 1962 Fawcett Publications, Inc. Copyright 1963 The Reader's Digest Ass'n., Inc.

The unforgettable woman is like that. You know that she is aware of you. Her mind is hospitable to your ideas, her heart to your joys and sorrows. She is not an onlooker on life. On the contrary, she is in the middle of it. She *cares;* things happen to her; she happens to them.

Everything a man does with such a woman becomes a memory. Because she was delighted, intrigued, curious, he remembers the morning he took her to the Fisherman's Market for breakfast; because she made it fun to walk in the rain the night the car broke down, he remembers her every time the rain falls. She can eat happily in a rowboat or in the most exclusive restaurant. "She belongs to the moment she is in," said a stockbroker. "She gives herself to the thing she is doing." Almost all greatly loved women have had this quality of joy in the moment.

Since she is responsive, the unforgettable woman has a genius for discovering what is worthwhile in another person. This one is witty, but his shyness prevents people from knowing it. She sparks that wit and sets it flowing. Under a hard-boiled exterior, this other one is a dreaming idealist. The responsive woman comes quietly on this hidden bloom and rejoices in it.

Paradoxically, the unforgettable woman has a deep core of "aloneness." She is a person in her own right. She is not lost in the crowd, and this is not to say that she stands out as the life of the party. It is rather that she has a sense of serenity and personal security, that some of her joys are inward, that she has a satisfying existence in her own mind and imagination. This integrity and inward richness keeps such a woman from any slavish desire to please. It gives her a wonderful simplicity and protects her from fussiness and pettiness.

The unforgettable woman is also feminine, but she is not necessarily assertive about it. Recently a young dance instructor, who sees hundreds of women a year, made a remark that struck me as illuminating. "The woman who keeps pushing her femininity isn't really feminine at all," he said. "The really feminine woman isn't proving anything. She isn't always getting into the conversation. She doesn't try to make you notice her and her clothes. It's just that when you are with her you feel like a man."

Other men agree. This feeling, they say, is induced by the fact that the very womanly woman has a tenderness for a man. She never thinks of herself as engaged in a hand-to-hand struggle to get what is coming to her. She likes men, respects and admires what they are trying to achieve, hopes to make them happy. It is not sexual prowess or a fawning helplessness or the ability to wear clothes that makes a woman feminine, but tenderness and concern and the willingness to sacrifice for others.

Must the unforgettable woman be intelligent? "Yes," say an astonishing number of men. Intelligence can flower into a rich and mellow wisdom, a magic something that helps us get the most out of the world we live in; or it can be a weapon with which to destroy. If a woman's intelligence is the whetstone on which she hones the little barbs that destroy a man, she'll be unforgettable all right — but not in a way that can give her much joy. But if her intelligence is an adjunct to the subtler understanding of the heart; if it helps her to build a bridge between a man's thought and hers; if, when he talks to her, he finds himself thinking more brilliantly and profoundly than is his wont, then he will remember her with warmth and delight.

What else? Well, Victorian though it may sound, a woman is unforgettable because she is good. To be sure, some very unvirtuous ladies, both free with their favors and stingy with their love, have lodged themselves in men's minds. But, to an astonishing degree, the women who have lived in history as unforgettable have been "good" women; not always conventional, perhaps, but honorable, loving, courageous, and generous.

Indeed, the woman who lacks these qualities has a short

tenure on charm, for goodness is more imperishably beautiful than anything else. Pettiness and hatred, meanness and greed take very little time to inscribe their unlovely handiwork on a woman's face.

Finally, the unforgettable woman makes other people feel larger than life. She gives a man the sense of being more than he thought he was, leads him further than he thought he could go. "When you're with a woman you really know and trust," said a thoughtful acquaintance, "you say and do things you've always wanted but somehow couldn't bring yourself to say and do with your everyday friends. In the end, the most unforgettable woman is the one who leads the spirit out of its hiding place."

Not many women can blaze through the pages of their time bright in the memory of thousands of people. But every woman could be unforgettable to the man who loved and chose her. For the woman a man remembers in the end is the woman he needs, the one who comforts, the one who can give him security and fruitful experience. And the more a woman seeks to live naturally by the best of herself, the more she loves, the more gentle she is in her judgments, the richer her inward life, the warmer her responsiveness, the more she will be the woman needed and, therefore, the woman unforgettable.

•-•--•-•--•-•--•-•--•-•--•-•--•-•--•-•-

Most of the beautiful things in life come by twos and threes, by dozens and hundreds: plenty of roses, stars, sunsets, rainbows, brothers and sisters, aunts and cousins, but only one mother in the whole world.

— KATE DOUGLAS WIGGIN

Hike the Price, Husband

by Earl Nightingale
Radio commentator

Back in the year 1619 when the colonists were trying to settle the stretch of beach now known as our Atlantic seaboard, a wife could be purchased for 190 pounds of tobacco. While it was as impossible then as it is now to place a value on a human being, particularly a female human being, in that time and place 190 pounds of tobacco was the going rate. That was the cost of transporting a woman from Europe to the Colonies, and wives were available.

Not too long ago a leading industrial psychologist said that a good wife can be worth a quarter of a million dollars in hard cash to her husband. This is in addition to bearing and raising his children, taking care of his home, and giving him the love and care he needs. I agree with this man wholeheartedly. There is just no way to determine the value of a woman who works with her husband and helps him reach the goals they have decided are important.

A friend of mine was having a difficult time with his business: it had been going steadily downhill despite everything he tried to do. Finally, after months of backbreaking work, worry, and lying awake nights, he realized he was going to have to tell his wife that he was almost broke. He asked her to sit down in the living room, and then told her the whole story. He was just about ready for the net by this time. When he had finished and felt that at last his world had come to an end, she went over to him, put

---

Copyright 1966, 1967, 1969 Nightingale-Conant Corp.

her arms around him, and said, "We'll just start over again."

For a moment he sat there, stunned. Then it dawned on him that he *could* start over, and his mind began to review the mistakes he had made and could avoid the next time. Somehow, this had been the one thing he had never considered. He had been stewing for months, afraid to tell his wife about the condition of his business, afraid that she might think less of him. He should have known that most women are at their best when the chips are down. Women operate best when they are needed. The fact that this wife might have to move to a small apartment and give up the home she had grown to love was not nearly as important as letting her husband know that she was perfectly willing to go back and start at the beginning again. The way it worked out, they didn't have to sell their home. Although things were pretty rough for a while, he was a good man and a hard worker and pulled out in fine shape.

How can you place a value on a wife like his? If she had not been the kind of person she was, there is really no telling what that husband might have done, or the seriousness of the situation which might have developed. He promised himself never to keep her in the dark about the condition of his business again, because he realized that when things were not going well, he could benefit from her strength and her ideas. Women are practical and have a way of thinking right to the middle of a problem. More men should talk over their jobs and business difficulties with their wives, and pay attention to their advice. Women often display an intuitive knowledge of just the right thing to do in a particular situation.

There is no question about it. A good wife can be the difference between a man's just drifting along or really accomplishing something.

5

PREPARING FOR PARENTHOOD

Partnership before Parenthood

by J. Allan Petersen

"Perhaps the most significant element in the dissolution of long-standing marriages is a consequence of living in the century of the child." So says Dr. Alfred A. Nesser, of Emory University School of Medicine in Atlanta, as he warns of the dangers of a child-oriented home. Yet we often pride ourselves on being the "nation of the child," and have become a society of child-watchers if not "child-worshipers." Psychologist Armin Grams explains that no other era has seen so much progress in the care and protection of children. The amount of information available to parents about child rearing is staggering. Child rearing could get to be a full-time job for a mother and could occupy all of a father's available time at home as well. But that is an unhealthy situation. This amount of attention is bad for children. If children need anything today, they need "healthy neglect." When we tend them too closely, we are contributing to the demise of childhood. Many parents feel they are doing themselves and their children a favor by letting their own lives revolve around child-centered activities that drain them dry. They may discover that in the process they did a very poor job of preparing these children for marriage responsibility and risked the "twenty-year fracture" in their own marriage — divorces that occur when children become independent.

How has this condition developed and what are its dangers? First, we have become afraid of our children. Let Jean Laird describe it: "Most of us want our children's love more than anything else, and feel it represents proof that we are doing a good job of being parents. In former years, the majority of parents wanted mainly respect from their children, which made things considerably easier. They weren't afraid to be momentarily disliked by children during the act of enforcing the rules. Now, a psychological revolution is taking place in many homes. Parents feel weighed down with a sense of guilty responsibility. They have been made acutely aware of the complex emotional relationship between parent and child, and are thinking in terms of psychological cause and effect. We parents are led to believe everything we say or do to our children will have a lasting effect for good or evil. As a result, many of us have become uneasy, embarrassed, inarticulate, and frightened — the first generation of immobilized parents who are letting their children practically take over their homes." So, many modern parents are afraid to demand respect from their children or their children's friends.

Second, we have surrendered to a permissiveness that is both unworkable and devastating. Reacting against the Victorian way of rearing children — rigid and authoritarian — we have become weak, passive, and indulgent. We are continuously giving and the children never stop taking. Instead of giving them experiences, we have given them things, so the middle-class child comes to feel that he should have everything he wants, that he should never be frustrated, and that he should never have to work for anything. University presidents are now gravely concerned about the intelligent young men and women on the campus, many of whom learned at home to rebel against authority and to take a casual attitude toward laws. Juvenile delinquency is directly traceable to parents who do not fulfill their moral obligation.

Third, we have adversely reacted to our own failures and deficiencies. How often I have heard this theme repeated in different ways by parents: "I couldn't when I was a child, so I'm going to see that they can." These are parents who want their children, however ill qualified, to go to college because they couldn't; who want their children to be thin because they were fat and suffered for it; who want their children to be athletic because they weren't — mothers who push their daughters into unwanted careers because they themselves can't stand housework; the mother who still remembers she had few boy friends so pushes her daughter into silly and premature "steady relationships" and then is so shocked by the teenage pregnancy; fathers who demand that their sons prepare for a profession that will salvage their own crumbling self-esteem; the parents who were deprived as children, so they feel they must send Johnny to that private school they really cannot afford. They have saddled their children with their own frustrations and hangups. These parents don't learn from their experiences — they compound them into their children.

What can be done about this unhealthy child-centered situation? There are several basic principles that must be indelibly inscribed in our thinking.

Note well, partnership is more important than parenthood. How you treat your mate is more important than how you treat your children. You can't really love your partner and neglect your children. A child's most basic security is in knowing his parents love each other — more important than their love for him. He is assured by this that he will never be abandoned, and is part of a strong, satisfying relationship. The Bible always speaks first of marriage responsibility between partners, before it speaks of family responsibility to the offspring (Ephesians 5:22-33; Colossians 3:18-21; 1 Peter 3:1-8).

Also, a radiant partnership is necessary for the right marriage example. The only course on marriage most children ever take is the one at home, and the most potent influence in child culture is imitation. That they will emulate us is evident.

Where does a boy learn the privileges and responsibilities of a husband but by watching his father? The greatest gift a man can give to his son is a strong image of stability and tenderness, a daily example of courage and integrity, a balanced combination of leadership and love — all enhanced by his dedication to Christ.

And what does a girl need to see? A supremely happy wife, beautiful with the charm of a gentle and quiet spirit, attractive because she is still in love with her husband, she has joyfully embraced her home responsibilities as a stimulating challenge and realizes that to be the "queen of the castle" demands her finest efforts and brings her greatest reward.

Our children will carry in their character the subtle impressions of our marriage and home. We are determining the quality of future marriages by strengthening the quality of our own.

Lastly, marriage is permanent while parenthood is only temporary. The Bible says, "For this cause shall a man leave his father and mother and shall be joined unto his wife and they two shall be one flesh." This leaving-cleaving relationship of a man and woman is the essence of the family. There is no evidence to support the assumption that "children hold a marriage together." Dr. Grams says, "Children were never meant to be the hub of the family. Their place is on the periphery, sheltered and loved but respected as children and expected to behave that way. The center of a family is the relationship between the husband and the wife. All else revolves around that. In this way, when children leave the family they can do so with the least disturbance to the family unit. If they are in the center of the cell, they cannot emerge without a serious rupture of the whole. Our function as parents is gradually to make ourselves unnecessary, to equip and to permit the child to orbit the family in ever-widening circles, until he establishes himself in society as a fellow adult."

A marriage begins with two people and will end the same way. It runs the cycle of parenthood and returns where it started. It starts with a couple in love but doesn't necessarily end this way since there are more divorces after twenty years of marriage than any other time except the first three years. Often this is because of a child-centered home, and when these children are grown and gone there is no more common center of interest. And these parents, in their efforts to do the best for their offspring, have actually allowed their children to come between them — to the detriment of everyone involved.

Four practical suggestions will help us keep in balance and protect us from the tragedy of the child-focused home.

1. *Determine to keep your partner first in your affection — ahead of your children.* Revive your love, renew your vows. Show affection at home — in front of your children. Speak your love — let them hear it. Call your wife what you would call her if you had no children. Learn her first name again — vow never to call her "Mother." Let the children do that. Recall the names you called her when you were courting, and put them in use again . . . and learn some new ones. Cook and dress for your partner, not your children. Find your emotional satisfaction and support in your sweetheart, so you won't need to seek it from your children. Continue the courtship. "The lack of affection between father and mother is the greatest cause of delinquency I know," says Judge Philip Gilliam.

2. *Plan for more adult times — just the two of you.* Have more second honeymoons and more activities in your role as spouses rather than in your role as parents — the symphony, the Sunday school class party, a retreat, a con-

vention. Take an overnight trip together — something spontaneous . . . and plan something special for the children while you are away. When you return you will find everyone appreciating each other more and your children will have learned some self-reliance.

I am not advocating taking the time the children should have, substituting for the family vacation, or neglecting family rituals or togetherness. Too many parents already give their children everything but themselves, but the extras for husband and wife alone must not be forgotten.

3. *Don't allow yourself to become a slave of your children's activities.* Don't let the Little League, nursery school, music lessons, athletic events, and parties make you into little more than a chauffeur with a marriage license. Creative planning and scheduling is absolutely necessary in today's busy and complex society. Children must learn that not everything others do is necessary to full living. You cannot afford to sacrifice the important for the urgent — the permanent on the altar of the immediate.

4. *Always take the long look.* The future is the result of the past. What is done now will determine the quality of your relationship later. Your children will be gone before you realize it and you will be back where you started. It can be bliss or boredom. Are you growing closer together now by improving your communication? Is your love deepening because you are taking the initiative in showing and telling it? Are you learning now to pray together and share your dreams and ambitions with each other and God?

Marriage is not wrecked by a blowout but rather by a slow leak — continued negligence and inattention. Marital vegetation can take place even while a couple lives, eats, and sleeps together for years if that is all they do. But what you generously and diligently invest in your partner will be returned with interest in your children now, and you will eliminate the risk of the "twenty-year fracture."

Why God Gave Children Parents

by W. Robert Smith
Professor of Philosophy, Bethel College, St. Paul, Minnesota

God could have brought our children into the world in an entirely different fashion. He could have caused them to be full-grown and developed in a few months or even weeks. Animals and birds mature in a very few days or weeks or years at best. But it takes long years for the development of a child until he becomes what he ought to be — mature in Jesus Christ. A child is given parents for these reasons: to provide for the child and to guide the child. Both are necessary in order that the child's whole personality may develop in all its intended richness.

First we need to provide for our children a proper physical body. We need to give our children the proper kind of physical food. We have to see that the child eats first things first. Don't give him dessert unless he's finished his meat and vegetables. And stick to your guns. No child is going to starve himself to death. He will eat.

Not only should we as parents be concerned about our children's physical well-being, but we should provide opportunities for them to develop in cultural areas as well. By providing the right kind of story books, classics, works and lives of great men, we can influence our child's literary growth.

Now the Lord gives children to parents not only that they may be provided for, but that they might be loved and disciplined. And they go together. Love without discipline is pure sentiment. Discipline without love is tyranny.

What do we mean by loving children? Well, first, we're to tell our children they're loved. When was the last time you said to your son, "Son, I love you; you are a gift from the Lord Jesus Christ and we love you"?

Many a rebellious child grows up that way because he feels he was never accepted, appreciated, owned, or loved.

Do we love our children? If we love them, then we can discipline. But if you try discipline without love, you are going to have rebellion on your hands.

1. *The first and most basic rule is*: *"Be consistent."* If you mean it, say it; if you don't mean it, don't say it. But when you say something, stick to it!

2. *Teach the child that whining and screaming gets him nothing.* The first two temper tantrums are the child's fault. After that it is the parents' fault.

3. On the other hand, *don't always be correcting your children.* The Apostle Paul says, "Fathers, don't overcorrect your children or they will grow up feeling inferior and frustrated." Many times parents expect too much. Children expect discipline in an atmosphere of love. Have a few simple rules and let the child wobble around inside and make up his own mind on lots of things. But the few rules you do have, apply.

4. *We must teach them that all discipline is under the dear Lord.* A little boy in my home who was disciplined one day said, "Fathers are always right, aren't they?" I said, "No, my son, fathers are not always right. As a matter of fact, fathers have real limitations and weaknesses and fathers sin; and your father sins against you at times and has to ask your forgiveness. But I'm the only father you have, and you have to learn to be obedient to me or you'll never learn obedience to the Heavenly Father." Now, if you sin against your children, be honest enough to ask forgiveness. When I talk to my children about asking forgiveness, they know how to do it because they've seen their father do it. Can you do it, or are you too proud?

5. We can do far more for the child's development than we realize if we *show appreciation by encouraging them,*

bragging on them, and putting support under them. Our children go bad because we say only, "Don't! Don't!" and they think all of life is negativism. Now there are some things we don't do, but what do we do? Do we give them a joyful experience of understanding; do we appreciate them? And when they do a good job, do we brag about them? Or do we wait until they do wrong and then cuff them? Children rejoice in our love and appreciation and praise, and we are building a basis of confidence in real love and yet in honesty.

Now, you instruct the child. You can't palm off religious instruction to the bishop, vicar, pastor, or anyone else. Where did I learn about Jesus Christ? From my father and mother. Where have most children learned about Jesus Christ? From their fathers and mothers.

If your child isn't doing well in school, you, as a father, ought to take over. A parent has to spend time with the child. We should take a keen interest in our child's school work and homework: whatever he is studying in class, how much he comprehends, and where he stands in reference to his classmates. Your child may be doing poorly, and you don't know why because he has a high I.Q. and studies hard. Maybe he needs glasses — he may not be able to see the blackboard. Or your child may have a hearing defect and cannot hear all the teacher says. All these factors have to be considered and are part of our responsibility as parents.

We ought to encourage our children, bless them, provide for them, discipline them, instruct them, and set before them a Christ-like example. A Christ-like example is the greatest educational influence in the lives of our children. My sons and daughters know whether I love Jesus Christ or whether this is pure form. They know whether I'm greedy or whether I'm not. They know these things because our lives demonstrate our values to them. We have to examine ourselves. Are we as parents placing most of our emphasis on things on earth? If you want your children to become in love with Jesus Christ and his kingdom, then demonstrate the divine Law by the generosity of your heart. Do you have missionary biographies in your home? Do you read about missions? Do you and your children support missions financially? In your Christian home are your children breathing in the kingdom of God in love? Are you giving them the instruction and example?

The last consideraton is: do we protect our children from the encroachments of society? Sometimes our children grow up in Christian homes where we advise, "Don't, don't . . ." and then turn them over to a dark pagan world without providing any facilities for recreation. Then we wonder why they slip into darkness. "There are certain things we don't do, my son, and certain things we do." If you have a home of love, then they understand. I remember one day when my son said to me, "Dad, would you fix my bicycle chain?" I said to myself, "I've had a busy day at school and I have to go to a banquet. I don't have time to monkey around with a bicycle chain." But I didn't tell him that. I said, "Dear Lord, I don't have time *not* to monkey around with a bicycle chain. That's far more important than another banquet." I went to the hardware, got two links, put on some old clothes. The hardware man made a mistake and gave me two different sizes so I had to go back to the hardware again — half a mile — and finally got the chain fixed. After my son drove it around and came back, I said, "How's it going?" He said, "It's going wonderfully." And I said, "That's great! I'm glad I could fix it for you." He said, "Daddy, it's wonderful you fixed my bike chain. Lots of fathers don't have time to do things like that for their boys." I gave him a hug and said, "Son, one of these days I'll ask you to do some things that may be hard, and not to do other things which are wrong, but when I do, I want you to know that this is because your father loves you." "O.K., Father."

Are we concerned where our child goes and what he does in society? Do we say, "No, you can't do that"; "You must be home at a certain time"? Do we protect the child from his own wrong choices until he is mature enough to make the right ones?

The responsibilities we have as parents may seem at times to be overwhelming, but remember that in all these things we have the help of the Lord Jesus Christ. He wants us to seek his grace and guidance and to enjoy our children and our homes, for they are meant to be a foretaste of the glory of heaven. He is far more concerned about your child's growing up to be mature in him than any father or mother could be. And if we love the Lord, if we live as men and women in Christ, our children should grow to become what we want them to be — mature in Jesus Christ.

.•··•··•··•··•··•··•··•··•··•··•··•··•··•·

When God wants a great work done in the world or a great wrong righted, he goes about it in a very unusual way. He doesn't stir up his earthquakes or send forth his thunderbolts.

Instead, he has a helpless baby born, perhaps in a simple home and of some obscure mother. And then God puts the idea into the mother's heart, and she puts it into the baby's mind.

And then God waits.

The greatest forces in the world are not the earthquakes and the thunderbolts. The greatest forces in the world are babies.

— E. T. SULLIVAN

It Makes the Home Go 'Round

by Lars I. Granberg

President, Northwestern College, Orange City, Iowa

Does your Christian faith affect your family life?

"Ah!" you say, "it does affect it. I attend church regularly, go to midweek service, tithe my income, sing in the choir, teach Sunday school, and avoid worldly forms of amusement."

But if that is the limit of the effects, you have a false understanding of the Christian life. This is one reason why we so often have the wrong kind of family life. And this is one reason why Christian homes so often fail.

Do not misunderstand. Of course it is important to attend worship faithfully, exercise responsible Christian stewardship, and contribute one's talents and energies. But to regard these as the hallmarks of Christian living is to fall into the Galatian error. This is a heresy as old as mankind. It creeps out in one form or another in every generation, but always with the same aim: to let me keep spiritual score on myself and my neighbor, so I can tell God where I stand. This false view of the Christian life substitutes rules for relationship, demands for understanding, and judgment for love. And in so doing it badly misses the point. The great words of Holy Scriptures are love, forgiveness, reconciliation and fellowship. These constitute the message of the gospel. They set the tone for how we do what we do, and make clear that it is the spirit in which we relate to God and live with each other that differentiates the mind of Christ from its pious-appearing counterfeit.

Copyright 1964 *Church Herald*

The false view leads to a spirit of judgment. There is much emphasis on appearances, on blame, on avoiding criticism. In a home dominated by such an atmosphere people become defensive. Some pull into a shell. Some stay away from home as much as possible. Others fight back in countless subtle and obvious ways. They suspect the worst motives in what others do and say, look for things to criticize, nurse grudges, and try to hurt before they get hurt.

It is just this kind of self-satisfying bitterness and vengefulness that our Lord came to heal. The life-giving force is that special kind of love which helps us work constantly at understanding, forbearing, forgiving, consideration, and courtesy — and not only at such times as we feel the other is deserving. It is a love which places warm fellowship higher than one's own ego. It prompts the Christian to take the initiative to keep things right rather than allowing us the luxury of nursing an injury or insisting that because we feel wronged the other must make it right.

Probably the biggest problem among our staunchest Christian families, however, isn't open strife within the family. Nor is it a matter of family members' harboring deep bitterness or resentment toward one another. These family members are loyal to each other, quick to help one another build a barn or a garage, and they stand by one another during times of serious need. In one sense we would have to speak of them as close families. Nevertheless, many members of such families feel lonely and uncertain. They express a real hunger for love and compassion. Listen to one fine young person from just such a home:

"One thing I regret about my home is the fact that love was very rarely expressed openly. I am certain that deep love was felt for the other family members, but somehow it was seldom put into words. I think this has stood in my way as I have tried to enter into deep personal relationships."

This young person regards the home in which he grew up as a good one in most ways. Physical needs were met. There was faithful Christian instruction. Parents were thoroughly dependable. But they were somehow unable to express their love directly.

Many evangelical Christians seem to feel embarrassed about their tender feelings. Sometimes they teach their children that these are personal and not to be worn on the sleeve. There is suspicion that those who openly express love are shallow or false. (On the other hand, they do not quit spending money because some money is counterfeit.) They insist that when children are given plenty of good food, shelter, warm clothing, care when sick, proper training and discipline, and many other needful things, it should be obvious that their parents love them.

Alas, it isn't that simple. Actions are open to more than one interpretation. The home situation described can be explained on the basis of duty as well as love. Most children — most people, for that matter — are uncertain enough of their own loveableness to need at least an occasional unmistakable declaration of affection, for they know they often disappoint those they love.

When you think about it, there is a strange inconsistency found in these situations. Parents are distant and hesitant about expressing love, but rarely do they feel the same about expressing disappointment or disapproval. When the child or spouse is deemed to be in need of reproof, there seems to be no hesitancy at all about "wearing one's feelings on his sleeve." Disapproval is expressed clearly in words of one syllable. Why is this? Why is it important to be clear and unmistakable about disappointment and disapproval, while the other person is left to guess about approval and affection?

A usual result of an inconsistent approach such as this is to leave a child quite clear on what is wrong, but rather fuzzy regarding what is right. This creates the kind of morality which is preoccupied with avoiding what is wrong rather than upon achieving what is good: the morality of the Pharisees, leading to the Galatian misunderstanding of the Christian life.

A few suggestions: the key to understanding companionship begins with the desire to communicate love, respect, understanding, and forgiveness. Such love recognizes human frailty, hence does not make extra trouble through unrealistic expectations. Neither does it wait for the other to take the first step in healing broken or strained relationships. It is necessary always to bear in mind that it is not easy to convey accurately one's thoughts and feelings to another, for each of us has his own private world through which we interpret what we see and hear. Therefore we need to take pains to make our thoughts, feelings, and intentions as clear as we can. Above all, give the other person the benefit of the doubt — even when there doesn't seem to be any doubt. Most family members respond to this kind of generosity.

This is not easy. No wise person expects it to be. There is risk. People do get hurt. But it is richly rewarding. Through such efforts one learns what the biblical statement means when it says that a man who wants to save his life must be willing to lose it. *Learning to give* when we'd rather receive, *forgive* when we'd rather nurse a grudge, and *love* when we'd rather be loved moves us toward Christian maturity. And in such a family atmosphere, your Christian home will not fail.

Small wonder that when the Apostle Paul set down the qualifications for leadership in the church, he put great emphasis upon a man's having first learned to shepherd within his own household (2 Timothy 3:4-5). To create a family situation where people feel mutually responsible for shepherding each other is to make Christianity real at home.

The Difficult Art of Parenthood

Time *magazine editorial*

War between generations is nothing new. . . . All through history, denouncing the young has been a tonic for tired blood. More important, defying elders has been hygienic for the young. . . . Growing up is a . . . process that requires things that one can push against in order to become stronger. It takes limited war against worthy opponents; a child matures by testing himself against limits set by loving adults. . . .

Can that be true?

To charge that American parents are flunking the job is to ignore the stunning fact that most American youngsters now work harder, think deeper, love more and even look better than any previous generation. . . . Americans revere children, and they must be doing something right in the process. "Everything for the kids" is a U.S. creed that moves GIs to feed every war waif in sight; that goads concern for the country's ghetto schools; that has already provided most American children with good medical care, free education, antichild-labor laws and unparalleled freedom from adult repression.

And yet something is clearly wrong in Eden. Quite a few . . . youngsters . . . are spectacularly discontented . . . too many are withdrawing. . . . While flower children go to pot, the new disease of alienation drives elite collegians into private exile. "Children are not fighting their parents," says author-sociologist Edgar Z. Friedenberg. "They're abandoning them."

Copyright 1967 Time, Inc.

At the heart of Eden's anomaly lie vast technological changes in Western culture that have steadily lengthened childhood and sharply diminished communication between generations. . . . Until recently, puberty occurred at about fourteen or fifteen, marriage two or three years later. . . . Today the pressure is to stay in school to be better prepared for life in a complex society. Meanwhile, better nutrition has ironically quickened puberty; the young are now biological adults at twelve or thirteen, but they usually cannot legally work full time . . . until at least sixteen . . . they are often economically dependent on their parents until twenty-four or twenty-five. In effect, they may stay children for more than a decade after becoming "adults."

Nothing is wrong with segregating youth . . . to strengthen them for highly complex roles. . . . This is just what happens to the vast majority of American youngers. Even so, the failure rate is big enough to ask why some of the most privileged children are so unready for adult life. One reason is the lack of self-shaping experience; part of the hippie syndrome is a quest for adventure and competence. They did not have the benefit of those cattle-boat jobs that might have helped to slake the thirst for adventure; they rarely got a chance to help their father at work.

To a startling degree, American parents have handed child-raising to educational institutions that cannot or will not do the job. . . . More than one third of U.S. mothers work at least part time, and some fathers hardly see the kids all week. According to psychiatric social worker Virginia Satir, the average family dinner lasts ten to twenty minutes; some families spend as little as ten minutes a week together. Studies show that father absence has baneful effects (especially on boys), ranging from low self-esteem to hunger for immediate gratification and susceptibility to group influence. Hippies commonly flee from father-absent homes in which despairing mothers either overindulge their children or . . . overpressure them. . . .

With their own uncertainties, U.S. parents lead the world in gobbling child-care books . . . producing a good many faddishly permissive parents. Often a father is more involved in living up to his child's expectations than the child is in living up to his. To avoid "hurting" children, he shields them from adult power and indulges their impulses. . . . In panic, some weak parents . . . hush up serious misconduct and bribe miscreants with new cars. Still others, incredibly, flee on vacation, leaving their kids to stage monster open-house parties. Then there are swinging parents, who even try LSD with the kids, another form of child abandonment that robs children of adult limits to test themselves against. . . .

From foolish permissiveness to foolish repressiveness, too many American middle-class parents career downward from the joys of birth to the final whimper, "What did we do wrong?" The hard answer is that failed parents tend to be failed people who use children for their own emotional hangups. They never stop, look or listen to the kids; they never grasp that parenthood is a full-time job, perhaps the most important job in a chronically changing America. They never see the challenge; teaching a child integrity — the self-respect that makes for strong, kind men and women who can cope with life's temptations and who are willing to face the fact that life is a set of problems to be solved.

How to be a good parent? . . . The key is communication. . . . Many parents have no idea what their children really think because they never give them a chance to explain. "Can't you see I'm busy?" is a put-down that ought to be banned from the parental lexicon. "Listen" ought to be tattooed over every parent's heart. Regular "time alone" with parents so that children can unburden themselves is vital. As educator Clark Kerr advises, "Spend time, not money. . . ."

Basic to communication is the art of helping children to express . . . and thus handle, their inchoate feelings. It seldom pays to condemn or reason with an angry child; strong feelings vanish not by fiat but rather by the clarification that occurs in a child's mind when a parent "mirrors" or states his problems for him. To spank a tot who says, "I hate you," is to store up his anger that will augment future misbehavior. A skillful mother listens, says, "I know just how you feel," and the child's feeling that someone understands shrinks the anger to a size that he himself can subdue. Reassurance rather than reprimand is often the best medicine for defeat or failure.

However, good parents draw a sharp line between free speech and illegal conduct. . . . How and when to set limits depends partly on the child's age. Nothing makes a small child more anxious than being asked if he "wants" to do this or that. Dr. Benjamin Spock, sometimes accused of permissiveness, firmly advises, "Just do what's necessary." In short: time for bed, lights out, no chatter.

Limits certainly require reasons but once clearly stated, they should be enforced without exception. Letting a child get away with something that he knows is wrong or dangerous makes him feel that his parents don't love him . . . and rightly so. Old-fashioned as it may seem, children still need discipline and guidelines. . . . In Seattle, a permissive father's 14-year-old daughter, who had been slipping out at night to date a paroled convict, was straightened out only after a community-relations officer bluntly told her father that he had to show some stern authority. "The girl was screaming silently, 'Help me; make me stop this,'" said the officer. . . .

"Discipline comes from being a disciple," says psychoanalyst Bruno Bettelheim; both words come from the Latin word for pupil. Children become disciples of parents who enjoy and back up one another; whose mutual respect and ungrudging praise for work well done makes children draw a positive picture of themselves. But the approach must be genuine; the young mind is quick to spot the phony.

In disciple families, "No" is said as lovingly as "Yes." The children learn to wait; the parents refuse to buy them this or that until they prove themselves mature enough to use it wisely. Allowances are given not as a dole, but to train children in budgeting necessary expenses. Little girls are not pushed into premature dating; the parents couldn't care less that "everybody else does it. . . ."

One way to help build a disciple family is to make sure that parents and children never stop doing meaningful things together. Family games, hikes, building projects, and political debates — such activities underline adult skills that children then naturally want to have. Just because evening meals get tense is no reason to quit them: there is no better ritual for spotting and curing the tensions. One San Francisco family has no fear of the kids' trying drugs; all its members do volunteer work together at the narcotics-control center. . . .

Enterprising families can still find ample superordinate goals. The possibilities range from tutoring slum kids to organizing block councils, restoring old houses . . . . running Pop for political office. . . .

Many eighty-hour-a-week executives might try something else: rejoining their families. In recasting themselves as fathers, they might recast their values and change their lives. Making a living is important, but selling more soap should not destroy the process of raising sons. And why not attack age segregation by putting teen-agers to work teachings tots and nursing old people? . . .

In a country that offers more different life styles than any other, there is no reason for viewing the generation gap as insurmountable; no reason why parents and children cannot learn how to fight for rather than against one another. The fact that America is full of disciple families — despite seemingly enormous odds against them — is a counter weight to the relatively few pathological cases that get all the publicity.

Is Jesus at Home?

by Paul A. Jongeward
Public school teacher

My experiences over the past few years in working in public schools as a teacher and later as a psychologist, and in Christian youth programs, have led me to an inescapable conclusion: Jesus Christ is a "missing Person" in the majority of "Christian" homes. His living presence and love have been replaced by a rigidly enforced, but largely meaningless, habit pattern.

During my years in the public schools I saw little, if any, difference in moral behavior, attitudes, and values in the children of Christian parents. Although Christ should be making some vital differences in their personal lives and in relationships with their children, he was embarrassingly missing.

In working with high school young people in the church (those who were still coming) I found that Christianity had little relevance to the pressures and frustrations of their teen-age world. Most of them came because they were coerced by their parents. They confided that Christianity was not exciting to them and they saw little relation between what they were doing in church and their everyday life. Christ was not a reality to them and many termed Christianity "a real drag."

I found that as the Christian young adult becomes independent he either (1) culminates his rebellion against the hypocrisy and discards the "Christian life"; (2) quietly puts away what he has experienced as Christianity with

Copyright 1969 Evangelical Foundation

other childish things; or (3) continues to practice "habit Christianity" and soon begins teaching his progeny to do the same.

As I began to search for ways in which the Lord could use me in a crusading attempt to change Christian homes, the Lord instead began showing me that he was not the living reality he wanted to be in my own life. As I began honestly to examine my Christian life I saw that it, too, was basically a habit pattern. I attended certain scheduled church services, did what I felt to be my part in "service" to the church, used ecclesiastical jargon, mixed socially with a circle of Christian friends, didn't partake of certain worldly vices, etc.

At this point I was faced with a dilemma. During my growing-up years and even after college I had always felt that becoming "serious" with Christ meant becoming a stereotyped personality — the thought of which I abhorred. Over the years this misconception kept me from genuinely desiring a vital relationship with Christ.

However, through intimate contact with a few others in a weekly Bible study group, I began gradually to see how erroneous my concept of the "serious Christian" was.

Through individual and corporate study of Scripture, honest discussions, prayer, and reading books by Keith Miller, O. Hobart Mowrer, Watchman Nee, and others, the light began filtering through. My wife, Lila, and I began getting excited with the Person of Christ, his love for us and the kind of life he wanted to live through us.

As we gradually began seeing Christ and the Christian life from this exciting perspective, we determined that Jesus Christ was not going to be missing in our home, and that Curt, our three-year-old, would grow up knowing his reality.

I began asking myself, "What is Curt seeing and experiencing that is indelibly teaching him that Christ is making Mom and Dad different people — that he is for real?"

As a result of honest prayer and study, my wife and I began to find ways that, for us, help to bring Christ into our Christian home. Jesus Christ is extremely concerned with how much time I'm spending with my child during the day and what we do together. He wants to be a vital part of my professional and social life and wants me to have his perspective on people and tasks throughout my day. He wants my wife to be abiding in and enjoying him in even the most routine household duties. It is now natural for us anywhere in the house or car to seek Christ's guidance, confess a sin or just thank him for something, using the same language we use when we talk to each other. Our boy understands this and it becomes meaningful to him.

He now accepts and enjoys my grabbing him up in my arms, sitting down with my wife and "talking to Jesus" about whatever might be relevant to that situation. Unitedly praying for things that fit into his little world is especially important. Recently we were concerned that he had no playmates that live close to us. When the house over the fence became vacant, we prayed together that Jesus would bring in a family with children of appropriate ages for him to play with, knowing that Christ loved us and was concerned with the details of our lives — Curt's as well as ours. Within two weeks a family with three children (two pre-school) moved in. Curt has become fast friends with them and enjoys them immensely.

Weekly home Bible study with two or three other couples has been a definite part of our Christian life style for several years. Our boy now assumes that any time we get together with others it is for "Bible study."

In recent years psychology has put increasing emphasis on *honesty* in interpersonal relationships. Here is a scriptural principle that we Christians are tragically neglecting. Christian husbands and wives rarely confess to each other or to their children. Of all people we Christians should be the most honest. Recently I confessed to Curt that I had been cranky with him earlier in the day. He then asked me in complete sincerity if "Jesus was now going to help Daddy to be a happy boy." The message hit home.

During the past few months my wife and I have implemented something that we have found to be the single most effective method for making Christ a reality in our hearts and in our home. The method incorporates many of the principles already discussed in what we feel to be a wonderful manner.

Following an illness which the Lord used to show me that the priorities of my life had become disordered, I determined that I would daily attempt to make Christ the first concern of my life and place other concerns and activities in this context. My wife and I decided to take the promises at face value that if we delight ourselves in him and seek him first each day, other aspects of our lives would fall into natural place because of his direction. In attempting to come up with some practical technique to assist us, we resolved not to go to sleep any night until we had a time of sharing and prayer. This nightly time together has become the highlight of our day.

We have no structured plan, but use the time in a very flexible manner to talk over problems we've had during the day, share an idea that came to us, discuss a concept we ran across in our reading or share something exciting that we saw for the first time in a verse of Scripture. Sometimes we read together and discuss a book or article and attempt to make practical applications to our lives and home. If one has provoked the other at some point during the day, this is an ideal time for honest confession to each other and to God.

The communication, honesty, and "closeness" my wife and I are enjoying are beyond anything we have ever experienced before. We are seeing aspects of each other never before perceived. The communication and introspection are helping to "free" us to realize more and more of our potential as individuals and as a Christian couple. To give a prime example, Lila was recently able to share something with me that had bothered her terribly for many years and had hindered her spiritual and personal growth. The changes that are occurring in her life since she was able to share this with me have been thrilling to behold.

Sometimes we find ourselves at the end of our rope, only to find the Lord pointing us back again to something we had learned from him before but had forgotten. However, we've never enjoyed living more — in every realm life has become stimulating and exciting. The other night, after praying with Curt before bed, he looked up to us and said in his sweet, three-and-one-quarter-years-old manner, "Curtis sure loves Mommy, Daddy, and Jesus!"

.•-•--•-•--•--•-•--•-•--•--•-•--•-•--•-•-

There is but one way to eliminate juvenile delinquency — that is by providing each child in America with competent parents.

— J. Edgar Hoover

The Crime against Children

by Oswald Hoffmann
Radio speaker, The Lutheran Hour

I feel sorry for a lot of young people these days. Their parents have simply washed out on them.

Some parents have failed their children because they were just too self-indulgent, too selfishly interested in their own affairs to pay any attention to their children at all. Others really loved their children and thought they were doing the young people a favor, allowing them and even encouraging them to do as they pleased without any consistent instruction, direction, or restraint. The effect in both cases was the same: young people grew up like weeds instead of the cultured and cultivated products they could have been. The results can be seen all around us in the price society has had to pay for the overpermissiveness of a whole generation of parents.

Men and women in the teaching profession tell me that it's tough to be a teacher these days. Recently a teacher walked into a principal's office and announced, "I just can't take it any more." Every attempt at discipline on her part was met by a consistent and obdurate refusal on the part of children to conform to the most elementary rules, often encouraged by parents to consider themselves beyond the rules. When a girl or boy winds up dishonoring himself and the whole family, parents frantically look around to find someone whom they can blame for what is really the result of their own permissiveness, their own lackadaisical, "anything-goes" attitude toward the training of their own children. Even to call it training is a laugh.

Overpermissiveness is really a crime committed by parents against their children — a costly crime — costly not only to parents but also to children who deserve something better than this encouragement, this inducement, to underachievement at school, causing many young people to blow their opportunities for a genuine education and often for a satisfying life.

Nowhere is the permissiveness of parents more evident today than in the area of what some people are disposed to call "sexual freedom." Actually most of this sexual freedom is just plain, stupid misuse and abuse of one of the glorious powers given to man by God. All too often the result is a slave addiction which does not permit a man to be a real man or a girl to become a real woman capable of the mature emotional attachments and downright physical enjoyment that make a marriage such a satisfying achievement, such a circle of joy and such a comfort in time of trouble, for both young and old.

Taking a good hard look at some of this so-called sexual freedom at which the overpermissiveness of parents winks an eye, the headmaster of a fine preparatory school in the United States has said: "After a few years of this freedom, these boys and girls are like robots in heat. Watching them, one wonders: what will there be for them to look forward to at twenty? Is there anything left that will entice this boy to take an adult emotional and domestic responsibility? Can this girl have a honeymoon?"

The jaded appetite that can no longer be attracted by what is fine and noble and good is a high price to pay for the permissiveness of parents who never made any demands upon their children and, consequently, never contributed to their growth. A good deal of the rebellion among young people today is not against the overrestrictiveness, but the overpermissiveness of parents. Young people rebel against parents who don't care anything about their children, or don't care enough to employ parental authority in enforcing elementary responsibilities that help to make a man a man and a woman a woman.

Addressing himself to the problem of helping young people to become mature men and women in a materialistic age very much like our own, St. Paul turned to the Ten Commandments. "Children, obey your parents," he said, "for this is right. Honor your father and mother (this is the first commandment with a promise), that it may be well with you and that you may live long on the earth."

The apostle was not telling young people that they have to approve of everything their parents are or do. Parents make mistakes too. Whatever mistakes parents make, they are still parents, privileged by God to have children and responsible to God for those children. This is true of all parents, no matter who they are. Children do honor to themselves when they give honor to father and mother, no matter how uneducated they may be, no matter how poor, or how limited in their ability to fill the role God has given to them. They are still parents.

The apostle also had a good word for parents, a practical word in an overly permissive age: "Fathers," he said, "do not provoke your children to anger, but bring them up in the discipline and instruction of the Lord." What he said to fathers he knew would get through to mothers too. But he talked especially to fathers, because fathers need to remember that mothers can't do it all. Mothers can't take care of the religious upbringing of children when fathers spend all of Sunday morning at the golf course, or use Sunday morning to sleep off either the worries of the week or a long Saturday night spent with the boys. There is more to being a father than bringing home a paycheck.

Children are not impressed with the kind of parental permissiveness which makes it quite clear that parents don't care what their children do or how they turn out. Nor are they impressed with parents who do not have the inner strength to make the hard moral decisions that have to be made.

All too often parents are too permissive with their children because they are too permissive with themselves. Children have an instinctive feeling about this. They don't respect parents who are not willing to demand a price of their children because they are not willing to pay that price themselves.

We live in an age when people demand instant satisfactions for themselves. We know all about instant coffee, instant oatmeal, and instant dinner. Now we want to have instant satisfaction of every little desire that happens to pop into our little minds. The price of instant satisfaction, we ought to have found out by this time, is too high to pay. Centuries ago the prophet said, "The fathers have eaten sour grapes, and the children's teeth are set on edge."

The plaintive song sung by the Beatles runs something like this, "She's leaving home after living alone for so many years." The story of the girl in that song has been written largely by parents who were more interested in themselves than they were in their children, listening to all the baby care books and forgetting about the Bible.

St. Paul told parents to quit betraying their children by refusing to pay any attention to them. Bring up your children, he said. Train them with discipline and instruct them with faith. Don't imagine that you are helping your children by letting them do as they please. Be a father, he said to fathers, and be a mother, he said to mothers. You can't excuse yourself with the plaintive plea: "We gave our children everything money could buy." That isn't enough. The price of that permissiveness is too high to pay.

If I read the apostle correctly, he cautioned parents against rushing from foolish permissiveness to foolish repressiveness. Fathers, he said, do not provoke your children to anger and rebellion. Be fathers, yourselves practicing the art of faith in Jesus Christ, and bringing up your children in the discipline and instruction of the Lord.

Parents can't take a popularity poll every week to see how they are doing with their children. Parents who follow Jesus Christ are very conscious of their own shortcomings and of the fact that they have been forgiven by God. Forgiven people will treat their children as human beings. It is not at all out of place for parents to discuss matters with their children before reaching a decision on what must be done in a particular situation. Lack of intelligence or information or insight never made a contribution to a wise decision. Bringing up children with discipline in the instruction of the Lord demands a lot of understandng, a lot of good common sense, and a lot of faith, along with a lot of patience of the kind that the Lord has to show to us all.

Fathers, you are not running for an office. You hold an office. It is your duty to fill that office.

A young friend of mine told me what happened to him one day when he ran into a father who exercised the responsibilities of his office. This young man had made a date with a certain girl. His friends had warned him, "Wait till her old man gets through with you!" But the boy made the date, anyway. He went to the house, and was met by the girl's father, an Irishman, stern but kind. The father sat down in the living room with the boy and asked him a few questions: Who are your parents? Where are you going this evening? Are you going alone or do you have a double date? How long have you been driving a car? Where do you go to church? That's the way the conversation went for about a half an hour. Then the father said, "Well, I better call Pat and see if she's ready." The girl and her mother appeared immediately, probably having been waiting in the wings all the time. Many years have gone by since that evening, but this man tells me that he never forgot that half hour and he always respected the father of that girl. He wasn't running for office either with this boy or with his daughter. He had an office, and he did what he was expected to do.

Good parents are the salt of the earth. They invite the respect of their children. They help to make our world a better place. They are the promise of better things to come. They help young people to grow up as young people must. Good parents are the agents of God, not willing to pay the price of permissiveness but ready to pay the price of love.

·●··●··●··●··●··●··●··●··●··●··●··●··●·

Before my father died he turned his face heaven- ward with the happiest, most beautiful smile. Someone leaned over the bed, and asked, "Dr. Rader, how can you smile like that, when there is not one of your children that is serving the Lord?"

He smiled as he answered: "That doesn't matter a bit. It was settled long ago. I brought them up as he commanded me to do. They will every one be brought in. They are a strongheaded group, but God will lead them; yes, every one!"

And every one of them is walking in his way to- night; yes, every one!

Oh, for praying fathers in our nation, and moth- ers who pray for their children! I tell you, God hears them! He hears! He hears!

— PAUL RADER

6

UNIQUELY CHILDREN ⟍

Understanding Age Growth

Sacred Design Associates

The chart on the following pages traces child development from ages five through eighteen. It includes the physical, social, spiritual, and sexual aspects of the child's growth.

In using this chart, the reader should remember that there is no "normal" or "average" category. These are characteristics which the majority of people may experience, and exceptions are to be expected.

Resources for this material include the Minnesota Department of Health, as well as the writings of Arnold Gesell, M.D., Dr. Kent Gilbert, Frances L. Ilg, M.D., Milton I. Levine, M.D., John Lewellen, and Willard C. Olson.

	PHYSICAL	SOCIAL

AGE 5
(Kindergarten)

PHYSICAL

Child can run, jump, climb. Learns to hop and skip this year. Child grows approximately 6 inches and gains about 10 pounds in weight. Can dress self, tie shoes, brush teeth, button clothes. Gains reading readiness.

SOCIAL

Children learn to relate to others outside the home. Activity with others is very important at this age. Children should learn give and take in preparation for life. The child likes to be at home with mother, or to know she is near.

AGE 6
Grade 1

PHYSICAL

Child continues high energy. Coordination improves. Can turn somersaults. Begins to lose front baby teeth. Difficult to sit still for long periods of time. Attention span short. Learns to read and gets numbers concept.

SOCIAL

Social adjustment must be made at this age. Child learns to interact with others in higher grades. He gradually learns how to control his emotions and behavior. Looks to adults for approval of actions.

AGE 7
Grade 2

PHYSICAL

Child continues high energy. Coordination improves still more so now can handle writing and drawing tools, etc. Still has short attention span. Child is usually noisy, active. Growth is slow.

SOCIAL

Child at this age needs help in becoming self-confident member of society. Often is dreamy and extremely sensitive to approval or disapproval of others. Child likes competition in group play, but always wants to win, is a poor loser.

Copyright 1968 Sacred Design Assoc., Inc.

SPIRITUAL

SEXUAL

Accepts fact of God as Creator and loving Father. Sometimes confuses names and persons of God and Jesus. At times worries over ideas that God sees everything he does. Likes stories from the Bible. Usually enjoys being in the church school class.

Child is usually curious about "where he came from". Asks many questions about babies. Is curious about the difference between male and female. Family unit is good beginning for basic sex information, which should be gradually progressive at each succeeding age.

AGE 5
(Kindergarten)

Just beginning to develop a sense of values. God is important. He can accept the fact that God sees him, but the opposite is not true. He expects his prayers to be answered in a literal way, and immediately! He is ready for more Bible stories, the activity of dramatization. His ideas are concrete, not at all abstract as yet.

Concept of family as basic unit is of continued importance. Child is interested in new members in their family, sex differences, how they arrived, etc., as was true in Kindergarten. Child is interested in "how" of reproduction. Asks questions about animal mating.

AGE 6
Grade 1

Thinks carefully about God and heaven. Is able to participate in class discussions using more abstract concepts. The Bible heroes seem very much alive to him. He enjoys stories from the Bible. Is able to begin making decisions for his life's actions.

Child of seven begins to grow more firmly from egocentricity to being a member of the community with accompanying notice of sex differences. Frequent handling of sex organs may be noted. Children might disappear into the bathroom to laugh about toilet functions, they may touch each other on buttocks or genitals.

AGE 7
Grade 2

	PHYSICAL	**SOCIAL**
AGE 8 Grade 3	Coordination such that they can skate, do simple folk dances, etc. Grows quite a bit this year. Attention span increases so can work for longer periods.	Boys learn it is important to be brave in any situation. The child wants to appear grown up and yet depends on parents and teachers. He is inclined to be bossy. Clubs are usually of one sex. Beginning to be aware of self as a person.
AGE 9 Grade 4	Growth is slowing down for boys and there is usually a growth spurt in girls. Coordination is excellent. Some girls have the appearance of breasts and pubic hair, though most still not developing.	Clubs and group activities important. Each club stays with own sex. These groups help form good behavior patterns. Enthusiasm runs faster than his abilities. Wants to be like his peers.
AGE 10 Grade 5	Girls begin to pass the boys in height. Team games more important now.	Boys and girls seem to dislike each other during 5th, 6th grades. Their humor is funny only to their peers, it seems. Girls have best friends, often several. Relationships are more involved than previously.

SPIRITUAL

His world is expanding and the mission interest can be introduced. He has many questions about things which were previously accepted on faith. Can read for himself now, from his own Bible. He can accept forgiving love in class experiences.

SEXUAL

Modesty becomes very important to the child. Sexual questions become less frequent. A change in the sex glands occurs at this time; growth hormones become more active while sex hormones quiet down. Boys interested in "dirty" jokes and vulgar words. May ask about father's part in reproduction.

AGE 8
Grade 3

This age child can grasp the history of the Bible. He looks up to heroes and can be motivated greatly to Christian character and action by teachers who know and understand him. He can understand service to others and can also comprehend the idea of the worldwide Church.

Period of getting ready for adolescence from now until thirteen years of age. Sexual development not very marked. Girls might start menstruation. Discussion of sex with friends may occur.

AGE 9
Grade 4

At this age the child is responsive and able to discuss his Christian faith. He can continue learning the facts of the Bible and apply them in his own life. He is able to find meaning in Christian stewardship.

Majority have learned about menstruation. Some interested in details of reproduction. (Girls) Some have experienced normal sex play. Have heard of intercourse, interested in "dirty" jokes. May experience a spurt of curiosity about sex.

AGE 10
Grade 5

	PHYSICAL	**SOCIAL**
AGE 11 Grade 6	Competitive spirit is strong. Team sports are very popular. Quite a difference this year in physical development of girls, most have begun to show breast development and most have reached 90% of mature stature. Boys still don't show sexual maturation.	Interest in Scouting and similar activities at its height now. Still has a strong family attachment, though seems to disparage family in conversation. Still has friends of same sex and relationships more emotional and complicated.
AGES 12, 13, 14 Grades 7, 8, 9	Girls maturing more quickly than boys. Boys mature about the ninth grade usually. Some seventh grade boys have pubic hair and growth of genitalia. Girls read romance stories and dream, whereas boys are more interested in sports and physical activities. Girls' breasts begin to fill out, underarm hair develops, menarche tends to occur. Awkwardness common.	Boys still interested in gang or group activities. They enjoy sports and hunting with other boys. Both sexes are trying to break ties with parents. 8th and 9th graders more interested in opposite sex to some extent.
AGES 15, 16, 17, 18 Grades 10, 11, 12	Most of these youth have reached sexual maturity. Boys are extremely well coordinated in sports activities. Girls become more visibly feminine. It is important to watch for good diet in order to be strong and have good complexion. Acne is a problem.	Although it is wisest to "play the field" at this age, youth are inclined to "go steady." They find security in a regular and steady date for school affairs. They find their activities outside the home for the most part.

SPIRITUAL

The eleven-year-old begins to think of his life occupation and can be encouraged to relate his faith to this choice. He will respond to group activities at the church and enjoy them. He is able to create tangible expressions of his faith and should have opportunity for these creative activities.

SEXUAL

Most girls know about reproduction and intercourse, though on a factual basis, biological rather than relational concept. Most boys know about masturbation and have had some experience with it. Some have erections from non-erotic stimuli.

AGE 11
Grade 6

The Junior High youth is beginning to master abstract thinking so can be led into ethical discussions. He begins to wonder and to ask questions about religion. This experience should be encouraged and should be guided by a sympathetic and able teacher. They sometimes think of Christ as a courageous hero who was brave to die on the cross. They need guidance in applying it personally to their own lives.

Sex education should be honest and should have reached completion factually. Build now on strong relational aspect. Boys may experience emission of semen during sleep. Most girls will be menstruating. Teen-agers wonder how to use their sexual capacities; they joke about it and try petting on dates.

AGES 12, 13, 14
Grades 7, 8, 9

The youth of this age has an expanding horizon and wants to structure his own activities. An understanding leader is invaluable. This age youth is capable of deeper abstract thinking. He needs help in understanding the problem of ethics. His life is before him and the subject of Christian vocations is timely. He is capable of deep emotional response to worship and Christian leadership. The church can take advantage of this situation.

Need for adult guidance in sex education extremely important at this age. Strong sex feeling and urges are felt.

AGES 15, 16, 17, 18
Grades 10, 11, 12

sacred design ®

"Understanding Age Growth" chart, reprinted from *Sex Education*, Approach/Program/Resources/For the parish. Copyright 1968, Sacred Design Associates, Inc., 840 Colorado Avenue, So., Minneapolis, Minnesota 55416.

This chart available in wall size (18" x 35"). Can be purchased for home, church, or school use. Order from Sacred Design Associates, Inc.

The American Institute of Family Relations reported a survey in which mothers were asked to keep track of how many times they made negative, compared with positive, comments to their children. They admitted that they criticized ten times for every one time that they said something favorable. Teachers apparently do a little better, for a three-year survey in the Orlando, Florida, public schools found that the teachers were only 75 percent negative. The study indicated that it takes four positive statements from a teacher to offset the effects of one negative statement to a child. Parents, take note!

•-•--•--•--•--•--•--•--•--•--•--•--•--•--•--•-•

The home should be to the children the most attractive place in the world, and the mother's presence should be the greatest attraction.

— ELLEN G. WHITE

Wise Parental Love

by Hazen G. Werner
Bishop, Methodist Church, Taiwan-Hong Kong

The attitudes of parents and other adults determine to a great degree the concepts a child forms of himself, of life, and of God. A child who has never known the full and real love of parents will find it hard to trust completely in the love of God. Leslie Weatherhead says, "Children have so often been made to feel that their parents will not love them unless they are good that they inevitably project onto their Heavenly Father the feelings they have developed about an earthly father and mother. . . . They cannot believe in unconditional love, but only in a love which depends on the attainment of moral standards. . . . The glorious truth is that God loves us whatever we do and our 'rights' are the rights of a love-relationship, that of sons and heirs, not the right born of achievement in the moral realm."

The simple, homely virtue fundamental to the happy maturing of the life of your child is love. Someone asked a mother, "Do you think all children deserve the full and impartial attention of the love of a mother?"

"Of course," she said.

"Well, which of your children do you love the most?" the inquirer asked, hoping to catch her in a contradiction.

"The one who is sick until he gets well," she answered, "and the one who is away until he gets home." The love felt for one another in the family — this is the fulfillment of God's plan.

Genuine parental love, naturally demonstrated, comes

Copyright 1959 Abingdon Press

nearer to being the cure-all for all the problems of child care than anything else that one could possess. Your love as a parent is most important to your child at the very moment when he is least lovable. This parental love is as needful to the spiritual and emotional growth of the child as food is to the body.

Ardis Whitman refers to the work of Dr. Rene Spitz, a New York psychoanalyst. He spent three months observing the reaction of babies in a foundling home where the nursing staff was so busy that each child "had only one-tenth of a mother." Dr. Spitz estimates that 30 percent of the babies died before they were a year old. "Without emotional satisfaction, children die," says Dr. Spitz. "Emotional starvation is as dangerous as physical starvation. It's slower, but just as effective." "There can be no question of the fact," says Dr. John G. McKenzie, "that to be loved and to love does give that sense of belonging to someone, that sense of security which is necessary to the possession of confidence. Without confidence we cannot face life."

Parental love must be a love for the child's sake. When parental love is real, it is a love that wants happiness and fullness of life for the one loved. "Infantile love," says Erich Fromm, "follows the principle: 'I love because I am loved.' Mature love follows the principle: 'I am loved because I love.' " Mature love means that a mother or a father is ready to share in the life and growth of the child, and to release the growing person into the ever-enlarging orb of existence.

Subtract parental love from the parent-child relationship, and the child lacks the feeling of acceptance. Here is the great danger. For this lack, the home today must bear its share of blame for delinquency in this country. Without parental love and the approval and acceptance which it implies, a youngster lacks a sense of self-worth. He feels frustrated in his desire to belong. For him it is as though he had been shut out and not wanted by those who should have stood by him.

A study was made of the twenty-one GIs who went over to Communism after the Korean War. Analysis of that study revealed some plain reasons for this defection. Nineteen of the twenty-one felt unloved or unwanted by fathers or stepfathers. Sixteen had withdrawn within themselves. Eighteen took no part in school activities or sports. Only one was ever chosen by his classmates for anything. It is quite obvious that we have here more than a lack of patriotism. The roots of the weakness of these boys run deep into early life. Home and society must accept its share of the blame.

There are parents who condition their love upon a child's good behavior: "Mother won't love you if you aren't good"; "If you aren't a good little boy, I'll just give you away." When the child comes to feel that he is loved only so long as he is suppressing his own individuality and letting himself be stamped with the pattern of other people's demands, he loses hold on himself as a real person.

There are parents who condition their love on a child's willingness to please. Children grow up trained to the one chief aim of pleasing their parents. The mother lavishes affection on her children when they do what pleases her. She is aloof or angry when she is displeased with what they have done. When she withdraws her love on such occasions, she lets her child down in such a depressed state of feelings he may respond in very undesirable ways.

There are parents who are perfectionists. It is unwise to force your child to strain after the stars. Children lose confidence in themselves and in life when they consistently fail to meet their parents' expectation. They end up with deep-rooted inferiority feelings. This kind of perfectionism can only result in devastating frustration.

There are parents who continually compare a younger child with an older sister or brother. A younger child who grows up under the shadow of a brilliant brother or sister has a hard time of it. It is unfair and injurious to hold up the superior abilities of these older members of the family in order to coerce a child to perform as parents want him to perform.

The important thing is to love this child of yours because he is yours. You love Johnny not because he knows all the answers, not because he plays the clarinet well, not because he is getting good marks, or has an unusual vocabulary. You love him because he is Johnny. You love him for himself and because he is yours. In all the world there is no security which can compare with that. With a love like that comes a sense of belonging, of being needed, of being sufficient. That's how a child grows up to be a sound, mature person.

There are unwise patterns of parental care that need to be examined from a Christian point of view. They may be accountable for the emotionally and spiritually underprivileged children of today.

Overindulgence. "I have had a hard struggle in my life. I'm going to see to it that my children have it easier." Nobody can dispute the kindness that may prompt such an assumption. However, the wisdom of it is certain to be subject to dispute. When parents overshelter or overshadow their child, the result is likely to be a partially developed personality. One finds in either instance the lack of the very security that is so much desired. He needs to face life and to be confronted with the necessity of choice-making; out of the latter comes growth and maturity. You can't do your child's thinking or concluding for him, but you can help him to achieve the right and the good. And when he does, he is more certain to try to do the right and the good another time.

Possessive love. "That love that possesses," says Peter Bertocci, "is the love that destroys more than it creates." Isn't it strange that the mother who gives life can also take it away? We've all known the mother who is very uncertain as to whether any girl is good enough for her son. There is the widow who implores her daughter not to marry and leave her alone.

Examine the consequence of possessiveness. When a mother completely dominates her child's life and treats him as a perennial infant, he has little chance to escape the dwarfing of personality. His life is like that of a seedling that unfortunately springs up too close to a large, full-grown tree. All of its life it is so overshadowed and so cramped that there is no room for the extension of its branches. Because of this constant frustration, the growing person becomes totally dependent. In all probability, a child growing into adulthood will seek a mate whose life bears this same characteristic, who gives promise of the complete care that by now has become utterly necessary.

A Christian parent, out of divine resources and with a will to provide for a child's individual growth, will love a child for himself, as a person. As a Christian parent, try to create in the home itself a proper context for the development of your child — a strong selfhood, useful and free. The most rigorous job in the world is being a parent. You have a life on your hands — a growing, changing, unfolding life. The greatest challenge that life can give is yours. With God's help, meet it!

.•··•··•··•··•··•··•··•··•··•··•··•··•·

Every child comes with the message that God is not yet discouraged of man.
— RABINDRANATH TAGORE

When to Say No

by W. T. Thompson

Author, Adventures in Parenthood, *and Professor, Union Theological Seminary, Richmond, Virginia*

For some years after the turn of the century, and long before, the advice to parents might have been, "Say no as often as possible." Discipline was stern, and punishment severe. More recently there was a sharp reaction from this viewpoint, and the caution then was, "Never say no," lest you block the child's creativity and prevent the development of his unique personality.

After a generation of this permissive treatment, it was discovered that to let a child run as his own impulses dictated might result in all kinds of harm to him. Unless we tell a boy no as well as yes, can he escape moral harm? How can he know what is right and what is wrong? If we always let him do as he wishes in the early days, he will build habits and attitudes that will make it impossible for him to adjust to others. He will become so selfish, so willful, so dominant, so arrogant, so lacking in manners, that people will not like him. In his resentment at being unable to get along with others he may break the laws which society has created for its protection and land in jail.

The surprising result of freedom, which was supposed to prevent emotional blocking, was that serious harm was done in the realm of the emotions. Our guidance clinics discovered these youngsters unhappy, tense, anxious, inferior.

Unlimited choice places an intolerable burden on the child. Furthermore, it is hard for a child to know that his

Copyright 1959 C. D. Deans

parents love him if they let him do as he pleases. The very fact that they have set limits, and are prepared to stop him, makes him sure that they care. Through obedience to rules recognized as wise and just which his parents have made, a child learns to trust his parents.

A child needs and wants help in controlling the strong, aggressive drives which at times frighten him by their intensity, and by his inability to cope with them. He feels, at times desperately, the need of help from someone older and stronger who will enable him to control these urges.

There are parents who say no constantly. But is it good?

A little child is created for activity. To say no all the time is not only irritating to him, but thwarts his interest in life, blocks his curiosity, reduces his eagerness to learn.

There are two periods in the child's life when we should reduce our no's to a minimum; when he is a year and a half to three years old and from thirteen through fifteen.

Several studies have shown that a high proportion of temper tantrums occur a half-hour before the evening meal. The boy comes in hungry and tired. Especially is he worn out if he has been playing hard with older children. He is on edge, the threshold of control is lowered, and he may be on the way to trouble.

It is advisable to be sparing of our no's when our youngsters are "down," when they haven't been doing too well in school or in games, or have been at odds with their friends.

When to say no? You have to say no, but say it as infrequently as possible, and about things that matter.

Say no unitedly. Parents must agree about their treatment of their children so that they say no together. If there is a chance to "divide and conquer," the child will take advantage of it.

Father may make a mistake; mother knows it, but she stands behind him at the time. Later she may talk it out with him, and they may plan a better strategy for the next situation.

Say no consistently. Children are confused when their parents say no today, and yes tomorrow, unless the situation has changed. If it has, they should make the child see the reason for it.

A promise should be faithfully carried out, so that there will be something the child can count on in this unstable world. Our yes should be something he can bank on.

As far as possible we should treat all the children in the same way, or let the children see the reason for any difference in dealing with them, and not let them feel that we are playing favorites, or that we love one more than the other.

Say no reasonably. We forget our own childhood so completely, or remember it so imperfectly, or have so little imagination as a substitute for memory, or so little knowledge of the way in which children grow, that we create difficulties for them and for ourselves by expecting more of them than they can do.

If we are to be fair we have to get at the cause of the misbehavior, or the motive behind it, so that it will appear to us as the boy sees it, or as it is; though he may not understand it. We see one boy striking his smaller brother. Our impulse is to send him to his room without any attempt to discover what lies behind their quarrel. He seems so clearly the aggressor. But his younger brother may have had a subtle way of provoking an attack with the intention of getting the older boy in trouble. He really is the culprit, all appearances to the contrary.

Sally failed on a test, and the teacher took her to task before the class. Condemning her won't get at the root of her difficulty. What she needs is a bit of praise, an assurance that she is loved, an opportunity to show that she can do something well.

As the children get older we can explain more fully the reason for our saying no, and the necessity for cooperative living in the home. Many a misunderstanding could be avoided and a new spirit created in the home if we would just sit down and talk things out.

It is a part of fairness to remember that a small boy is a person, with some sense of his own dignity and worth.

A father, feeling a bit piqued because his ten-year-old son was always quoting a man who lived in their neighborhood, asked, "What is it you like so much about him?" The boy hesitated and, reaching for words, finally said: "I guess it's because he talks with you as though you knew something, too, and weren't just a kid."

We must keep in mind also, if we are to be fair, a child's utter absorption in play. Especially is this true if others are in the game with him, and he feels that to drop everything would spoil things for them too. "It is nearly suppertime; finish your game in ten minutes, then I'll call you again" is so much better than waiting for the hour to strike and shouting, "Supper's ready, come at once!" Regardless of his age, we should be very careful about saying no or criticizing him sharply in the presence of his friends or of other people. He is a person, his feelings are sensitive, and his self-respect suffers if he loses the respect of others.

Say no expectantly. Arnold Bennett said that when you speak to another you speak twice: once through what you say; and again in the way in which you say it — the manner, the tone of voice; and he is sure that 90 percent of the friction in life is caused by the tone of voice. When we speak to a child, we may sound as if we had no idea he would do what we are asking him. The threat of punishment is in our voice. "I want my ice cream," a boy says. "No, you don't — not until you have eaten the rest of your dinner!" We imply: "We don't think you will eat your dinner; we are sure you will not have your dessert." What a different atmosphere we would create if we should say, "Of course you will, when you have eaten your dinner." He feels we believe he will eat it, and get his ice cream. Already the taste of it is in his mouth by anticipation, and he is encouraged to devour the potato and cabbage which he doesn't like. A relaxed attitude, a light touch, a bit of humor, instead of tenseness and sternness, will work wonders.

Say no firmly. He must know we mean it. Often we toss off so many no's so carelessly that he is confused. If we say no thoughtlessly and forget it, and never check on it, we encourage him to disobey us the next time we say no.

Say no lovingly. Love is the basis of all our dealing with our children; not silly sweetness, weak sentimentality, but a deep, strong, selfless devotion. Such a love enables us to say no firmly, and mean it.

There will be resentment at times, perhaps bitter. He would have a feeling of relief, and a new appreciation of us, if our love were so understanding that we could let him express some of his bitterness.

If we have to punish him, we must let him know by our actions that while we disapprove what he is doing, our love for him has not changed; he is not cut off from the family.

Is obedience something our children owe us because we are their parents, or is it a means to the development of their lives, leading to self-mastery and a wise use of freedom? Shouldn't our purpose be to enable them so to discipline themselves, that increasingly they will have the judgment and strength to do what is right, and will become free from our control, or any other outside control? To put it differently, shouldn't we try to prepare them to choose Christ as their rightful Lord, and in freedom and joy to obey him?

We must examine ourselves to find our own hidden motives for seeking implicit obedience based on our no's. Is it for his sake or for ours that we are saying no? Will what we are doing bring him to the place where on the basis of his own accepted ideals he will not need us to say no to him, because he can now say no to himself, and also yes?

Pleasurable Discipline

by Henry R. Brandt

Author, Build a Happy Home with Discipline, *and Consulting Psychologist*

Child discipline can be a pleasant task. There is a genuine joy in guiding a child toward becoming a mature, happy adult. You are a partner with God in making disciples of your children. It is your great privilege to lead your children to become followers of your example and of the Lord Jesus Christ.

We think of a disciplined person as one who has voluntarily chosen a certain way of life. To "discipline" a child is not to punish him for stepping out of line, but to teach that child the way he ought to go. Discipline therefore includes everything that you do in order to help children learn. It is the challenge and the privilege of training children.

Discipline involves a twenty-year process. The parent does his part along with the school, church, other community agencies, and society in general. During those twenty years you very slowly relinquish complete control in favor of the gradually developing inner strengths of the child that enable him to take responsibility for his own conduct and its consequences.

If you can do this and enjoy the process through each swiftly passing phase, then the "discipline problem" will become a pleasant task of leading your children to an abundant life.

All forms of discipline, to be successful, must be based on the foundation of love. The puzzlement of many parents

Copyright 1966 Henry Brandt

over the place of love in guidance of their children is reflected in such questions as:

"Should I withdraw my love when I punish my child?"

"Should I show that I love him after I punish him?"

Parents asking these questions usually are thinking in terms of overt acts such as the withholding of or the giving of hugs and kisses.

The biblical standard of love is described in 1 Corinthians 13:4-8. It has nine components: patience, kindness, generosity, humility, courtesy, unselfishness, good temper, guilelessness, and sincerity.

Such love is a matter of the spirit; it is something within you. In love you help your child to repeat acceptable behavior and in love you restrain him, if necessary, from repeating unacceptable behavior.

From a heart of love you can say to your child, "No, you can't do that," because you know such action is not good for the child. Conversely, you can lose your temper and snap, "No, you can't do that!" Your spirit makes the difference. You know the difference — and so does your child.

When, in a spirit of hostility and anger, you strike at your child, you fail to help him and you hurt yourself. This striking need not be physical. It can be sharp words or a stinging silence, yet be just as painful to the child as violently administered physical punishment.

Admittedly none of us can claim perfection. What then shall we do when a hostile spirit grips us? Repent, and seek God's forgiveness and his grace and patience.

For the Christian parent, the major task is to teach your children from the beginning that you are followers of the Master, that your children need Christ as Savior, and that they should keep God central in their lives.

Mark Fakkema makes these three points:

1. Begin as early as possible to teach your child to fear God. Since "by him were all things created . . . and by him

all things consist" (Colossians 1:16, 17), it is clear that parents have ample occasion to inspire awesome reverence for him who alone is worthy of all love and all-out devotion.

2. Begin as early as possible to teach your children respect for God-given authority. Since there is no power but of God (Romans 13:1), parents who exercise authority must do so under God's orders, in God's name and in the greatness, the power, the majesty, the glory, the righteousness and the justice, grace, and love of God.

3. Be sure that your commands to your children are expressive of God's will. It should be ever apparent that your commands are God inspired. To teach God's will without knowing the Bible is to teach your own will — and to fail in the teaching of obedience.

You can count on your children's resisting your training and correction. They will sulk, pout, throw tantrums, cry, and argue.

The question is: How do you show love for the child when he acts like that?

Is it a sign of a lack of love when you make your child do something he hates to do? Or when you say no? Do you show your love by giving in to your child's resistance? Or by saying yes?

The Bible does not teach us to fulfill the desires of our children. It says to train them in the way that they should go. It does not imply that they will welcome your training. The fact is, they may stubbornly disagree with you every step of the way. Remember, you are the trainer; they are the trainees. As such they do not decide the rules; they follow them!

And what if they don't? Then you help them until they do. The challenge and test of parenthood comes when the parent faces defiance, resistance, screaming, tantrums, rebellion, and similar reactions.

Uncertainty on the part of an adult about the direction

that guidance should take indicates a lack of proper study and consideration. A sure sense of direction — so sure that the adult conveys it to the child in word and deed — is essential to effective guidance. Look at the biblical view: "The rod and reproof give wisdom: but a child left to himself bringeth his mother to shame" (Proverbs 29:15). "Correct thy son, and he shall give thee rest. Yes, he shall give delight to thy soul" (29:17). "As many as I love, I rebuke and chasten; be zealous, therefore, and repent"(Revelation 3:19).

Adults who leave the child's achievement at the level of getting his own way, and his development within the limits of his interest of the moment, are not guiding. Such adult action — or inaction — is irresponsibility, not guidance.

What makes a child thrive physically and socially are adult-decided responsibilities which are gradually given over to the child as he shows himself capable of handling decisions and responsibilities effectively. There is no magical formula on procedure. What you do and the way you do it is a compound of your knowledge, your values, and your inner strengths.

One of the basic principles for happy family living is the setting of limits. Whenever two lives cross, it is necessary to establish certain well-defined boundaries to make possible friendly relations. Your children need to know what is permissible and what is prohibited.

Specific limits ought to be as few as possible, reasonable, enforceable, withdrawn or modified as the child grows older.

Limits placed upon your children amount to responsibilities. When these are fulfilled adequately they form a basis for granting privileges. If these obligations are neglected the privileges may be reasonably withdrawn.

When a privilege is no longer deserved, or if a request cannot be granted, the decision should be made promptly and clearly. A child of any age can accept a negative answer more easily than a halfhearted or a postponed answer.

It should be made clear to your children that privileges are not rights. Teen-agers, for example, may regard use of the family car as their right. Other such privileges are choice of clothing, the hour to get home, and the time to be in bed. Limits need to be established for these areas and any failure to meet the limits should involve automatic curtailment of privileges.

When you set up even the simplest system of limits, you can be sure your child will want to break them. He will test you, put you on trial, to see if you plan to enforce the limits. On the other hand you should understand that children will never maintain limits perfectly. Your task is to set reasonable limits and not become overanxious when your child resists or complains that the limit is not reasonable. Whether a limit is sensible or not is a decision that belongs to the parents — not to the child, whether he's eight or eighteen. See to it that you say no in a spirit of patience and gentleness, rather than in a spirit of exasperation or anger. The way you react will make a difference in the results.

Parenthood, and the discipline which is such a vital part of it, is a twenty-year-long job. If you have done your job well, your children will go forth to tend to their own families or careers. While they are in the process of training their own children, you'll be establishing a new and fruitful life in new areas of living.

You can train your children with this goal in mind. You can anticipate the day when your children launch out on their own and you will both rejoice that you have trained your children in the way they ought to go (Proverbs 22:6).

Demand Their Best

by Arthur Gordon
Magazine editor

We had a minor crisis at our house the other morning. The nine-year-old had been told several times the night before to attend to a certain chore before going to school. Just as she was putting on her coat to run off, she was asked if she had done her chore. Her answer was a startled look. She had forgotten; but never mind, she promised she would do it after school.

No, her mother told her, she would do it right now. But this, she cried, would make her late for school! Too bad. She just would have to be late.

Tears, lamentations, despair. Rather than be marked late, she sobbed, she would not go to school at all.

Yes, she was told, she would go to school, late or not.

The chore was done right then and there, to the accompaniment of heartrending moans. The reluctant scholar was escorted to the sidewalk, given her lunch money and a gentle shove in the direction of the school. We watched her go with love and pity, a forlorn figure. We knew that she would come back after school, as cheerful and as fond of her ogre-parents as she had ever been. She did.

Just a routine family episode, unimportant, insignificant, except for one thing. We probably wouldn't have handled the situation that way five or six years ago.

Five years ago we would have taken the line of least resistance. We would have avoided a scene. "All right," we'd have said, with mild exasperation, "so you forgot. Do your

Copyright 1961 Fawcett Publications, Inc.

chore when you come back from school." But in the last five years our concept and conduct of parenthood has changed quite a bit. Let me tell you how this change happened, and what brought it about.

Five years ago the oldest of our four children (we have five now) was ten. Aside from the usual intramural bickerings and scufflings, we had no great behavior problems with them. But when we tried to look ahead, to project the children's lives a few years into the future, we found ourselves getting worried.

What alarmed us was the mounting evidence that something was seriously wrong in a critical area of American life: character formation in children, and particularly in adolescents, or young adults. It didn't seem to matter where we looked. At the decline of simple good manners. At the increasing permissiveness that seemed to tolerate such activities as drinking and smoking at far earlier ages than formerly. At the prevalence of — and indifference to — classroom cheating. At the much publicized rise in juvenile crime. At the less publicized, but just as sinister, rise in the venereal-disease rate, mainly — heaven help us — between the ages of fifteen and nineteen. At reports of shaky morals and poor performance in the armed services. We looked at these things and we didn't like what we saw.

I don't mean that we held a solemn conclave and decided that the entire younger generation was coming apart at the seams. We knew some admirable teen-agers. But the overall climate into which our children were heading did worry us. And we asked ourselves, very seriously, what we should do about it.

We knew, to begin with, that we couldn't change the climate; social trends are too massive, too inexorable, too slow. The problem, then, was how to weatherproof the children, how to give them the resistance, the resilience, and the high sense of purpose that they would need.

The more we looked at the situation, the stronger our

conviction grew that American parents were giving their children too much and not requiring enough of them. That was the basic fault.

I remember very well the moment when this thought crystallized for me. I happened to be reading an anecdote in which a famous schoolmaster in England, J. H. Bruce Lockhart, was asked what his formula was for producing superior youngsters. "I demand," said the old headmaster. "And then when I have what I demanded, I demand still more. The more you demand, the more you get, and this is the secret of schoolmastering."

"Demand," a strong word. A subtle word. And a word rusty with disuse in the vocabularies of too many parents. Schoolteachers, after all, were faced with much the same problems as parents. If this demand technique worked in one area, why shouldn't it work in another?

And so, gradually, we began to tighten up on discipline and insist on better performance all along the line. Better table manners. Stricter rules where bedtime and television and homework were concerned. More household chores. Insistence on being kept informed as to whereabouts and plans. At the same time, we cut down on some of the services that we had been performing for the convenience of the children. We stopped chauffeuring them almost entirely. If they wanted to go somewhere, they were told to walk, or ride their bicycles. We reduced the amount of canned entertainment and watched to see if they would begin to invent their own amusements. They did. We also watched to see if they would resent this change from a climate of relative permissiveness to a climate of demand. Apparently they didn't.

I don't mean that they welcomed the dishwashing with cries of gladness, or enthusiastically dropped whatever they were doing whenever bedtime came. But in a curious way they seemed reassured by the stronger framework of discipline in which they found themselves.

It also seemed to us that by demanding a certain amount of thoughtfulness in small things from the children, we knocked a few chips off the granite of their inborn egotism. Last Halloween, surveying the loot she had acquired trick-or-treating, the ten-year-old began worrying about "the kids in the hospital who couldn't go out and have fun the way we did." On her own initiative, she called the hospital and got permission to go through the wards, with one little friend, giving her candy away. Perhaps we were seeing cause and effect where there was none, but something weakened the wall of self-centeredness that surrounds most youngsters and let this ray of light shine through.

Perhaps, in part, that "something" was a desire to win praise or approval from her suddenly-more-demanding parents. The human being is a unique creature in that he will often make more effort to please someone else than he will to please himself. To recognize and use this principle in dealing with children is probably the most effective and subtle way to demand.

Looking back, I can see now that my father was a master of this. He demanded a good deal, but he did it entirely without pressure. He never "laid down the law" to us children. He never exhorted us to get good grades, or become good athletes. He simply let us know, in his quiet way, that if we tried to excel it would make him proud and happy.

The whole object and purpose of demanding, of course, is to bring the child to the point where he will start demanding the best of himself. "Our chief want in life," said Emerson, "is someone who will make us do what we can." During a child's formative years, this is a function that only the parents can perform. But a lot of parents seem to be afraid that if they do perform it, their children will dislike them.

Military discipline has never been very popular with us stridently individualistic Americans, and certainly I did my share of griping about it when I was in uniform. But it seems to me that in their evaluation of human nature the armed services are a good deal more realistic than many modern parents. Ask any admiral or general how to persuade young people to face up to the strain and unpleasantness involved in putting aside their personal convenience and desires to meet the demands of duty. The answer will be prompt and simple: you're not going to "persuade" them. You must demand and you must enforce.

In other words, the military, despite the growing number of letters to congressmen from anguished rookies and their mamas, has not lost its capacity to demand. If it ever does, we are finished as a nation.

Many thoughtful police officers see a direct and unmistakable connection between juvenile crime and parents who are so afraid that their children won't have everything that they deprive them of nothing. The excuse such parents often give is that they want their children "to have the things we didn't have." Last November, in a letter to the local newspaper, Lt. Robert Funk of the Savannah (Georgia) police department addressed himself to such parents.

"Of course we want our children to have all the things we didn't have, but what are some of these things? Our parents didn't let us stay out all night. We were not allowed to be disrespectful to people. We were not allowed to eat 'junk' all the time. We were not allowed to throw our clothes around. We were not idle; we had jobs to do at home. We didn't receive money unless we earned it. We didn't enter a room without knocking on the door. We didn't fail to attend religious services. . . . It's not too late to set down some rules," he concluded. "Our children are starving to death for some real leadership. Help your child today, for he or she will be the citizen of tomorrow."

It is precisely this flame that each parent must look for in a child, and breathe on, and nurture, and never dampen. Only then are we going to produce strong people, proud of themselves and the job they do and their reasons for doing it.

Mature men and women have always known that there is no feeling in the world like the exhilaration that comes from attempting the difficult, achieving the doubtful, and mastering self in the process. But children are not born with this knowledge. They have to be taught. And the best way to teach them is to demand from them, until the shining moment when they begin to demand of themselves.

·•··•··•··•··•··•··•··•··•··•··•··•··•··•·

Sound family life is the largest factor in mental health, broadly speaking. Apart from definite genetic conditions, the early upbringing of children, largely centered on the "atmosphere" of the home, is more significant than any other single influence in determining whether an individual will be able to develop mental and emotional normality, be able to relate usefully to other persons, marry successfully, and produce children who, in turn, grow up with good mental health and make a constructive contribution to the work of the world.

— PAUL POPENOE

Angry Children

by Stanley E. Lindquist

Director, Department of Psychology, Fresno State College

The average American boy today has one chance in five of ending up in court as a juvenile offender.

This is the assertion of Roul Tourney, author of the shocking book, *Kids, Crime and Chaos.* As answer to the problem, the author, whose research was sponsored by the W. M. Armistead Foundation, insists: "Let's take juvenile delinquency away from the experts. It's time to give it back to the amateurs — the parents, the teachers and the ministers. . . ."

Parents can control the juvenile delinquency problem in most cases, but it takes warmth and understanding in handling their children. When love prevails in the home the situation is largely solved.

Paul realized this many years ago and exhorted the New Testament Church: "Provoke not your children." In Scripture this exhortation is used twice — first in Ephesians 6: 4 and again in Colossians 3:21. Why has he placed such emphasis on this particular concept of child rearing?

There are many possible explanations, but I wonder if Paul was provoked as a youngster by his own father, and as a result he accented this aspect of child rearing. His own background may have made him especially aware of this problem.

Children should not vent their anger at parents when corrected or punished. This could be the beginning of a later rebellion against society — and a subsequent juvenile delinquency problem. But many do. Why?

Copyright 1962 Christian Life Publications, Inc.

Lack of explanation regarding the reason for punishment is probably the most important factor. Correction is part of the growing-up process, and should not be eliminated or neglected. But children feel they have the right to know the reasons for punishment. When the parent goes to the trouble of helping the child understand the reasons, he more readily accepts and learns from it.

Another problem is: When should we punish a child?

Usually punishment occurs when talking has failed; the youngster misbehaves until the parent is goaded beyond the capacity to contain himself. It is important to tell the child that you are helping him remember not to misbehave. One way to do this is to create some pain.

Some authorities say you should never strike a child in anger. I feel that a parent who postpones and carefully plans punishment has something wrong in his personality that needs investigation. The time to punish is at the time of misbehavior, but if anger causes you to lose control, you'd better wait and seek help for yourself.

At this point, it should be emphasized that mother should not wait until dad comes home to have him do the punishing. This makes dad's homecoming something to be dreaded rather than looked forward to with anticipation. Worse, the child may not connect his original act with his punishment. Father then becomes an unjust punisher.

Often the frustration of the parent is vented on the child. When you punish your children severely, ask yourself: "If I had felt better, would I have punished in this way?" If not, your own frustrations are interfering with the lessons you are trying to teach your children. As a result they are provoked to anger.

Another reason for a child's becoming provoked is "unfair" punishment. If a younger child is not punished for the same thing as the older child, this seems unfair; nevertheless, punishment should fit the misdeed and the age of the child involved. The older child may not be able to accept this fully, but the parent's patient explanation will encourage understanding.

Sometimes there is a feeling of unfairness because neighboring children or friends are not punished for the same things. It is important to help a child realize that each family has different rules, and the rules of your family are the ones to which he must conform. This will build family cohesiveness, and the child will recognize that he is a treasured member of a special family.

One of the most insidious, and horrifying, types of punishment a parent can inflict is to tell a child that God doesn't love him if he disobeys.

I believe this kind of early training has alienated more children in Christian families than almost any other factor. If God's love for us were dependent on our doing what pleased him, none of us would be recipients of his love.

To try to bludgeon a child into conforming to our ideas by such a threat will either cause bitterness toward God, with a resultant lack of faith, or it will result in the insecurity so evident in people who cannot do anything spontaneously or freely. These people are always troubled that God might punish them for real or imagined error. This is inverted anger, focused on oneself, and causes discouragement which extends beyond childhood to adulthood.

Sometimes parents threaten children by quoting ominous scriptural passages. Such a procedure creates resentment toward the Word of God. The use of threats does not teach a lesson. Scripture is given for "reproof, correction, and instruction in righteousness" (2 Timothy 3:16), but it accomplishes this purpose only when the application is made in love. It must not be used by the parent as a threat to force a child into obedience.

The tragedy of this procedure is that the child's thoughts are focused on the letter of the law and not on its spirit. This kind of training kills rather than giving life (2 Corinthians 3:6). The child who learns Christianity through negatives will have a false conception of the abundant life Christ promised.

Another way to provoke children is to tease them incessantly. The child is stimulated beyond his capacity and the resultant anger is punished, but his own attempt to tease his parents meets with rebuff. The result is a nervous, discouraged child!

Often parents ignore the age level or ability of the child; they expect him to do things in the same fashion and skill as an adult or another child. When he can't, irritable criticism creates severe resentment. Parents must be patient and understanding in their instruction and help. Not to do so is to seriously violate Paul's exhortation to us.

The alternative given by Paul to provoking your children is to "bring them up in the nurture and admonition of the Lord" (Ephesians 6:4). Scripture can teach each of us important concepts for helping us develop a rich personality. From this vital source, we can learn much to bring up our children "in the nurture and admonition of the Lord."

·•··•··•··•··•··•··•··•··•··•··•··•··•··•·

Whatever parent gives his children good instruction, and sets them at the same time a bad example, may be considered as bringing them food in one hand, and poison in the other.

— JOHN BALGUY

7

CREATING THE ATMOSPHERE

Worship, Family Style

by Howard Hendricks
Professor of Christian Education, Dallas Theological Seminary

I referred to the "family altar" during a talk and a lady came up afterward and said, "Dr. Hendricks, can you buy these in the bookstore?" She had come out of a Roman Catholic background, and I think this was an intelligent question. In any Catholic bookstore you can buy the equipment to set up a little family worship center. But I've been amazed by the number of people who have never heard of a family altar or a family worship time.

Remember in John's Gospel when Jesus engaged a Samaritan woman in conversation and led her on into spiritual insight? "The hour cometh, and now is, when the true worshipers shall worship the Father in Spirit and in truth; for the Father seeketh such to worship him." God is in quest for my soul to worship him.

Worship is a personal response to a divine revelation. God has revealed himself and I am responsible for responding. Arthur Gibbs called it "the Christian's highest occupation." But, alas, it's the lost chord of Christianity. It's a lost art in our churches. But worse — and probably the reason it is — it's a lost art in our homes.

Copyright 1966 The Navigators

Let's look at the crutches — excuses often pawned off as reasons why we do not have family worship.

"I don't have time." This is a problem of priorities. You don't have time for what? To do that which God is seeking? We're living in an activistic society that unfortunately has rubbed off on us Christians. Have you learned anything of the barrenness of busyness? There's a sterility to activity, and much of our activity is nothing more than an anesthetic to deaden the pain of an empty life.

"It's not convenient to get the family together." This is a problem of scheduling. The average American is looking for a religion that is comfortable and convenient. And there are plenty of them on the market. You cannot take cost and conflict out of Christianity and have the same thing left. Family worship time is something you have to make as a sacred appointment and keep.

"I don't know how." This is a problem of technique, and probably the most legitimate. Maybe you didn't come out of a Christian home. This was my problem. When I recognized my responsibility I was like a babe in the woods, but I just forged it out.

"I don't need it." This is a problem of vision. A man said to me, "You're going overboard on this thing. Isn't it enough to go to church on Sunday?" Compartmentalized Christianity — the little religious compartment on Sunday with the Lord on call in case of trouble.

But you know, these excuses evaporate upon examination.

What goes into a family worship time? First of all, *prayer,* a time when you talk to the Lord. A number of years ago a scholar who was visiting us sat in on our family worship time. In typical style my children prayed for the fence and thanked the Lord for the tricycle and other sundry items. Afterward he took me aside and said, "Professor Hendricks, do you teach your children to pray for these things?"

I said, "Certainly."

"You teach them to pray for the fence?"

I asked, "Do you ever pray for protection?"

"Yes," he answered.

"Well, that's exactly what that fence is to my boy. He looks outside and sees all those big dogs and he's real glad Jesus gave him a fence." I said to him, "Do you ever pray for your Ford?"

He said, "Certainly."

I said, "What makes you think your Ford is more important to God than my boy's tricycle?" We've gotten educated years beyond our intelligence.

Our family keeps a little notebook. On one side of a page we put: "We ask," and on the other side, "He answers."

About six years ago when we met a financial crisis the six of us got down to pray. And as we asked God to supply, the doorbell rang. Someone had wired me over a hundred dollars. When I relayed the news to my family, one of the youngest said, "Daddy, why are you so surprised?"

A second component to family worship is *the Bible.* In prayer we talk to the Lord, but in the Bible God talks to us. We have made it a rule in our family not to read the Bible meaninglessly. This is particularly true for children. We need to take the Word of God and translate it into words they understand.

Another is *music.* A great tragedy of the day is that our children are not reared in the hymns of the faith. We have taken as a project in our family to learn the hymns. What a treasure house this is for one's future.

Devotional materials are a fourth component. You may be familiar with the Moody Press *Our Home Bible Story Book.* If you have any small children, this is an excellent translation from an original Dutch version. There is also a helpful book by Ken Taylor, put out by Moody Press, called *Stories for the Children's Hour.*

Let me give you some of the characteristics of a good family worship time.

The time is not important, but *regularity* is. I know families who have it in the morning. I know families who have it in the evening. The important thing is to find a time when you can get all the family together — a time you can keep.

Try to be *brief,* but not rushed. Some people seem to think that to have something that's holy, it must be an hour and a half. That isn't true.

Keep it *varied* — and believe me, this demands creative planning. In talking with seminary students who have come out of Christian homes I have discovered the one thing they resent about a family worship is that it was boring — always the same.

We have a different theme and prayer subject for each day. Monday we discuss what we learned in our church the day before. We pray specifically for our witness in the community and for the children's witness at school.

We have two days for missionaries. We read missionary stories in serial fashion. We correspond with our missionaries by tape. Why, Africa is closer to us than some parts of Dallas. Our children save their pennies and nickels to support a little boy in a school overseas who talks to them in his own language by tape. They get excited!

On another day we pray for our relatives. My father, a retired Army colonel, came to see us. When he got off the plane my youngest boy ran up to him, jumped in his arms and said, "Hey, Granddaddy? Do you know Jesus yet?"

My father said, "No, son, I'm afraid I don't."

"Well, we're praying for ya and pretty soon you will," my boy replied. I'm convinced that when my father comes to Christ it will be through the faith of the children's prayers.

We review memory work. We pray for family problems

and needs. On Sunday we usually paraphrase a portion of the Bible. We pray for the Lord's day — for our pastor.

And finally, it should be *informal*. It doesn't have to be preachy. Keep it primarily child-centered. Every one of the children can participate and their needs can be met.

Richard Baxter was a great man of God who took a very wealthy and sophisticated parish in England. For three years he preached with all the passion of his heart without any visible response. "Finally one day," he wrote, "I threw myself across the floor in my study and cried out to God, 'God, You must do something with these people, or I'll die.' " And he said, "It was as if God spoke to me audibly and said, 'Baxter, you're working in the wrong place. You're expecting revival to come through the church. Try the home.' "

And Richard Baxter went out and called on home after home. He'd spend an entire evening in a home helping people set up a family worship time with their children. He moved from one home to another until finally the Spirit of God started to light fires all over that congregation, until they swept through the church and made it the great church that it became, and him a man of godly distinction.

We hear a lot about revival these days, but it's always in connection with the church. I wonder if God is not saying to us, "You're working in the wrong place." Ask God to bring revival in your home. If he does, I'll guarantee you, it will infect the church. And I believe it begins when you and I establish a value system — a priority system — to meet the Lord every day with our families.

·•··•··•··•··•··•··•··•··•··•··•··•·

Blessed are those who can give without remembering and take without forgetting.
— Elizabeth Bibesco

Kazoku

by Roland Conlon

Kazoku is our thing. Family work schedules, recreation activities, and just about everything else is decided and programmed by the Kazoku Club. Each natural member — my wife and I and our three children, ages 8-13 — has an ID card, sealed in plastic with his own picture. Each associate member (visiting relative) also receives an ID card, while honorary members (family pets) get only an ID necklace.

The club's officers change every six months by popular vote. These include a secretary, treasurer, and a publicity chairman who publishes a monthly newspaper and a semi-annual magazine. In addition, one permanent officer (Dad) is the special projects chief. He prepares a monthly calendar, and sort of coordinates things. We feel that the father image is not only a biblical requirement for a Christian home, but a necessity for the stability of any family. Finally there is a program chairman, who rotates weekly. He is responsible for family night games and refreshments which are purchased from his own income or allowance.

Kazoku has been a family tradition since well before any of the children were in school. As the children have matured so has the curriculum, but so slowly that they have not recognized the change. Instead, they have grown up with it. It is a way of life that had its beginning when our first child, Danny, was born thirteen years ago, and we realized that we were responsible for the mental, physical, and spiritual growth of that tiny bundle of goo's and slobbers.

Copyright 1970 Christian Life Publications, Inc.

"Such a precious little thing," my wife, Margie, would say over and over. Then one day we asked each other, "Why do so many sweet babies grow up to be ugly and selfish?"

It was then that we determined that we would do everything possible to make our children loving, kind, and thoughtful. That would require more than just a plan on how to raise and discipline them. It had to go deeper, beyond our children. It had to involve us as parents. Therefore, we resolved before God to give ourselves 100 percent to each other so that we might be an example of love for the children as they matured. Next, we resolved to allow nothing to divert our attention from the one calling in life that we could attribute directly to God: that of parenthood. This done, we were ready to become parents in the true sense of the word.

Our program developed gradually, often by trial and error, but steadily. Before the children were able to read or write we began a Friday family night program. It was simple, usually amounting to nothing more than a few games, making pop corn, or engaging in some other fun activity, followed by a Bible story from a book with lots of pictures. After the story, the children repeated what they remembered. But this was not nearly as important as the fact that they were able to curl up on my lap, to experience the security of love and affection, and to learn how to communicate. Even in the middle of a story lesson, if one of the children innocently grabbed my nose, I realized it wasn't because he was mean or bored, but because he felt he belonged, that he was wanted, loved, and needed.

In addition, when the children were four or five, we set aside several hours three evenings each week to teach them their ABC's and, finally, to read and write. This always was followed with a few thoughts from the Bible and a goodnight prayer.

Finally, we knew we needed a name for our program. Because the Orient seemed mysterious and fascinated the children, we invaded the language of Japan and came up with Kazoku, Japanese for "family." The children liked the word, and we formed the Kazoku Club, or, in translation, The Family Club.

Since then, each of our children has committed his life to Jesus Christ and has proved his understanding of this act by the life he lives. We have never experienced a generation gap. If a child has a problem, he doesn't run to a counselor, but brings it to Mom or Dad.

Our children trust us, and they trust each other. When one has a job, he freely shares a portion of his or her income with the rest of the family. It's not an obligation, but each receives a real joy in giving.

Study nights (Monday through Thursday) include home work, or special education projects designed by Margie or me. Study time follows the evening meal and lasts until bedtime. The purpose of the special projects is to build reading comprehension, an ability to express oneself in writing, and concepts of arithmetic. Much Christian literature is used in the reading, but most of the projects are tied in with school activities and are later introduced by the child at school for extra credit.

Thirty minutes before bedtime, the children bring their Bibles into the family room and I read two or three verses while they follow in their Bibles. Then I explain the meaning of what I have read. Following this, the children close their Bibles and write in their own words just what they are able to remember from the short text. This session is closed with prayer, and it is then bedtime. TV, radio, or stereo are not even a part of the children's weektime vocabulary.

Friday comes once a week, but Tommy, eight, wishes it could be every night. After our Friday Kazoku Club meeting, we play games. One week Sara, eleven, is in charge, the next Dan, thirteen, and so on, until everyone has had his turn. Then we start all over again.

Games are an excellent way to get the family to work together, think together, and react together. Regardless of the location, sharing time, adventure, and even money makes a family's love for each other grow, and gives them that bit of seasoning required for a sweet flavor.

I wonder if there is a time in a child's life when he or she becomes too old to kiss both Mom and Dad! Children of all ages need affection, love, and a feeling of belonging. A goodnight kiss — even just a peck on the cheek — is reassuring. It seems to me that it is more important in the development of a child than giving him a new car, a bank account, or any number of other material gifts. We have decided to let our children tell us when they think they're too old for this type of thing. So far, none has felt it out of place.

Fun and frolic begin the evening, but the most important moment, and really a primary reason for family night, is Bible study. One of the misfortunes of much Christian Bible study in the home is that many parents think of it as an obligation. But in our home, it is eagerly anticipated. After the games, prizes, refreshments, and business, we sit around the fireplace, or on the floor, and sing. Sarah is learning to play the violin and soon will be accompanying us. Danny's favorite song, "Wonderful Grace of Jesus," has just about become our theme song, but Tommy's, "When the Roll Is Called Up Yonder," runs a close second. Then, of course, we have made up our own "hash" chorus (a composite of many favorites all run together). We sometimes get to singing so hard I wind up with a sideache.

Following the song service, the children recite their memory verse and explain its meaning. Those who have it letter-perfect and fully understand the meaning receive a prize. Then we read the next week's memory verse, and, as the children make notes, we open the Bible to serious study.

We don't just read a chapter at a time or follow a sequence of verses, book by book. Instead we study the Bible by themes. For example, as I am writing this, our subject for the coming Friday evening is the Sixth Commandment, "Thou shalt not kill." As we discuss this subject, we plan to examine Matthew 5:21-24; Luke 23:34; Psalm 120:6-7; Revelation 13:10; Matthew 5:43-44; and Exodus 20:13.

The material itself is not chosen arbitrarily, but usually to answer questions or problems the children may have.

Our last Friday night study was on the Fifth Commandment, and between Sarah's and Dan's questions it was past midnight before we finally had prayer and went to bed.

Once these Friday evening discussions get rolling there's just no stopping them. But then, we really don't want to stop. We want to communicate. When they talk about drugs, sex, dating, future careers, or whatever, we want to be involved. We want them to trust us for advice, and then take that advice so they will avoid some of the pits we had to crawl out of. If the children did not gain something to live by, then we would feel Bible study was a waste of time.

Discipline is not dreaded, but eagerly participated in by the children because the family works, plays, eats, and prays together. We have a page of Kazoku Regulations which lists the "daily routine" (chores, hours, etc.) and the "point system" (with its penalty for infractions such as leaving clothing on floor, failure to perform daily chores, etc.). For each five points of penalty, 25¢ is paid to the treasury.

In all matters, we have agreed to accept the authority of the Bible as our standard of conduct and our example in planning the future.

Every family may not be able to follow this exhausting schedule, but to us, as I said before, it is a way of life. Alterations to fit each need would require only small adjustments, but the greatest adjustment is the attitude of the family itself. They must commit such a move to God, and trust him for the time and energy. The spirit of the idea is not to exact "the letter of the law which killeth," but to close the generation gap and make an honest effort to bring Christian training into the home. This training must be so natural and uninhibited that the child feels it is as normal as five fingers on each hand.

Our Kazoku Club has helped us achieve this.

.•··•··•··•··•··•··•··•··•··•··•··•··•··•·

What is the difference between a home and a house? Anybody can build a house; we need something more for the creation of a home. A house is an accumulation of brick and stone, with an assorted collection of manufactured goods; a home is the abiding place of ardent affection, of fervent hope, of genial trust.

There is many a homeless man who lives in a richly furnished house. There is many a modest house in the crowded street which is an illuminated and beautiful home. The sumptuously furnished house may be only an exquisitely sculptured tomb; the scantily furnished house may be the very hearthstone of the eternal God.

The Bible does not say very much about homes; it says a great deal about the things that make them.

It speaks about life and love and joy and peace and rest! If we get a house and put these into it, we shall have secured a home.

— JOHN HENRY JOWETT

The Family That Plays Together

by Ken Anderson
President, Ken Anderson Films

You've heard it said, "The family that prays together stays together." From rather disheartening observation, however, my wife and I have come to the conclusion that the family that "prays" together may yet go shipwreck unless that family also "plays" together.

If this sounds like the watered-down philosophy of a too-modern evangelical, hold steady for a few paragraphs. And if you are also a parent, take brief inventory of your own family activities and the results of them.

We have seven children. While we make no pretense of knowing all there is to be known about the "do" and "do not" aspects of Christian parenthood, we have learned lessons which may prove helpful to some of the less initiated.

If any one rule for being a successful mother and father has emerged from the trial and error of our family life, it is this: to win your children, you must make them feel you are the most wonderful people in the world. Discipline them, of course, but give discipline meaning because it comes from two people who put legs to their love, and give heart to their happiness.

We have fallen far short of the ideals which hindsight now gives to us. But we thank God for the evidences of success in mixing fun with faith to lead little minds out of the wonder-world of childhood into the reality of Christ-centered youth.

Both my wife and I have taken note since our own childhood of Christian homes which have succeeded, spiritually speaking, and Christian homes which have failed. Without exception, we have found that children go astray from homes where the solemn truths of the Bible are proclaimed as dynamic law, but where the parents, however sincere, fail to add that warmth of genuineness which must be seen for the Christian faith to ring real in a child's calculating mind.

There is not time here to speak of negativism, except to say that any parent is on dangerous ground if the things he says no to are not outbalanced by the things to which he says yes. But I do want to emphasize that, in my opinion, successful Christian parenthood involves identification with the child in all the details and delights of life.

From our children's earliest years, we have found time to fill each day with at least a few moments of family frolic: long hikes through the woods which surround our house, picnics along some nearby waterway, parlor games, and a family fun night, whenever my hectic schedule would allow. Among these bright threads we have interwoven the more somber strands of family responsibility.

The result? One by one — and to God be all the glory! — we have seen our children come to the Lord and identify themselves as positive Christians.

Call it coincidental if you must, but I add that not one of these children made a profession of faith in a public evangelistic meeting. Each met the Savior either at my wife's knee or at my own.

We have traveled thousands of miles together, on a budget that did not so much as permit the renting of a lakeside cabin for a week. Instead, thanks to the American procedure of so much down and so much a month, we bought an inexpensive tent. With it, we've camped in the mountains, at Niagara, out in the desert, and alongside Grand Canyon.

Some of our most memorable occasions in family devotions have come out in the fresh breath of nature, a Christian family enjoying together those profuse magnificences the Lord has provided, but which so few take time to enjoy.

One morning, for example, a giant sequoia tree formed the background for: "But grow in grace and in the knowledge of our Lord Jesus Christ," as we told our children, "It gives the Lord much pleasure to create one of these great trees, but not nearly so much pleasure as when he sees the building of a beautiful Christian life."

Discipline, too, has come as a natural course. Five, then six, and then seven youngsters make up a sizeable safari; and more than once wary shopkeepers have watched askance lest something go splintering to the floor.

We'll always remember, however, the day we went through Ashland Manor, the home of Henry Clay in Lexington, Kentucky. The lady in charge followed us through several rooms. But we had experienced this before, so we weren't overly embarrassed. After a bit, however, she disappeared. She was sitting at her desk in the lobby, as we concluded the tour.

"I must tell you something," she said as we left. "Never in my life have I seen such a large group of well-mannered children."

I winked at my wife. Two of our older children grinned. Outside, one of them said, "Boy, Dad, it's a good thing she doesn't see us sometimes!" But, to this day when we go out together — those who yet remain with us — the very mention of "Ashland manners" brings immediate meaning and results.

Even in our family worship we have tried to intersperse the aspect of play. Instead of reading the Bible without comment, we relate it to the natural events of childhood, and of the rapidly passing year: the excitement of a ball game, the fun you can have at a friend's house, or when he comes to yours — any event of the day which casts a shade of meaning upon the portion being read. For, again and again, the introductory light touch would gain and hold attention for the deeper meanings which might otherwise be missed.

Sometimes, frankly, we have wondered if our emphasis on taking the happiness approach might be overdone. Like the time, for example, when one of our boys exclaimed: "You don't seem like our parents sometimes! You're just like one of us!"

But there was also the day when another of our children, in a solemn moment, said, "You sure feel sorry for kids who don't have a family like ours. No wonder they can't understand why us kids are all Christians."

Draw your own conclusions. Rest assured, too, that our family life has not been spared of its share of blemishes. But do be wise enough to face, as we have faced, the fact that a long, long bridge spans the gap between childhood and you. Only as you reach across the bridge to your children can you lead them safely across.

My wife and I believe you undergird your children when you pray. You lead them in moments of serious counsel, of course, but you give meaning to that counsel, and to your prayers, when you take time to play.

•••••••••••••••••••••••••••••

Successful family living strikes me as being in many ways rather like playing chamber music. Each member of the ensemble has his own skills, his own special knack with the part he chooses to play; but the grace and strength and sweetness of the performance come from everyone's willingness to subordinate individual virtuosity and personal ambition to the requirement of balance and blend.

— ANNIS DUFF

Character Building Blocks

by John R. Rice
Author, Home, Marriage and Children, *and Editor*, Sword of the Lord

When God provided that children would take nearly twenty years to grow up, he clearly intended that parents should use those long years in growing Christian character in the child to make him a godly, strong, happy, moral man, adequate to do the work, to master the difficulties, to meet the problems, and decide the choices that he must face.

Daniel, a lad of high school age carried into faraway Babylon and tempted with the enticing meat and drink from the king's table, had courage and judgment to purpose in his heart that he would not defile himself. That strong character was developed in his youth and doubtless in the home of his father and mother. Daniel lived a life of high principle and self-control and godliness, with no essential change from the time of his youth until he was an aged man, the counselor and prime minister of kings.

Young Joseph was put over the affairs of Potiphar's household down in Egypt. When tempted by Potiphar's wife, though he was but a lad, he had the strength of character to refuse her and the good sense to flee from the temptress. The integrity of the lad had already matured. Joseph could be trusted in later life because he was already trustworthy by the time he reached maturity. Who can doubt that his character was developed in the home of his father Jacob?

The greatest single influence on character, of course, is conversion, that is, coming to repent of one's sins and taking Christ as Savior and Lord of one's life. Then after one

———
Copyright 1946 Sword of the Lord Foundation

is a child of God, the constant use of the Word of God, learning the precepts of the Bible and becoming accustomed to following them, is a great source of molding godly character. However, I should like to mention here some necessary elements of character building in the home, aside from winning the child to Christ and teaching him the Word of God and teaching him to pray.

1. *Obedience, the foundation of character.* Children should be taught to obey without question, and when necessary, without waiting for any explanation. Good citizens obey the laws because they are good citizens and because laws are to be obeyed, not because they have weighed out every problem involved. And likewise, a child who does not give unquestioning obedience is really not giving any obedience at all.

Obedience must be instant obedience, without argument. Any real obedience accepts it as fundamentally true that the one in authority knows best what to do, and so the one under authority submits and obeys, not in his own time, but in the time and way he is ordered to obey.

What child is wise enough to weigh whether a drink of beer would do him any harm or not? What teen-age girl is wise enough to judge as to whether she ought to be home at a certain hour at night? Real obedience is unquestioning, and instant obedience.

Teaching obedience requires real character on the part of parents. The parent who would teach his child to be steadfast must himself be steadfast in his requirement. And along with justice there must be mercy. Children are only human beings. Fathers and mothers must distinguish between willful disobedience and the natural frailty which must be overcome by a combination of firmness and kindness. And more important still, parents who are to act for God in the home, with an authority that is tremendous, must see to it that they are never capricious, that they always have reasons for their demands, and that love and good sense and reasonableness are back of every order given.

2. *Children should be taught to work.* See that every child has work to do. The mother may feel that she would rather dry the dishes herself than to watch the children mishandle her precious china or crystal ware. Never mind; that boy or girl is more important than the china or crystal ware! Perhaps the mother can make the beds and sweep the floors in less time than her daughter can do it under her mother's supervision. But happy is the mother who takes the hard way, temporarily, and supervises the work carefully and teaches her daughter to do the work. Remember that the Word of God says, "If any would not work, neither should he eat" (2 Thessalonians 3:10). A good habit and conscience about work is an essential part of Christian character.

3. *Children must be taught regular habits for happiness and usefulness.* One who does not have well-developed habits for the routine of daily living will have a miserable time trying to get in all his duties. Happiness, success, character — all these depend very largely upon a good set of habits developed in childhood. Therefore I suggest that parents take particular pains in having regularity in the home and that children be taught to do regular things at regular times and without many exceptions. I suggest the following matters that need regular attention: to go to bed at a regular time without complaint; to have good habits of personal cleanliness; to be trained in orderliness and neatness about their clothes and belongings. The mother who is wise in helping her children form good habits is not simply teaching them to put away toys and clothes but is teaching them to be responsible for their acts, to carry their part of the burden of Christian living in a home and in society.

4. *Children must be taught courtesy in the home.* Cour-

tesy begins for the child in "Please" and "Thank you!" It ought to be a well-established rule that the child who does not say, "Please," does not get the food he wants. Young people should be taught deference for old people. Boys and young men should be taught deference toward ladies.

And children should learn to be courteous to one another, each to respect the rights of the other. Each should be glad to wait until the other is served at the table. Children should be taught to "love as brethren, be pitiful, be courteous." That is a part of Christian character.

5. *The art of living peaceably with others should be taught at home.* The child who is taught obedience and courtesy as we have advocated above, will not find it so hard to learn to get along with others.

No fighting should be allowed. No child should be allowed to force his own way upon a younger child or a weaker one. Of course there will be arguments and good-natured scuffles, but children should be taught to keep the peace.

Children must be taught to respect one another's possessions and not to take what is not their own. It is an unhappy home where everything of value has to be moved out of reach of children because they are not taught the difference between "mine" and "thine," are not taught what they have a right to touch and handle and what they must leave alone. Some children are a terror to every home in which they visit because they have never been taught to leave alone what does not belong to them.

Children should be taught to share their property. Big sister must let little sister play with her doll for a little time, carefully watched by mother or by herself to see that little sister does not pull the dolly's hair off her head, or punch the little eyes out. Mercy must be taught as well as justice, and charity as well as honesty.

Children must be taught to forgive and to ask forgiveness for a wrong. "I am sorry" — those are about the hardest words in the language to say. A child must be taught to be sorry for mistakes or sins, and to try to make it right by an honest confession.

Children likewise must be taught to forgive. Let no little child go to bed with a known and deliberate sin unconfessed, and make sure that no child goes to bed with a black grudge in his heart against anyone.

Oh, how tender and forgiving mothers and fathers ought to be at this point! Little feet stumble so easily! Little tongues wander so naturally from the truth! Little hands drop so many things and break them, and take so many things they ought not to touch! Godlike mercy and kindness in forgiving and teaching forgiveness ought to be the part of every mother and father.

Let every father and mother bear well in mind that character must be built in the home, day by day, line upon line, precept upon precept, here a little and there a little.

•●••●••●••●••●••●••●••●••●••●••●••●•

The conscience of children is formed by the influences that surround them; their notions of good and evil are the result of the moral atmosphere they breathe.

— GENE PAUL RICHTER

Christian Training, When?

by Theodore H. Epp
Director, Back to the Bible radio broadcast

"Train up a child in the way he should go, and when he is old, he will not depart from it" (Proverbs 22:6). How early should one begin this spiritual training of a child?

The Apostle Paul wrote in his second letter to Timothy concerning Timothy's faith: "When I call to remembrance the unfeigned faith that is in thee also . . ." (1:5). This passage, of course, tells us that Timothy was a third-generation believer. His mother and grandmother both had had a vital testimony for Christ. Timothy followed their example. But at what age was his training in faith begun? This is stated in 3:14: "But continue thou in the things which thou hast learned and hast been assured of, knowing of whom thou has learned them; and that from a child thou hast known the holy Scriptures, which are able to make thee wise unto salvation through faith which is in Christ Jesus."

The mother is the key person in this. She holds the child and cradles it, so it is at that early age when all of this should be started. The children's thinking should be molded from the very beginning. We need to use the right words and state the right truths even before the little ones can understand them. They learn by hearing things over and over again. The point is to be sure that the children hear the right things and thus learn to repeat the right things.

So far as my family is concerned, our children began to attend church as soon as Mother was strong enough to take them. In those earlier years we did not have nurseries in

---

Copyright 1966 *Good News Broadcaster*

which to leave the little ones, so the baby went with Mother. When the child was old enough to sit, he or she sat with Mother. And there was discipline in the pew also.

It is true that a small child can hardly be expected to sit quietly all the time, but the mother can take along things to interest the child but that will not distract others. At the same time she should insist on good behavior.

We made it a rule with our children that if we had to take them out of church because of their behavior, they were disciplined when we got home. This is something that needs to be done only once or twice, as a rule. They soon learn that they are expected to behave themselves while in church.

There must also be a time when a parent begins to read Bible stories to a child. This must be done as simply and clearly as possible. You will be surprised how much these little ones understand. At first they may not comprehend a great deal, but by the telling and retelling of these Bible stories, their young minds are molded into Bible patterns of thought. So we need to start with our children before they begin playing with the neighbors. The time to begin is before the child can even walk.

There is also a time to begin memory work. This can be done just as soon as the child begins to talk. At this stage verses must be very brief, perhaps just two or three words at a time. But persist in teaching them to the children.

My wife used to stay with our children for a half hour in the evenings at times, going over the Bible verse with them before they were tucked in for the night. I can still remember that when they had learned their first Bible verse, they would come and repeat it for me. They were delighted with their accomplishment.

There is also a place for gospel songs in training children. This is something that should be done for them before they hear the noises of worldly music that come over the radio. They will learn to recognize hymn and gospel song melodies. Some children will even be able to hum the tunes before they can speak.

So far as factual knowledge is concerned, children know nothing when they first come into this world. By the time they are three years of age, they have learned a lot. Certain facts are impressed on their minds by that time. Certain attitudes are in their hearts. What impressions of soul and life have we Christian parents implanted in our children by the time they are three years of age?

The mother, of course, will be responsible for much of this. However, the father bears a great deal of responsibility also.

The father has the responsibility with regard to discipline. Too often in the modern home the father is called in when the mother has reached a point of frustration and does not know what to do. Then the child is left with the feeling that the father's place in the home is that of a disciplinarian only.

Fathers must be careful in this respect. The Bible makes note of this where it says, "Ye fathers, provoke not your children to wrath: but bring them up in the nurture and admonition of the Lord." The father must be fair and kind in discipline.

Begin early in impressing on the children that they are part of the family. Be practical in their training. Do not be satisfied to merely talk about Jesus and the Bible, but apply the life of Jesus to them and show them how the Word of God fits everyday life. They will come to see that Christ is not only an example, but that he is their very life and lives in them.

The path of least resistance is that of letting the children do what they please. We do not have to train them to do the wrong things. It is true that corn when planted will grow by itself, but it grows better when it is cultivated.

There is no need to cultivate weeds, for they will come almost in spite of us.

The depraved nature which we inherit is like the law of gravity. It constantly pulls us down to lower moral and spiritual levels. There is nothing we can do about it of ourselves. We need divine help to overcome it. If we overcome the law of gravity, we need power to do so. So it is in the spiritual realm. All we have to do to do wrong is to let go. If we want our children to walk on the broad way which leads to destruction, we do not have to do anything about it. That is the road they would naturally follow. But if we want our children to be trained for the Lord, then we must take a definite part in this training and we must begin early.

The Bible is full of illustrations concerning this subject. Moses was destined to spend many years in the court of Pharaoh. Yet Moses was so well trained in the early, formative years of his life that he finally reached the decision to suffer affliction with the people of God rather than enjoy the pleasures of sin for a season.

Samuel is an example of another godly man who was started early in the things of the Lord. His parents took him early to serve in the house of God.

Let us seek to mold these children of ours in the way they should go. Then when they are old they will not depart from the correct paths mapped out for them.

•-•--•--•--•--•--•--•--•--•--•--•--•--•--•--•-•

They do not love who do not show their love.
— SHAKESPEARE

8

CLOSING THE GENERATION GAP

Needed: Growing Parents

by Anna Mow

Author, Your Teen-ager and You *and other books*

Many parents do very well with their children when they are small, but run into real confusion with them as teenagers. The chances are that too many parents have not matured in their own love for one another and have thereby lost the secret of harmonious relationship — if, indeed, they ever knew it. They are ill prepared to be a help to their adolescent offspring when they are as confused as the children.

Teen-agers need love and want to know about love more than anything else. Where are they to learn about love — from the movies and a sex-ridden culture? Where are they to learn about the relationship of the physical to the spiritual phases of love — from the biology class? Where are they to learn about what makes a good marriage — from a magazine column?

You, the parents, carry the first responsibility to *show* your teen-ager what genuine love is. Your differences and even your conflicts won't hurt him at all if he sees you resolve them. If you can maintain an unbroken relationship through whatever happens, you will have given your child

---

Copyright 1967 Zondervan Publishing House

the greatest gift of life: courage — a courage which is an integral part of the security of love. Courage is the faith and hope with love of the abiding qualities of life.

Teens need security, but this security is not necessarily in things. The greatest security is in relationship, in a relationship that does not change with circumstances. This includes a growing relationship with God, recognizable relationship between father and mother which is never broken even by differences and misunderstandings, and his own relationship with both parents which is never broken whatever happens.

Within this security of relationship teens need independence too, or they will never grow up. Often a small child is pushed to independence before he is ready, when some mild indulgence would not hurt him. It is hard for parents to wait until he can stand, walk, and talk.

Then, when he is a teen-ager and often wants more independence than he is ready to be responsible for, the parental attitude is reversed. Out of their fears the parents do not grant even the freedom an adolescent thinks he can handle. He does need bonds, but not bondage. The parents must be the first to distinguish between the two. "Smother love" is in the bondage category and it will, of course, lead to rebellion — and it should. If teen rebellion is against sudden overprotectiveness, the parent must first look to himself to see if he has been unwise. Then the parent must consider how he can help to prevent negative and destructive rebellion.

Maturity and real love are required to face a child's rebellion objectively. It helps greatly to remember that rebellion is a normal part of the growing process. The child is unconsciously crying out that he is a real person in his own right, that he is not the property of his parents, but that he is their responsibility. Within him is the God-implanted yearning to know who he is.

The child's rebellion may be the unconscious effort to

protect his innate yearning to develop his own individuality, which will make him react against domination. This is first of all something fine and strong in him and not something personal against his parents. Whether this rebellion remains healthy or becomes actual rebellion depends upon how the parent reacts to it. The parent who reacts as if his authority were rejected will set his child in a competitive attitude which may lead to dangerous rebellion in adolescence. But the parent who can help his child find himself will know the truth of Tagore's statement: "Let my love like sunlight surround you and give you illumined freedom."

Everything we do for our children, from infancy on, works toward making them more dependent or more independent. The successful parent works himself out of a job but never out of a relationship.

A continued and unbroken relationship with a child depends on what is happening to and in a parent during the process. Is the parent growing from one experience to another? One mother complained, "It seems that no matter what I say to my teen-agers, it is the wrong thing. I looked forward to the time when I would have four children in their teens at once, but now I find it a terrifying experience."

As a mature individual, this mother began to take stock of herself. She decided she talked too much. To her teenagers it was "nagging." Disciplining her tongue helped her discipline her irritations. To her surprise her children began to change too. They began to show appreciation for her in many little ways. The crowning experience was the Sunday the youngest and most rebellious one responded to the pastor's invitation for rededication of life. The mother followed and together they knelt before God. That day began a new relationship which inspired them all.

These devastating experiences of rebellion and parental shock taken creatively become tests of the quality of parental love. Love can never be taken for granted; it is too easily perverted to self-interests.

I like C. S. Lewis' discussion on "need-love" and "gift-love" in *The Four Loves*. He says that need-love is not necessarily selfish because our highest love, our love for God, is need-love. It is, after all, the only love a baby can have. Every succeeding year in life we all need love. This love is perverted only when it grasps solely for its own benefit when the time for gift-love has come.

We think of gift-love as being like the maternal instinct. As C. S. Lewis points out, it is a love that needs to give and therefore needs to be needed:

"But the proper aim of giving is to put the recipient in a state where he no longer needs our gift. We feed children in order that they may soon be able to feed themselves; we teach them in order that they may soon not need our teaching. Thus a heavy task is laid upon this gift-love. It must work towards its own abdication. We must aim at making ourselves superfluous. The hour when we can say, "They need me no longer" should be our reward."

The perversion of gift-love is much more subtle than the perversion of need-love because it is so easy to justify that which gives for another. It will take a higher love to tame "the ravenous need to be needed" which will "gratify itself either by keeping its objects needy or by inventing for them imaginary needs."

Teen years are years of natural frustrations. It is unfortunate when these natural growth frustrations are complicated further by frustrated parents. One mother wrote recently, "How did we ever come to the point where we feel threatened by our young people?" Why are parents frustrated and threatened by their own teen-agers? That is what the parents must find out if they want to be a help and not a hindrance. How do those teen-agers irritate you? That "how" is your point of frustration. Is it because you do not understand them? Or do you feel thwarted by them? If it is in your own feeling, then you can do something about it, for your irritation is your frustration and your responsibility, not theirs. Until that is clarified and conquered, you can do little for your child who is now old enough to do some discerning for himself.

In fact, you are back where you were when they were very young. Again, but in a deeper sense, what you are counts more than what you say. Many parents find that now words seem useless; they only antagonize and raise barriers. Of course, the silence of those parents might do the same thing! But this is no time for despair. It is a time for inventory to find out what we really are. Every jolt a rebellious youth gives a parent is a challenge to the parent to look into the mirror to see who he himself is, what he is and if he is growing. The youth's problem, indeed, is too often merely the reflection of the parent's own problem.

Too often the parent's problem is basically not with his child but with his mate. Overpossessiveness toward the child, domination to the point of meddling, grasping for love-response and appreciation are almost certainly from unmet needs and unsolved problems between the child's father and mother. When they were babies, mother alone could give security, but for a teen-ager it takes father *and* mother. An unhappy relationship between father and mother is the greatest cause of a teen-ager's problem. If parents can solve their own problems they will find that many of youth's problems have disappeared into thin air.

Young people cannot be fooled. They always know what the basic parent relationship is. A mother of teen-agers was talking to me not long ago; she said her own parents were very different from each other. Not only were they different, but they differed verbally with each other on many issues, often quite vehemently. She said, "I am surprised that as I remember my teen years I never felt any insecurity because my parents seemed to quarrel. Their disagreements never seemed to do anything to upset their love for one another."

If the days do come when it seems there is little one can

do about any problem, there is still a whole field to work in. Dr. Fritz Kunkel called it the "area of free choice." Parents can always work for improvement in the area of their own lives.

Let me suggest that you do not know how much you love your teen-ager until you can be satisfied with the way you love your mate.

·•··•··•··•··•··•··•··•··•··•··•··•··•·

Marriage is a life work which some scarcely begin and only a minority ever fully achieve.

— VERNON GROUNDS

Coping with Rebellion

by Warren W. Wiersbe
Pastor, Calvary Baptist Church, Covington, Kentucky

There are two kinds of teen-age rebellion: the normal, that leads to maturity; and the abnormal, that usually results in anarchy and destruction. Normal rebellion is constructive; it helps the teen-ager "shed his cocoon" and start to use his own wings. Or, to use another image, it means cutting the apron strings but not the heartstrings. Normal rebellion actually opens communication between parents and teen-agers and gives them opportunity to explore problems, understand one another's feelings, and all grow together. It is an occasional thing and it is varied in its expression. One week Tom will fuss about clothes; the next week he'll argue about the merits of joining the Foreign Legion or the Communist party!

But abnormal rebellion is quite another matter. It closes communications between parents and their teens; and instead of being a varied, occasional thing it becomes settled and specific. It is always about the car, or dates, or money, or friends. A "cold war" settles down on the family and mom and dad dare not mention these areas of concern. Abnormal rebellion actually turns a teen-ager away from life into some narrow detour, while normal rebellion helps him better understand life and his own role in the family. Normal rebellion is creative; it makes a man out of a boy. But abnormal rebellion is destructive; it can make a criminal out of a son or daughter.

I believe the spread of lawlessness in our day is directly

Copyright 1968 Moody Bible Institute

connected with the predicted decay of society in 2 Timothy 3:1-7. Young people without Christ are "children of disobedience" (Ephesians 2:1-3) and under the control of the lawless one. And our present social situation, with its ample supply of cars, money, and leisure time, makes it easier for young people to do what they want to do. Add to these the permissiveness of parents and teachers and the seeming paralysis of law-enforcement agencies, and you can understand why today's young people are doing what they want to do.

I'm not going to deal with youthful rebellion in general; I want rather to discuss your teen-ager, or the young person in your Sunday school class, the fellow or girl who knows Christ as Savior and, generally speaking, enjoys a good life but for some reason is going through a period of rebellion.

There are several values to normal teen-age rebellion. As I have already mentioned, it helps the teen-ager mature. Someone has pointed out that our young people grow in three directions: they grow up, they grow away, and they grow toward. You can't become a swimmer by reading a book, and you can't become an adult by listening to teenage lectures on maturity. You have to live!

This leads to a second value to normal rebellion: it helps to draw teens and adults closer together, provided the adults are mature themselves and willing to face facts honestly. Most teen-agers do not create family problems; they reveal them. The weak father who for years has covered his insecurity with arrogance and bullying is going to have a rough time talking heart-to-heart with his teen-age son who has built-in radar and can detect a phony a mile away. And the social-climbing mother who is trying to relive her own life in her daughter's life will never have real communication with Suzy who wants to be herself. Normal rebellion is an opportunity for a mature parent and a maturing son or daughter to mature some more.

The key, of course, is communication. Many parents who spent hours listening to and talking with their children suddenly went off the air when John and Mary turned thirteen. We parents ought never to lose that heart-to-heart and mind-to-mind communication that we have with our own flesh and blood. If we do, it is usually because we are afraid to grow ourselves; we want to maintain the quiet status quo of the home and we want everybody to conform to our own ideas of what the home ought to be like. Or it may be that we see ourselves in our own teen-agers and we don't like what we see. Many a father doesn't actually reject his son; he rejects himself in his son.

There is a third value to normal rebellion: it gives our teen-agers assurance with their parents and with other adults. Teen-ager-parent conflicts do more than simply release pent-up emotions and tensions; they are an evidence to the teen-ager that he can be himself and still be loved and accepted. If Christ is in the home and heart, then these conflicts will actually be stepping-stones to new self-understanding and self-esteem, both on the part of the teen-ager and his parents.

What does this add up to? Don't be afraid of conflicts and rebellion if they fall into the normal pattern. If you are yielded to the Lord, these conflicts can result in creative growth and not chaotic destruction.

One of the main causes of rebellion is confusion: the teen is discovering who he is. He is also discovering who his parents and teachers are — what makes them tick. A teen-ager may rebel against your actions and answers, but he should never rebel against your attitudes. "I disagree with Mom and Dad a lot," one college freshman told me, "but I like their approach to our disagreements. They can disagree without becoming disagreeable."

Another root cause of rebellion is fear. One psychiatrist has said, "Violence is fear turned inside out." Rebellion is one way a teen-ager has to cover up his true feelings.

When a young person knows he is loved and appreciated, he can come to his parents as his true self and really open up his heart — fears and all.

Social pressure is a third cause of rebellion. The approval of their friends means much to maturing teen-agers. This is why it is important for parents to know and fellowship with their children's friends. Making it easy for our children to bring their friends home and have a good time is one of the best ways to build bridges, not walls, and to overcome the so-called "generation gap." When "the gang" has met mom and dad, they are less likely to criticize them for their standards and rules.

Now for some positive suggestions. Begin early to practice loving, consistent discipline. Young people want parental discipline, because it helps them discover "the limits" and feel the security of adult approval. Adult permissiveness leads to confusion and confusion leads to rebellion.

Along with discipline that is consistent and compassionate ("Whom the Lord loveth, he chasteneth . . ."), there must be a practical flexibility. The confident parent who has good communication with his teen-agers can afford to "give in" when the consequences are not significant. The give-and-take of a family situation is a great experience for adults and teens alike.

A third suggestion is: try to provide adequate substitutes. "Don't prohibit without providing" is the way one pastor friend put it, and I respect his words because he raised a godly family, all of whom are today in Christian service. We must give of ourselves and help to provide an adequate substitute for any activity that would really hurt our teens. This must be a consistent thing in the home — that the parents share themselves with their children and teen-agers so that the worldly substitutes have less and less attraction for them.

Most important, learn to listen and to care. Adults are used to talking, to giving orders; but when it comes to living with teens, adults need to listen with both ears and with their hearts. A modern writer has pointed out that there is a difference between being misunderstood, feeling misunderstood, and not being able to understand. Our young people need this practical insight. They must feel that we do care, that we are willing to listen without becoming angry or without interrupting or shouting at them. It's true that "the family that prays together stays together"; but it's also true that "the family that talks together, walks together." And this means talking together even when there are no problems: talking about the everyday things of life, the events of the day, how each family member feels. It means keeping the receiver off the hook so our teens don't have to figure out what number to dial to "get through" to mom and dad.

Last, but certainly not least, is a sense of humor, a Christian buoyancy that creates an atmosphere of acceptance and joy in the home. It's difficult to harbor both anger and joy in the same heart. When parents are walking with the Lord, reading the Word, living honestly before their children (and this means being willing to admit weaknesses and mistakes and to apologize), then teen-agers enjoy family living and learn to laugh with others and at themselves. To coin a phrase, "The family that has fun together will be one together."

All of this simply means that we as parents must work at this business of understanding, appreciating, and liberating our teen-agers. Sometimes we may need outside help — the pastor, the church youth director, the family doctor, the school counselor. Most of the time we just need open hearts and minds and lots of spiritual intuition, a generous helping of patience and fortitude and a steady infilling of God's grace. We also need a great deal of faith, not only in the Lord but also in our young people — faith that allows them to be themselves and not carbon copies of their parents; faith that gradually they will grow into Christian maturity, even though there may be problems and defeats along the way. After all, there are few convictions without "convulsions"!

The more I think about it, the more I believe that what Paul wrote about in Galatians 5:22-23 is exactly what we parents need as we face and solve these teen-age rebellions: "For the fruit of the Spirit is love, joy, peace, longsuffering, gentleness, goodness, faith, meekness, temperance. . . ." It's hard to believe that normal rebellion can long survive in that kind of home!

•●••●••●••●••●••●••●••●••●••●••●••●•

The real danger facing our nation is not turmoil on campuses but a national revolution. The seeds of revolution have been planted by parents who fail to teach their children moral values and patriotism. America's youth are not satisfied with "take-it-or-leave-it" answers to their questions. This new attitude, if understood and channeled constructively, can mean much to future American greatness. But constructive channeling requires a base of home emphasis on moral values and religious principles. Many of our restless young men and women learned at home to rebel against authority and to take a casual attitude toward laws.

— WALTER C. LANGSAM

Keep Talking!

by Leslie E. and Ruth Small Moser
Co-authors, Guiding Your Son or Daughter toward Successful Marriage

An earnest and often violent condemnation of modern parents has gone out through press, radio, television, and the pulpit. The word is that parents don't care any more — that it makes little difference to them what happens to their children, especially when they have reached the teen-age years.

Is there truth in these remonstrances? Unfortunately, yes. But certainly the truth has been colored by journalistic emphasis for the sake of sensational news appeal. Most parents do care. It is only that often they do not know what to do; their efforts are so severely rebuffed that they withdraw with wounded pride and feelings.

Fathers and sons who were so very open to each other as they shared their interests in fishing and baseball suddenly become strangers who survey each other with evident distrust. Mothers and daughters who laughed, talked, and even cried together over childhood hurts, often yield to an unseen and intangible force that creates a wariness seemingly born of a belief that they live in two different worlds. They seem no longer to share the same interests and may actually prefer to hurt one another rather than to bear one another's burdens.

What is the source of this jamming of communication lines? Can it be avoided? If communication lines cannot somehow be kept open, then the possibilities of helping your teen-agers with any problem become nil.

Copyright 1967 Baker Book House

The desire to grow up contributes to the difficulty. This time of growing up causes young people to wish to pull away from parents, in the interests of independent action and personal freedom. Generally, parents and teen-agers grow apart; there seems to be a shared feeling that to be independent and self-sustaining means to refuse help. Nothing could be further from the truth.

There is manifestly no reason why a shutdown of communications should be either necessary or desirable. What is responsible for this feeling that continued contact with parents is opposed to the process of maturing?

Parents sometimes refuse to modify earlier relationships. For the most part, parents are unwilling to change the nature of their display of interest, even though the maturing of their young people clearly indicates that many changes should be made. Whereas during childhood days it was necessary for parents to be rather authoritative, this dogmatic authority which grew out of a deep and justified concern for their safety must be supplanted by a desire to render help on terms that can be accepted by the maturing young person.

The greatest single complaint made by teen-agers against their parents is: "They continue to treat me like a child." We parents who wish to keep communication lines open simply must school ourselves in the task of regarding our maturing teen-agers as young adults rather than as the babies we sometimes wish they would continue to be.

Do not press for close relationships. The world is full of inconsistencies, and parent-teen-age relationships involve many paradoxes. Yes, they want to be treated like grown-ups; but even though they claim equal status with you, they may not cherish an earnest communion with you.

Even if you grant them the cherished desire to be treated like grown-ups, you must remember that they are only partially so, a segment of their adolescence still remains.

This segment is most clearly seen in their resistance to you, their most devoted friends. Sometimes such resistance really hurts. Whereas they welcome the advice and suggestions of others younger or maybe even older, they still have the immaturity that prevents a full acceptance of those people called parents. So, often they will desire and seek communication with other adults and will leave you confused and hostile.

It takes a strong constitution. Being parents of maturing teen-agers is extremely hard on the ego. We must develop some built-in shock absorbers; we must not be rejection-prone. That they will often turn your interest aside even when you have the best of intentions and have no desire to intrude or to manipulate is an absolute fact. But remember, you are the more mature; you must learn to take in stride the rebukes that come your way when they seem to want nothing from you.

We are often tempted to say that if they do not want our help, then we shall just let them alone. But we cannot afford to say or to feel that. We must not reject them — no matter how obviously they reject us. We must rather let them know that we stand always ready, never desiring to intrude but anxious to communicate when they are ready. Does this seem too much to ask? In a way, it does; but if you can be convinced that it is the only way to keep the communication lines open, then you may be able to tolerate the hurts and move forward with conviction that your maturity must reign supreme — it must not give way in the face of the most severe tests.

Remember, young people are not all alike. Every human is different from every other; this also applies to the teen-agers in your own home. What works to keep one happy and to keep communication lines open does not work with the other; you must learn the individualities of each. Furthermore, the same young person varies a lot from one time to another, often making abrupt changes without identifiable cause. As a general rule, teen-agers will be a little harder to reach as they enter the dating stage; as they approach the sobering reality of marriage they become more accepting of parents. So keep tuned in by a very sensitive touch.

Maintain an interest in what they are doing. When they want you, you have to be ready and available on terms acceptable to them — there is no other way. But whether your involvement (according to their wishes) is from near or far, your interest must not wane.

Even though your demonstrated interest may be from a distance, your interest must be genuine and never-ending. You must be content to express whatever level of interest they desire, but you must always be seen on the periphery of their activities, out of the way but available.

Your young people must feel free to come to you. Good communication with your young people does not necessarily imply a daily conversation, although it does imply a pleasant contact. Many parents mistake the lack of constant conversaton with the loss of communication, and this is an error.

The center of concern should be how they feel about you. They should feel completely free to seek your guidance in everything, no matter how trivial or how serious. They may not always seek you, because in the interest of their own maturing they choose to carry some things alone. But the freedom to converse must be kept absolute.

Free communication depends upon acceptance. If you wish to foster an open line of communication with your teen-agers, you must develop the capacity to hear with equanimity some rather threatening things. No barrier to communication is quite as impregnable as the openmouthed, horrified response to a revelation which is upsetting to you.

But consider this: What is the value to them of having a confidant if the confidant will hear only the nice things?

Young people need parents to share their joys and their heartaches; more than that, they need parents who will have the capacity to hear about their mistakes without going to pieces and shouting remonstrances.

Don't force them to be secretive. When young people find it necessary to keep secrets concerning their behavior, companions, etc., from their parents, a serious breakdown of communications has probably already occurred. There is little doubt that many parents need to loosen up their value systems somewhat to permit the acceptance of certain forms of teen-age pursuits against which they have built-in resistances.

Never be lax in standing against those things which are wrong, but be careful not to let your values which were arbitrarily arrived at within the cultural milieu of your upbringing stand between you and your teen-agers who are growing up in a different world — no better and no worse, perhaps, but different. You must lay aside foolish fanaticisms and live in their world while holding fast to the scriptural admonitions concerning righteous living. This is not easy to do. Your chief barrier will be the criticisms of your own peers who may say that you are going to the dogs along with your teen-agers. But we must all give intelligent thought to the overall problem. The setting of arbitrary standards is a chief reason for the breakdown of communications between young people and their parents.

Broken communications are difficult to re-establish. Suppose a young person is approaching marriage and earnestly desires communication with his parents. But somewhere back down the line there was a breach in communication, and this breach concerned objections of the parents to some teen-age fad. Now at the young-adult stage, neither parents nor the young person can remember what it was that caused them to lose communication, but neither is able to rise above the leftover hurts and reestablish the much-cherished relationship. A measure of tolerance and understanding would have prevented such a breach of communication.

Take the lead. The leadership must reside in the hands of the more mature person. If you are aware that communication has been lost, you must take the initiative in restoring it. You may be certain that the restoration is desired by your young person, and that if he is approached properly the past will be forgotten.

No matter what the provocation for your anger with each other was, you have been in the wrong in that you have allowed this chasm to widen between you and your son or daughter.

So make the approach. Do it by one means or another. You may accomplish this first move by doing something with a display of love for the young person — cook something special just for him, buy her something she has been wanting a long time. A few kindnesses will do more than words and will say in essence, "You and I have been very foolish to lose contact with each other. We need each other and I especially need you. Let's forget whatever it was that drew us apart. I am lonely for you and very much want to be close to you." Now, of course, you may actually say these things with very good results, but for most young people action speaks more eloquently than a thousand words.

Refuse to let communications be broken. If you have not experienced this problem of loss of communication with your young people, take it from those who have — it isn't a happy state. And you can often avoid it. Don't let little differences grow into big ones. Nip them in the bud. Don't let your young people be angry with you and keep their anger down deep inside, there to grow into sullen resentment.

"Don't let the sun go down on your wrath," say the

Scriptures. Heed this admonition — at least correct the flaws in the communication lines while the breaks are fresh and easier to mend.

If you are to be effective in helping your young people establish happy homes, you must be available to them — you must be in communication. Work hard to make it so.

•-•-•-•-•-•-•-•-•-•-•-•-•-•-•-•-•-•-•

There are two freedoms: the false where one is free to do what he likes, and the true where he is free to do what he ought.

— CHARLES KINGSLEY

I Trust You

by Bill McKee

Author, Shut Your Generation Gap, *and Missionary-at-large, Overseas Crusades*

"I trust you, but . . ." This statement has probably been made by all parents at some time in their relationship with their children. Sometimes the "but" is said out loud and sometimes not, but even the unspoken message comes through loud and clear.

Certainly this is the most tense and trying period of parenthood, involving the car, overnight outings, dates, etc. These are enough to send some mothers for the aspirin and a few fathers to the phone. The question for many is not, "Can the kids make it through these years?" but can we parents make it without ulcers or lifetime membership in the home for the weird.

Trust! Say it over a couple of times. It's a strong word. I like it! It's a man's word, with a powerful definition: "A *confident reliance* on the integrity, veracity, or justice of another."

I'd like to see a plaque with that definition placed in the kitchen and living room of families everywhere.

Do you trust your teen-ager? I've found that suspicious parents produce sneaky kids. Often their doubts are not based on actual facts but rather on their own past or on the stories of friends. It's surprising how many Christian parents will believe others and not their own. If ever there is a time to practice the democratic principle of "innocent until proven guilty" it's now. The tendency is to believe the reverse.

Copyright 1970 Tyndale House Publishers

Often the kids will do or say things that we inflate in our imaginations. For instance, Dad reads something about marijuana and his son says, "What's so bad about that? I know lots of guys who turn on. We can buy pot right at school." He's testing you! If Mother drops a dish in the kitchen and comes running in and Dad gets shook, he's pleased because he's shocked you . . . and he dies a little because he knows behind your reaction is a lack of trust.

Parents, let's face something honestly. If we are not really trusting God, in the strongest sense of the definition, we're going to have problems with our kids. How often we commit something to God in prayer and then worry and try to work it out our own way. We don't really believe that if we gave God more of our money than we could afford, he would find a way to meet our needs. We say we believe that principle but we don't practice it. We only trust him about our soul, heaven, prayer and "spiritual things," those things we can't touch and work out ourselves. And slowly but surely the beautiful trust God put within us at our rebirth slips away.

If I'm going to be a trusting parent, I have to be a trusting Christian. I have to continually commit my worries and hopes to God and demonstrate a daily, vital confidence in someone other than myself. Soon the practice will extend even to your kids.

Every young person has had a friend betray his trust: "If I tell you this secret you must promise never to tell." When the word leaks out, something in that relationship dies. The two may still be friends but the friendship can never be complete.

Don't ever allow your child to develop insecurity or cynicism because of your mistrust. This is serious! Of course he will disobey and betray your trust as he is growing up, but don't treat slips as criminal offenses; build character rather than tearing it down.

We sometimes hear of a "bad kid" from a "good home."

That is almost an impossibility. If you were in that "good" home for a while you would likely find unhealthy relationships between parents and consequent insecurities in the children.

The "good home" today is often measured by a monetary standard. But when parents trust in money to meet their need, their young people will never have enough to meet their needs.

If your trust is in intellectual ability, your child will put his trust in himself — and find frustration. He will attempt to solve infinite questions with the finite equipment of his intellect — and fail.

The truly good home demonstrates trust in God in all things, where children have heard your prayers and then seen your confidence in the God who hears and answers. Be careful to make your trust complete, or your children will not believe God can be fully trusted in all things.

Trust is taught; doubt comes naturally. So develop their trust in you and your Lord early. Then when they are on a date or out of your sight they will trust your confidence in them and respond accordingly.

Trust is also based on knowledge and experience. Work out the rules *together*. Be fair! Ask them to check the time their friends get in (don't you do this) and take their word. Also spell out the penalties for disobedience and let them know you mean it.

But don't take the place of the Holy Spirit. So many Christian parents rob their children of the privilege of knowing the Holy Spirit by usurping his work in their lives. They convict their children, guide them, "answer" their prayers, become their conscience, and superimpose their wills on them.

Parents, the best thing you can do for your teen-ager when he indicates he wants more freedom is to step back a little. As you allow him to make his own decisions and as the weight of personal responsibility is felt he will either grow stronger and sense the inner strength of the Holy Spirit, or he will indicate he isn't ready yet by coming back to you. If you try to restrain him, however, you'll invite his resentment. Make yourself available but dispensable. If the mother bird stays on the nest too long she'll be knocked off!

Tell them you trust them, then swallow hard if you have to, and *do* it. You'll need help, and you've got it: "My *security* I give you, not as the world gives . . . let not your heart be troubled" (John 14:27).

·•··•··•··•··•··•··•··•··•··•··•··•··•··•·

These difficult, mixed-up kids of ours are also the greatest, most lovable and exciting packages of potential that God could give to two parents!

— GORDON and DOROTHEA JAECK

9

UNDERSTANDING OUR TIMES

Changing Homes, Changing Nation

by Lacey Hall
Professor of Pastoral Counseling, Trinity Evangelical Divinity School

Change is inevitable in our society. Psychologists and sociologists who have studied the changes occurring within our society attest to this fact. Most people don't have to be told; they are involved in the transition themselves. Some are convinced the changes are for the better; some say otherwise.

As these changes are taking place, what is happening to the American family? For history has taught us that when the homes of a society begin to change, the nation begins to change.

Let me cite eleven areas of major change which are remolding the American family.

Mobility. Families are on the move. Since World War II about 20 percent of the U.S. population has moved annually. One-third of all families with husbands under thirty-five move each year. American industry today is demanding people who will move.

A best-seller on the white collar class compares these conditions to the nursery that advertised, "We move our trees every year so they won't grow deep roots." In other words,

---

Copyright 1967 Moody Bible Institute

the nursery deliberately kept the root systems on its trees shallow so they could be transplanted easily. But they did not warn that such trees, without deep roots, are not withstanding the storms.

The church today has new kinds of problems in the neighborhood, in its congregation, in the Sunday school, because of mobility. As families move, boys and girls especially are going to be insecure.

Urbanization. It's no new or startling fact that for years people have been moving from the farm to the city. In 1850, 65 percent of the American people were farmers; in 1960 that figure was only 14 percent. Since 1960, two of every ten rural families have disappeared from the farm scene. Meanwhile, the urban areas are mushrooming, until we now see developing what is called the "megalopolis." One such great metropolitan area may soon stretch all the way from Boston, Massachusetts, to Richmond, Virginia!

Now what does all this mean? For one thing, it means many of these people can lose their identity. I was raised in a small town and I knew that if I stepped out of line somebody would probably find out about it — and would also tell my family! But today our urban areas are filled with people who have tried to lose identity.

During a record Chicago snowstorm many residents admitted that as they shoveled snow together and talked about the storm, they discovered their neighbors for the first time!

If I'm to get to know my neighbors, and if they're to get to know me — and what I believe as a Christian — I've got to look for ways to rub shoulders with them.

Working wives. Women today represent 34 percent of the nation's labor force. This means many marriages are getting off to a wrong start. In the months when the husband and wife should be working out their marriage adjustments, the wife comes home tired and has to fix supper, or the husband has to fix supper, and you have the climate for trouble.

In my counseling I have had clients tell me, "I know my grandmother better than I know my mother, because my grandmother raised me." And it's interesting that some of these parents make the same mistake. Many accept the pattern — unless suddenly they see what is happening in the family and are willing to sacrifice some material status for the children.

Forty percent of U.S. wives married from six to ten years are also working, which means that after the children go into school or are old enough to be put in a day nursery or kindergarten, the wife goes back to work and she's not home when the child gets home. And I think the empty home is one reason why our public schools and our Sunday schools have so many problem children.

Family size. It is hard to compare the relative merits of large and small families. There are many controls which vary greatly, such as neighborhoods, stability of parents, age differentials of children, attitudes, etc. But in larger families there seems to be a certain give-and-take among brothers and sisters. In the smaller families there's much more focus on me-and-mine, give-me-what-I-want, me-me-me.

Yet we see the key in the parent. It has often been said, "Happy parents have happy children." Those parents emotionally prepared for and agreeable to having a certain size family can do the best job in rearing healthy, happy children.

Sexual promiscuity. In our day of the "new morality" and "situation ethics," there is a definite changing attitude which can lead toward involvement in illicit sexual pursuits.

Many of the stories of extramarital affairs today go something like this: "I didn't know what to do with myself. I went to such-and-such a club. I visited my neighbor and she wasn't home, but her husband was home. We sat down and had a cup of coffee and a friendly chat. These chats continued another day and another. I found this man was a lot more interested in me and my opinions than my own husband. . . ."

This is not a situation to which the Christian is immune.

Certainly, the child exposed to today's TV, movies, magazines, and newspapers is influenced. Unfortunately, many Christian parents and evangelical churches have failed to meet squarely the pressures of sex which face this generation. Yet it is one of the greatest opportunities for catching the ear of today's young — where they are — with the gospel and with the Bible's constructive view of marriage and sex.

Early marriage. Between 30 and 40 percent of all weddings today are teen-age marriages. Many are eighteen and under. In 1946 only 1 percent of married men were eighteen or under; today that figure is 11 percent. In 1946, 16 percent of all brides were eighteen or under. By 1960 the figure had spiraled to 38 percent.

Some of these marry early simply to get away from home. The teen-ager whose home is an unhappy one hopes to find in marriage that which was lacking in his own home but too often he does not have the emotional maturity for marriage. As a result, 37 percent of these teen-agers are divorced within the first year!

Divorce. At least twenty-five percent of today's married couples will divorce.

Outside the divorced group are those couples who would get a divorce if they could afford it or if their church would allow it.

Then we have the "emotional divorce" — those living in the same house, putting up a front but lacking the real involvements which should be a part of any acceptable marriage. Again it is hard to estimate but many in the field estimate 20 to 25 percent are involved in this type of a dilemma. In this home it's the children who pay the greatest price, for they have "tuned in" to what is really going on.

Schooling. In 1940, 35 percent of high school graduates went on to college. In 1965 it was 54 percent, and this did not include those who entered various specialty schools.

In high school the study load has been so increased that a Northwestern University professor contends many bright students are intellectually burned out by the time they get to college. Today's students are generally far ahead of where their parents were, and they're asking "college-age" questions at the high school and even grammar school level. One wonders how much evangelical churches have geared to this stepped-up educational pace.

Senior citizens. Greater longevity has expanded the number of senior citizens. One study in the Minneapolis area revealed that in the past ten years the number of people over sixty-five had increased 30 percent, although the overall population increase during that same time was only 7 percent. As a whole, neither the family nor the church has satisfactorily adjusted to meet this situation. Work in this area is a gold mine for our churches today.

Leisure. Many families today face a problem in the use of leisure time. The shorter work week, the shorter working day, labor-saving appliances, earlier retirement, and other factors have contributed to this. Of course, one can find all kinds of things to do with leisure time, but can he use this time constructively?

The challenge today is to use this time creatively to develop ourselves and our families, thus creatively developing all the institutions of society which we touch.

Changing roles. Many of the previously considered changes point up a confusion existing as to the role of the man or woman, husband or wife. Is he head of the home or do we have a matriarchal or equalitarian unit? Who does the housework, disciplines the children, etc.?

For the past half century dramatic psychological and sociological forces have been reshaping the American home. We must face these changes with an open mind — whether we like them all or not. And it may well be within the next few years that the dedication and example of our Christian families and the success of our evangelical churches in reaching the homes around them with the message of Jesus Christ could decide what happens to the families of America.

·•··•··•··•··•··•··•··•··•··•··•··•··•··•·

The sequence of new experiences is speeded up today. It is part of our affluent society. Kids are hurried through experiences once deferred. They get bicycles earlier. They get trips across the country and around the world. Dating starts as early as thirteen or fourteen years of age. Therefore, about the only thing left unsampled by the time they reach the middle teens is the sex act itself. Then we step in and tell them: "You've done everything else when you wanted to, but you have to wait for this for another five years." We should program the age at which each experience is granted a child — spread them out so he won't run out of new experiences too soon.

— Dr. J. M. Bobbitt

The New Morality

by Letha Scanzoni
Author, Sex and the Single Eye

It all started with the 1963 publication of Bishop John A. T. Robinson's controversial book, *Honest to God.*

Suddenly it seemed everyone was talking about "relativism," "situational ethics," "freedom from legalism," "the love ethic," "the new morality," "the relationship ethic," and so on. There were some who assumed mistakenly that this meant that anything goes — that now there was indeed a unique new morality giving license to do as one pleases without the guilt incurred by violating codes of moral absolutes.

But what is the new morality? Essentially, it is a humanist ethic which takes into account the value of persons instead of a blind reliance on rigid principle and inflexible rules. Love is considered the only "moral absolute" — love that cares about the needs and feelings of the other person and acts in the way thought to be most beneficial to him. Moral standards, they say, cannot be "pre-packaged." We must have a "person-centered approach." "The new morality, situation ethics, declares that anything and everything is right or wrong, according to the situation," writes Joseph Fletcher in *Situation Ethics.*

Those who set forth the new morality are thinking, of course, in terms of all sorts of moral-ethical decisions (e.g., is it ever right to lie?). Sex is only one of the areas they have in mind.

However, we will consider here the new morality ques-

Copyright 1968 Zondervan Publishing House

tioning the church's traditional teaching that "sex outside the bonds of marriage is always wrong." Situationists feel that such an unqualified statement is unrealistic — perhaps even cruel. Might there not be some circumstances for certain people at certain times, they ask, which could make permissible — even desirable — premarital, extramarital, or postmarital (i.e., in the case of a person widowed or divorced) sexual relations? Does the law or the church have any right, they argue, to dictate to an adult man or woman how he or she should satisfy normal sexual needs so long as no other person is harmed? "Whether any form of sex (hetero, homo, or auto) is good or evil depends on whether love is fully served," writes Joseph Fletcher.

Second, the new morality is deeply interested in interpersonal relationships. To "use" or exploit another person for gratification of one's own sexual desires is not considered fair play. It is a failure to apply the law of love and thus is to be deplored.

Third, the new morality puts much stress on motivation and attitude and is concerned more with the why of sexual behavior than the what of what does or doesn't take place in a person's sex life.

Many Christians seem to be more upset about the implications of the new morality as it applies to sex than they are about its application to any other area. One reason for this may be that traditionally among Christians, sexual sin has tended to be regarded as somehow worse than any other type of sin. This notion, though prevalent, is by no means biblical. Fornication, adultery, and homosexuality are lumped together in the New Testament right alongside such sins against God as envy, strife, gossip, deceit, boasting, disobedience to parents, anger, dissension, jealousy, slander, foul talk, and the like. Alert Christians have, of course, pointed this out long before the current discussions on morality.

The fact is that there are historical, social, and cultural

reasons which lie behind the church's contention that sexual transgressions are the worst kind of transgressions.

One reason Christians are disturbed about the new sex morality is that some of its proponents have used illustrations that strike many as being rather extreme and perhaps more sensational than illuminating.

Some new-morality pleaders ask why a woman with no prospects of marriage should be denied the experience of giving birth to a child of her own, whether by natural means or through artificial insemination, if she so desires. Fletcher suggests that there might be occasions where an unmarried couple might, "if they make the decision Christianly," decide to have sexual intercourse for some specific purpose, such as forcing a selfish parent (via the girl's pregnancy) to consent to their marriage.

One of the most talked-about illustrations of the book *Situation Ethics* is the avowed story of a German mother interned in a Soviet prison camp in the Ukraine during World War II, who found that the only way she could be released and returned to her husband and children would be for her to be discovered to be pregnant. After carefully thinking it over, the woman asked a friendly guard to impregnate her; and when her condition was verified, she was sent back to Berlin. Her family was overjoyed, despite her admission of how she had arranged her freedom; and the child born of this extramarital union was loved intensely because it was because of him that the family was reunited. Joseph Fletcher calls this "sacrificial adultery" and asks whether this mother might not have done "a good and right thing" in such a case.

These examples are cited only to give some idea of what certain situationists have in mind when they state that no code can satisfactorily deal with all circumstances.

The new moralists insist they are not arguing for promiscuity or any other form of irresponsible sexual behavior.

For the committed Christian who sincerely wants to

obey Christ, however, the new morality lacks an added and essential dimension. This is because, with all its emphasis on the worth of persons (which is certainly to be commended), the new morality somehow seems to crowd God out of the picture. It simply doesn't go far enough. "You shall love your neighbor as yourself" is the *second* great commandment. To love *God* with our entire being — heart, soul, strength, and mind — must take first place (Matthew 22:36-40). It is on these two commandments taken together that "depend all the law and the prophets," said Jesus.

Some proponents of the new morality parry this by saying that we love God through our neighbor — that God never calls for any love to be directed exclusively to himself, but is only interested in our love for our fellowman. Of course, it is true that a genuine love for God will prove itself in its love for others (see 1 John 4:19-21), but this doesn't rule out the fact that in addition God does want us to direct toward him our devotion, our worship, our adoration, our affection — in short, our love (Deuteronomy 6:5; 7:9; 10:12; 11:22; Matthew 4:10; Joshua 22:5) — a love so great that no other love should be permitted to equal it (Matthew 10:37-39; Luke 14:26-27). And Jesus Christ said, "If you love me, keep my commandments" (John 14:15).

Furthermore, Christ specifically stated that he did not come to abolish the law and the prophets, but to fulfill them. Never did he speak lightly of the Ten Commandments. In fact, he warned against relaxing them in the least (Matthew 5:19). Nothing and no one may have the worship, love, and service that belongs to God alone. Sex can so easily become an idol.

In sum, then, the new morality may be seen to possess a basic inherent weakness when one sees that its emphasis on a man-to-man relationship fails to take into account the importance of a man-to-God relationship and responsibility. When its spokesmen argue that we must brush aside the Ten Commandments on the grounds that Jesus said he was giving a new commandment ("love one another"), they ignore Christ's own teachings on the commandments. Other New Testament passages that speak of love as the fulfilling of the Law do so in a context that by no means abolishes the specific commands of that Law. (See, for example, Romans 13:8-10; Galatians 5:13-24; James 2:8-12.)

To toss out God's moral law as irrelevant is to throw away the measuring stick that shows how far short of God's standard of righteousness all of us fall. It is by our knowledge of our failure to live up to all that God's laws require that we become aware that we are sinners in need of God's forgiveness through Jesus Christ (Romans 3:19). "Indeed, it is the straight-edge of the Law that shows us how crooked we are" (Romans 3:20, Phillips).

In this modern, sex-saturated society, when a young adult feels he is privileged to make his own choice from among several ethical standards, he may flatly reject the Christian position, concluding that one of the other two (or something in-between) is better suited to his personal needs. How could he possibly expect to live up to all that Christianity requires? The answer is simple: he couldn't. No one can.

Christianity, however, is not a system of ethics to be auctioned in the marketplace alongside other moralities. Christianity is Jesus Christ. This means that one cannot choose "Christian ethics" or "Christian sex standards." One can only choose *Christ.* After opening one's life to him and entering into an exciting, vital personal relationship with the risen Lord, these other matters fall into place. (This isn't to say, of course, that one cannot choose chastity apart from Christ. Such a choice could be made on purely humanistic grounds.)

The redemption offered by Jesus Christ promises freedom.

"If the Son makes you free, you will be free indeed" (John 8:36).

The Scriptures, however, make clear a strange paradox: all freedom involves some kind of slavery! If one is free from God, he is a slave of sin. But if one is free from slavery to sin, he becomes a slave to Christ (Romans 6:15-22).

The freedom made possible by redemption offers us Christ's resources. It may not be fashionable these days to speak of the superhuman dimension of Christianity — yet apart from this, there is no Christianity. When a life is opened to Christ, he transforms that person! "For God is at work within you, helping you want to obey him, and then helping you do what he wants" (Philippians 2:13, TLB).

•-•--•--•-•--•--•-•--•--•-•--•-•--•-•--•--•-

Nothing is more devastating than getting to do what you please, and then not be pleased with what you have done. In such a moment there is no one to blame but yourself; and there . . . you stop all this clamor for absolute freedom and begin to ask for guidance, preferably from the One who made this world and thus knows best how one should live in it. The truth is, I am not wise enough to make either the best or the most of this life on my own. Why? Because I am a junior partner in the enterprise of life.

The prodigal son is a clear example of man out of touch with his own being. First he tried to be more than he was, and ran head-on into a world he did not make; and then he tried to cop out by being less than he was — a nothing, a cog in a machine. In both ways he was making the Great Refusal that our forefathers described by the word "sin."

— JOHN R. CLAYPOOL

Sex Education — Whose Responsibility?

by John M. Drescher
Author, Now Is the Time to Love, *and Moderator, Mennonite General Conference*

Sex is a difficult subject for most parents to discuss. You may shudder to think of the time when your child will come to you with the first question about birth or reproduction, or you may already feel you have failed when you had opportunities to teach him. You may be secretive about the whole subject of sex because of hangups you experience yourself. You do not feel free to share.

"At the same time," says Millard J. Bienvenu, Sr., head of the Department of Sociology at Northwestern State College of Louisiana and author of *Parent-Teenager Communication*, "we have come to realize that the best way to help children grow up with a healthy and decent appreciation of sex is to avoid being secretive about it. Today's youth have available to them more information and misinformation and are exposed to more sexual stimuli than ever before. . . . it is imperative that they get the information which will shape their attitudes from the parents first."

The majority of young people who get into trouble have had very little factual information about sex.

Two preliminary points are important as we begin to consider sex education in the home.

First, whether you know it or not, you are teaching sex. You cannot avoid it. One writer says, "Long before the time most parents feel they should talk with Sally or Freddie about the birds and bees, the mold of sexual conditioning

Copyright *Good News Broadcaster*

has been set." At an early age the child senses love and acceptance. He quickly learns to interpret the tone of a voice and the touch of a hand. But most of all, his understanding of sex stems from what he senses in the relationships between his mother and father.

When mother and father love each other and are not hesitant to show it and say it, children never need to be told that sex is beautiful. They see it, feel it, and know it. When there is tension between mother and father, no amount of talking about the beauty or sanctity of sex will get the message across. The child's attitude toward sex is also learned from the reaction of parents to statements about sex. By all of these means parents are always, each moment, teaching something about sex.

A second important point is that sex facts such as the physiological differences between males and females, the body functions and changes, as well as reproduction, ought to be shared as fully as possible before such facts can affect a child emotionally, before children reach adolescence, when young people have enough other problems to trouble them in the turbulent teens. Proper names for the different organs of the body ought to be introduced early. Why should some parts of the body be referred to in mysterious and meaningless terms? We do not learn foreign names for our fingers and feet.

An understanding of the sex act relieves the mind from ignorance and curiosity. It is curiosity and ignorance, according to one experienced counselor, which "gets most girls into trouble."

If a boy is told by a loving parent about such things as wet dreams, circumcision, and reproduction before he enters adolescence, when such subjects become highly emotional, he is well on the way to making correct and mature adjustments. His mind is also more at ease. And he is more likely to come to his parents for additional help later on.

If parents share facts early enough, much mental and emotional strain, as well as misinformation, will be avoided. Much inquisitive exploration, which usually produces guilt feelings, can be avoided.

In addition to these two basic guidelines, certain simple, specific suggestions are helpful.

Be biblical. We warp and twist life when we try to ignore something God has put within us and expects of us. God made us male and female. This fact is inescapable. God made us this way for a purpose, and he proclaimed his creation to be very good (Genesis 1:31).

The Christian attitude is that sex is neither something to be ashamed of nor something to be exploited. It is a normal and wholesome part of life, as normal and wholesome as any other.

Be loving. To help individuals understand themselves as persons and to appreciate the dignity of human love is the basic purpose of sex education. Only parents can teach tenderness, freedom, and abandonment which come in the presence of trust, protection, and love. So by the loving kiss, caress, and word, even the small child learns his first lesson in what love is. Later he learns that sex belongs to the whole picture of love, caring, and sharing.

One young man tells how his attitudes regarding sex were formed when he saw the love his father had for his mother and his sisters. "Often early in the morning my father would go out to find the most beautiful rosebud in the garden. He would place it at Mother's place to greet her when she came to breakfast. It cost only a few minutes of time and a heart full of love. As she picked up the rose, he stepped behind her chair, gave her his morning kiss, and the whole day was glorified. Even the child who had got out of bed 'on the wrong side' felt ashamed because life had been touched by love. Now I think I understand why I always feel repulsed by those who consider a woman a cheap plaything. My parents illustrated to me what love and personhood really mean."

Be natural. Small children are more curious than emotional in their questioning. Therefore, answer the child in a natural way. Parents never dare imply by attitude, word, or silence that sex is bad, distasteful, or less than beautiful and good.

Speak casually about love and affection and about pregnancy and childbirth in front of children. This produces the atmosphere that is conducive to easy questioning on the part of the child.

Be honest. Always answer a child's question honestly, directly, and accurately. Provide information suitable to the child's age and the question asked. A good guide to keep in mind is that expressed by H. Clair Amstutz: "When a child is old enough to ask a specific question, he has already proved himself capable of understanding a direct answer." If a parent is dishonest in explaining where children come from, why should the child not later question the honesty of the parents' explanation about the evils of illicit sex?

Be alert. Alert parents can provide sex education by using the natural opportunities that present themselves. Such opportunities to impart knowledge come gradually and repeatedly. Not everything needs to be told at once.

When the child comes with the first question, be glad and share with him joyfully and in a direct way. The child's coming shows a confidence which the parent dares not lose. "Where did I come from, Mother?" "You grew in your mother's body. I carried you close to my heart." Such an answer with an affectionate hug teaches much. As time goes on, more facts can be shared.

One of the best early opportunities for teaching is at bath time. It is not long until the child learns the names of his ears, eyes, nose, fingers and so on. One can also teach the child the proper terms for other parts of the body by talking while the bath is in progress. In this way every part of the body can be referred to in a natural way.

As the child grows, he is open to all kinds of things which can and will influence attitudes on sexuality. And don't assume your child is different from others in what he knows. He likely knows a great deal more than you did at his age because he is bombarded by sex in so many ways today.

Be happy. This means that parents should enjoy their respective roles if they are to teach the true meaning of sexuality.

A mother who complains of her role — the drudgery of housework, the nuisance of children, the misery of menstruation, the pains of pregnancy and childbirth — is teaching a lot about sex and is helping her son or daughter to be maladjusted.

One happy wife writes: "When I saw the satisfaction my mother had in making a home and caring for a baby and the way she enjoyed doing the things every woman needs to do, I felt the greatest thing in the world was to be a wife and a mother. When I sensed her attitude of love and freedom toward my father, I felt the greatness of what it means to be a girl and a woman and the goodness of relating to a man one loves. Also, as I saw my father's love and headship in the home, I decided upon what I desired in the one whom I would someday marry."

One happy young husband writes: "No one showed me more of what it means to be a man and what it means to respect and love a woman than my own father. If he lacked many of the things some would call greatness, he was great in that he enjoyed being a man in his work, in his pastime activities, and as a father and husband in the home. His example is a challenge to me when my own family relationships seem frail."

In the words of Vivian Ziegler, "The reassuring fact is that if you as a parent accept your own sexuality and find joy in using it as a method of expressing love to your mate, you have very actively been giving sex education to your children since their birth in a positive, spontaneous, healthful and God-intended way."

.•..•..•..•..•..•..•..•..•..•..•..•..•..•..•.

In early life I had nearly been betrayed into the principles of infidelity but there was one argument in favor of Christianity that I could not refute, and that was the consistent character and example of my own father.

— Francis Quarles

Homosexuality Begins at Home

by David Wilkerson
Author, Parents on Trial, *and Founder-Director, Teen Challenge*

Homosexuality is one of the greatest social problems of our modern world. When I first came to New York City, I did not grasp its full significance, but after nearly a decade of counseling with homosexuals and trying to understand their problems, and after accepting many homosexuals in residence as patients at our centers, I have become acutely aware of some of the more tragic aspects of this deviation. An addict would tell me, "I want to kick the junk habit, I want to stop drinking, but I still want to be 'gay.'" Out of more than five hundred homosexuals I interviewed, only ten indicated that they actually wanted help.

This is a problem shared by thousands of teen-agers, male and female, in cities large and small. Whether people admit it or not, the problem is there.

I have encountered it in almost every city in which I have conducted a youth rally. Once in Boston, where I appeared on a radio program, I was told by a young caller that he attended a high school where the students had designated each Thursday as "queers day," at which time all boys and girls so inclined wore orange so they could recognize one another. I have heard of this being done in other cities as well.

For parents or ministers who would suggest that I am overstating the extent of this problem, I think you should know that I have prevented young people from committing

---

Copyright 1967 Hawthorn Books, Inc.

suicide because they could not cope with this influence upon their lives.

Society, particularly the church, must face up to this problem and offer some kind of help, if not a solution.

Perhaps we can at least shed a little light on the subject by indicating what the Bible says is the cause, and suggesting that the church must believe and preach that there can be hope for homosexuals.

The rise of homosexuality among our youth is one of the major failures of American home life. It may even become one of the major failures of American civilization. There was a time when people believed that the homosexual was born that way, that he was not a product of his environment. Now it is generally agreed that, except in the rarest of instances, the human shortcoming that contributed to the downfall of Greece and Rome is a result of childhood experience, often fomented by a too-doting mother and a disinterested or negligent father (with perhaps the reverse true in the case of lesbians), but also nurtured by a society that increasingly indicates acceptance of this aberration.

"Homosexuality is a problem as old as the world," an eminent psychiatrist said, "yet it is now so extensive it bears comparison to the decline and fall of the Roman Empire."

There was a time when we ministers pretended homosexuality did not exist. Now the church is being forced to take a long look at this social cancer. It is interesting to note that while many church members have refused to recognize homosexuality, the Bible speaks clearly about the matter. First, there is grave spiritual danger, as we see in Leviticus 18:22 and Romans 1:24-27. Please read these carefully.

Doctors warn of other very real dangers in homosexuality. The most threatening is potential suicide. Judge John M. Murtagh, a distinguished New York jurist, in his book *Cast the First Stone,* said that probably 50 percent of all suicides and homicides in a big city can be attributed to homosexuality. Other authorities agree, adding that the homosexual's life is characterized by deep loneliness, desperation, guilt, and frustration. Also, because they are never really fulfilled they are constantly seeking new thrills, which can lead to their becoming masochists or sadists. Crimes of arson and theft often have been linked directly to homosexuality. There is always the danger of alcoholism. One psychologist has gone so far as to say, "Not every alcoholic is homosexual, but every homosexual is alcoholic."

Venereal disease is another danger. In New York alone 3,500 new cases of veneral disease were reported among young people eighteen or under in a single year, "and it is safe to say that for every one reported, two were not reported — and that those two were cases of venereal disease contracted by young people consorting with older homosexuals."

Without doubt, the greatest threat that homosexuals impose upon our society is the seduction of children. The homosexual is constantly seeking someone young and "untouched." The tragedy is that most of those seduced are either led into a life of homosexuality or are seriously damaged psychologically by such an encounter.

Why do we have homosexuals? At least one cause for the rise in homosexuality is the increase in the feminization of men and the masculinization of women. The presence of women in the highly competitive business and professional worlds is one factor. Hair styles are a good index; young men with long hair and girls with short cuts, for example. Fashions in clothes are involved, too, psychologists agree.

The philosopher Nietzsche reminds us, "When there are no longer men, the women will become men." At the time this happens, our society will crumble. When Rome first conquered Greece, the Greek sculpture was predominantly feminine — as were many of its young men. At that time, Roman sculpture reflected the virility and power of manhood. Six centuries later, however, just before the barbarian hordes invaded Rome, the sculpture had become feminized, reflecting what had happened to many Roman men. It was Greece all over again. The softening of the empire's manhood was the prelude to downfall, bearing out Aristotle's comment, "A country is only as strong as each man in it and its civilization only as great as its dreams."

There are, of course, deep personal as well as sociological reasons for homosexuality. Homosexuals are made, not born. Homosexuality begins in the cradle, not in the womb. Dr. Clyde M. Narramore, in his excellent book *The Psychology of Counseling,* says the following types of parents can contribute to the creation of tendencies toward sexual deviation in a child.

The dominant mother. She stifles her son's masculinity, causing him to lose confidence in his own sex. He fears all women because of his mother and dreads the thought of intimacy with any woman. She may compete with her son for the father's attention and tell the child he was an "unwanted" baby. She says she planned for a daughter, dresses the boy in frills, insists that he play with girls, and subconsciously tries to make him fill the role of a daughter. By the time he reaches maturity, he finds it natural to play the role of a girl. The reverse sometimes happens to a girl. She was supposed to be a boy, so she is given a boy's name, and so on. Here the dominant father can be an influence toward lesbianism.

The weak father. Real tragedy results when a dominant mother is paired with a weak father. The son cannot look to his father for support in his struggle to be a man. The daughter loses respect for all men because of her father and is psychologically seduced by the masculine mother. Sexual identification is lost, and the child becomes confused.

The overindulgent mother. Just as harmful as the dominant mother is the one who caters to every whim of her son. She spoils him and when he is small may take him to bed with her when the father is away or relations are strained. Psychologically she seduces the child and tries to make him a substitute for her husband. Attachment between mother and son thus may grow to be very strong, so strong that he cannot break away. In many cases, the father is not much help. The boy feels, "Why get married? No girl could ever measure up to my mother." The thought of a normal sexual relationship seems repellent — "That would be like having sexual relations with my mother." Then, too, such mothers may tend to picture sex as something that is dirty and unnatural. They may complain about the pain of childbirth. Thus the door to heterosexual relationships is gradually shut and homosexuality results. Girls, too, can drift into homosexuality under the influence of such mothers, who make sex and childbirth seem unpleasant and who use daughters as buffers to keep their husbands at bay.

The cruel father. A son's fear of competition with other men can result from having a cruel father who subjects the boy to physical or mental punishment. A child has a deep wish to be accepted by members of his own sex, particularly his parent, and once a boy's father rejects him, he will turn to other males. He learns as he grows older that one way to win acceptance in the male world is to let other men use his body. Such youths are easy prey for older homosexuals, and once the pattern is established, it is very difficult to break. The daughter of such a father becomes afraid of men because of his cruelty. She may see herself in the role of the abused mother. Her fear of her father is transferred to all men. Since girls, like boys, crave love, she turns to members of her own sex.

Children reared in strong, happy homes will not grow up to become homosexuals, just as they will not grow up to become narcotics addicts or criminals despite the sociological pressures closing in on them. Thus an enormous responsibility is heaped on parents: those who find a son or daughter heading for or already involved in homosexual activity should refrain from asking, What is wrong with *him?* and inquire instead, What is wrong with *us?* What did we do that was wrong? How can we help this child? A leading authority on the homosexual problem commented recently: "The real tragedy of homosexuality is that with a little understanding, love, and help from the parents of these victims this would not have happened at all."

It is not necessarily true that once a youth has become a homosexual, nothing can be done about it, but it is true that the rate of "cure" is very low. The chief difficulty we encounter is the large number who do not want to change. They like the way they are! At least that is what they say.

It seems obvious that if the cure for homosexuality is difficult, we should devote our efforts to preventive action. There are strong guidelines in the Scriptures that could help stem the rising tide of homosexuality if we would but put them to work.

Parents who want to dress a boy in girls' clothing might find guidance in Deuteronomy 22:5. Parents should read 1 Peter 3 and Ephesians 5 and 6. Keeping in mind the causes of homosexuality, note what God says about a proper marriage relationship: wives should be in subjection to their own husbands; women should be meek and quiet of spirit; husbands are to give honor unto the wife, to respect her and hold her in high esteem; husbands are told to love their wives as their own bodies; the wife is to revere the husband; children are to obey and honor their parents; and finally, the children are to be brought up in the fear and admonition of the Lord.

The Bible allows no room for the dominant mother, the weak father, the overindulgent mother, or the cruel father.

Thus, if these admonitions are followed by parents, their children will have a good chance to grow up and be normal human beings.

•-•--•--•--•--•--•--•--•--•--•--•--•--•--•--•-

What a man is at home, that he is indeed, if not to the world, yet to his own conscience and to God.
— ROBERT PHILIP

The Turned-on Generation

by Gordon R. McLean
Co-author, High on the Campus

San Francisco spends $3.75 million annually for the hospital care required by approximately 5,000 teen-age drug users. New York City recently reported its youngest drug death — an eleven-year-old boy who had taken an overdose of heroin. Dr. Hardin B. Jones of the University of California at Berkeley comments that "drug abuse, which moved from the slums to our college campuses, has now infected the entire spectrum of our schools and is spilling over into the middle-class adult world as well. The extent of this drug craze is unbelievable and its projected increase is frightening."

For most students, the use of drugs is a once-in-awhile event. For others, it has become a way of life, perhaps because the experimenting can't be limited. These young people happen to be susceptible to certain drugs, become dependent, and get badly hurt from what may have started out as an innocent adventure.

Complicating the problem is the fact that we live in a drug-oriented society. We produce new alcoholics in this nation at the rate of fifty an hour. And millions of people are addicted to cigarettes, though they usually insist they can quit anytime. "It's easy, I've done it hundreds of times!" they say.

Truck drivers and students cramming for a test often will take pep pills to keep them awake, or persuade a doctor to give them diet pills to lose weight.

Copyright 1970 Tyndale House Publishers

For a growing number of adults, drugs are a way of life. They take pep pills to get up, tranquilizers to stay calm, a cocktail to start the evening, and a barbiturate to go to sleep. It can make for a very short day of rational thinking.

The young are also influenced by a growing number of movies and songs glorifying the use of drugs. The trend towards drug promotion and vulgarity in music is not a healthy one — dirty words used to be scrawled on walls; now they're flashed on screens or on "top 40" records.

Jim Smith and the editors of *Campus Life* magazine analyzed various student surveys and came out with eight reasons for student drug involvement.

"Man, there is just nothing else to do!" Caught in the monotony of living, a wild trip on drugs offers forbidden excitement. Without a healthy interest in the little things around him, and bored by routine, this student finds that moments of exhilaration and danger give life zest — for a little while.

"I lose all my worries and imagine many things." Drugs become a reassuring lollipop to suck on, a security blanket to curl up with. Retreat via drugs from the harsh — or imagined harsh — realities of life drives the user even further away.

"It blows my parents' minds. They just can't believe their little girl is on pot!" This is one way students hit back at parents — to shock them. One psychiatrist says, "It is fun for them to see their parents get put on. Drugs give them something with which to get their parents enraged and incensed."

"I just can't take all the tension." The gigantic pressure cooker most high schoolers are in — the cooker which demands high grades, heavy participation, and being a social swinger — proves too much for some.

Dr. William Glasser comments, "Too much school material is unrealistic, unemotional and dull. . . . The colleges of America which admit primarily on the basis of high grades are major culprits in an unpremeditated plot to destroy the students."

"Me? I was just curious, that's all." Dr. Mitchell Balter found in his survey of teens that about a third who experiment with drugs do so out of curiosity. With all the talk going on about Yellow Jackets, Double Trouble, Giggle Smoke, Speedballs, and Speed, even though the dangers are clearly pointed out, the desire to "try some and see" becomes tragically strong for some otherwise levelheaded kids. Educational programs, poorly presented, sometimes add to this problem. One student commented, "If drugs were worth canceling classes to talk about, they were worth trying!"

"I don't mind saying it. I'm just a failure, that's all." If you could look deep into the thoughts and feelings of many students, you'd find they considered themselves "nothing much," and that their clumsiness or their being overweight or their low grades or their rejection by other students keeps them from feeling self-assured. They may quickly cluster with other students who don't feel they're making it either — but they all can get some "high and good" feelings through drugs.

"Drugs will help me realize my true potential." The hostile, the confused, and the inept seek instant transformation by way of drugs. All that is needed, they believe, is to swallow the magic potion and their true value will be revealed to a humbled world. So the alchemists dreamed of an elixir to make them wise; so bottled sunshine was peddled from the tailgates of medicine-show wagons.

"Drugs will help me find a new religious experience and forget myself." The goal of true religion is not to forget yourself. It is discipline of self. This is not the same as slopping through the cosmos with no identity. The Christian emphasis is on "mind," "attention," "find." These the drug advocates shrug off in favor of "no mind," "relax," "lose." Anybody can do that: it's easy. Exactly.

Alienation from the adult society is one of the strongest

factors in creating the insecurity for which drugs have become a way out, and it is a reason parents, teachers, and the community establishment have the hardest time understanding. In this alienation is wrapped up all the campus unrest, the so-called generation gap, and the problem of drug abuse.

And the problem begins at home. Parents often are afraid of their teen-agers, so no limits or disciplinary standards are set. "They all let their kids . . ." becomes a guideline for weak-willed parents and a rallying point for overbearing adolescents. Parents encourage sexual promiscuity, use of alcohol or drugs, and other problems by leaving children too much on their own with no supervision or even knowledge of their whereabouts. Unlimited access to the automobile is another strong factor in molding teen-age standards. For the more responsible, a car can be a step toward adult living; for the immature, it can be a ticket to disaster.

One important element in parent-teen relationships we want to stress here is *listen to your youngsters*. If you wait until Junior is on pot to decide it's time to sit down and have a little heart-to-heart talk, you are apt to find the going rough. This will be a new experience for many parents, and how to get through to adults has to rank as one of the biggest teen-age hangups. An anonymous fifteen-year-old wrote:

"Some parents don't really listen to their children. Their minds are not where their eyes are. Sometimes parents listen, but not open-mindedly. They hear you out, then throw it right back at you in a fiery tone of voice. Some parents could care less about thoughts of their children. 'After all, they're only kids. We will listen to them when they know what they are talking about.'"

Another teen-ager was looking for friends when she found help at Encounter, Inc. She gave some good insights on parent-teen relationships as they relate to the drug problem:

"When I was sixteen, I was in big trouble. For two years I had used pot, pills, LSD, ether — anything I could find — in my desperate search for some kind of happiness, some release from the constant pain of living. Then, suddenly, I got busted. I thought, Oh, no, it's all over, I'm lost. But what actually happened was I found a group of people who helped me slowly, slowly relearn what it meant to be alive, to love, to be loved, and to feel self-esteem. It's a high a million times better than a high.

"What would you have done if you had met me two years ago? Would you have realized I was lonely, confused, in pain? Or figured I was just another supposedly happy-go-lucky hippie? Let me give you some guidelines from my experience because there are an awful lot of things you can do to help a kid like me.

"First, one's behavior always gives him away. If I'm flunking out of school, taking drugs, withdrawing from people, or lying a lot, things just can't be going groovy with me, no matter how much I insist they are. It's up to you, if you are responsible, to confront me strongly about my behavior. Point out how stupid it is, and suggest how I can behave differently. If you feel angry, show it — in such a way, of course, as to let me know that it springs from genuine concern for me. That's what will make me change. And a change in behavior is the first crucial step. Sometimes to get me to do that you will have not only to confront me but to threaten me with serious consequences if you find I haven't stopped.

"Second, once I'm acting like a human being again, I'll need you more than ever. But before I can accept your advice and concern, I must trust you. To get me to do that, you must not pretend to be infallible, or to love everything about me, or to know all the answers. No. All you have to be is human.

"Third, in order to help me deal with the reasons for my former bad behavior so that I don't fall right back into it, you should be talking to me a lot about emotions. How can anyone who feels rotten all the time ever lead a successful life? To be able to recognize and communicate feelings, even the wholly irrational ones like anger over a tiny incident, is most important. This is why you should insist I delve deep into my gut and figure out exactly what it is I'm feeling.

"Fourth, once I begin to do that, you can help me deal with my feelings. The rule here is that bad feelings are to be dumped, good ones are to be cherished, and both are to be shared with friends. If I have just been dropped by a boy, chances are I'll be both hurt and angry at him. To dump the bad feeling, I should be encouraged both to cry and get mad, while you (or another close friend) are with me. Not alone in bed at night. Stress that. Guilt and jealousy can be dumped by confessing them to the person I feel guilty and jealous about; loneliness by crying with someone who cares for me. Good feelings, like love and joy, are maintained only by spreading them: loving others, giving them joy. Joy and love I can keep only by giving them away.

"Fifth, the last step consists of your being aware of my misconceptions. Question my values so I can learn to question them myself. Show me how to be honest and open, and confront me when I start sliding. Straighten up my misunderstandings about sex . . . and a million other matters.

"When I begin to feel good enough about myself to interact freely with others, life gets pretty exciting. Beautiful, even!"

Dr. David Smith adds some advice for parents:

"Parents I have talked with are hysterical. Unless we are willing to become totally honest we will only increase the drug problem rather than alleviate it."

For the company of committed spiritual believers, the youth drug problem represents a great challenge to kindly, patiently, and faithfully point those in need to the One who said, "I am come to bring them life, and far more life than before." If the young doper can grasp that message, it can become for him the greatest Good News he will ever hear! Only a personal encounter with the Son of God can transform a life!

·•··•··•··•··•··•··•··•··•··•··•··•··•··•··•··•··•·

Blessed is the Christian homemaker who walketh not constantly to and from club meetings, nor standeth in the department store running up her charge account, nor sitteth idly chatting on the telephone.

Her delight is in building a Christian home; she buildeth with a believing husband or despite an unbelieving one, and toward this end she worketh by day and dreameth by night.

She shall reveal loving wisdom in its season of necessity; her patience shall not wither because of the demands of her family; and her housework shall give her joy.

The homemaker without God cannot reveal loving wisdom, but she is as unstable as a piece of lint caught in a draft.

Therefore she shall be unprepared for calamity or even minor difficulty; however, her complaint shall fold up in the presence of the Christian homemaker.

The Lord hath fellowship with the Christian homemaker and guideth her in preparing her family to dwell in his eternal home.

— ALICE KAY ROGERS

Social Drinker to Alcoholic

by Jerry G. Dunn

Author, God Is for the Alcoholic, *and Director, People's City Mission, Lincoln, Nebraska*

Not long ago, in one of the group therapy classes in our New Life Program, the problem of alcohol addiction was being discussed. Each of the forty-five men present gave a different reason for his own addiction to alcohol.

"I drink because I'm lonely." "I've always been a failure, and I suppose I'll always be one." "A guy like me could never learn to live without alcohol." "I didn't have what it takes."

What these men said is what I have found to be typical of alcoholics. They have their problems all figured out. They reach the conclusion it is hopeless to try to change.

But when they were confronted with the facts that people can become addicted to beverage alcohol, they began to understand that their strange pattern of living was developed to satisfy their addictive drive and did not necessarily come from a personality defect. Hope of taking their places as useful, upright members of society was thus seen as within their reach.

There is a popular present-day theory that a person is an alcoholic due to a physical, moral, or psychological defect in his makeup. Due to this defect, the theory maintains, a person was an alcoholic even before he took his first drink. This takes all blame from alcoholic beverages and places it on the individual.

There are some who drink because of such defects, but the weakness that caused him to begin to drink was soon succeeded by the greater weakness of his insatiable, acquired thirst for ethyl alcohol.

Dr. Robert Flemming, one of the leaders in the World Health Organization, says, "Most alcoholics are not psychiatric cases; they are normal people. First, nobody is immune to alcoholism. Second, total abstinence is the only solution."

Dr. Andrew C. Ivy, former head of the Clinical Science Department of the University of Illinois, states: "Beverage alcohol is an intoxicating, hypnotic analgesic, an anesthetic narcotic, poisonous and potentially habit-forming, craving-producing or addiction-producing drug or chemical."

The fact that most people don't recognize the addictive qualities of beverage alcohol is the principal reason social drinking is so dangerous. They don't know what the results of a seemingly harmless activity can be until it is too late.

There are an estimated eight million known alcoholics in America, and their numbers are increasing by four hundred and fifty thousand each year. A survey of divorce cases in courts reveals that 60 percent of all divorces have drinking in their background. The increase in the number of illegitimate births each year is parallel with the increased consumption of alcoholic beverages among young people. And in the field of crime 75 percent of all crimes are committed by those under the influence of alcohol.

The Bible clearly teaches that the problem is with the product, not the individual: "Who hath woe? who hath sorrow? who hath contentions? who hath babbling? who hath wounds without cause? who hath redness of eyes? They that tarry long at the wine: they that go to seek mixed wine. . . . At the last it biteth like a serpent, and stingeth like an adder" (Proverbs 23:29, 30, 32).

There is still an underlying cause. Howard Whitman, a well-known science writer, after reviewing the subject thoroughly in twelve articles, made this final statement, "Alcoholism emerges as a sickness of the soul." Alcoholism is a sickness of the soul — a sin sickness, and it must be considered such.

There are seven distinct, well-defined steps downward from sobriety to alcoholism and complete deterioration of the human mind and body. They can be warning signals — stop signs in the progressive downward march to alcoholism and destruction by it, or they can be signposts to mark the distance a man has yet to go.

The first step is social drinking. Practically without exception, people start to drink because someone offers them a drink. The pattern for so-called gracious living includes drinking. The "hospitality hour" and the cocktail party become an accepted part of social life. Although social drinking is the first step to alcoholism, sadly, it is also the snare that traps many individuals who have fought their way back to sobriety.

A man we'll call Pete was such a person. The path had been long and difficult for him, but at last he had reached the place where he could stay sober. He won back his wife and family, got a good job, bought a new home, and was getting ahead again. It had been five years since he had had a drink.

Then his wife went to visit her mother, and while he was staying at home alone, the people in the block had a housewarming for a new couple who had moved into the neighborhood. Anxious to be hospitable, the newcomers brought a case of beer from the basement.

Pete hesitated a little. How could he explain to complete strangers that he didn't drink? How could he go into an embarrassing explanation of the reasons why? These were his thoughts. So he took a glass of beer.

The fires of alcoholism had not been put out. They had only been banked within him, and were still smoldering. The taste of alcohol in that single glass of beer was enough to send them racing out of control.

Although five years had elapsed, he started to drink again. You know the rest of the story. He lost his job, his home, his family, and he finally hit skid row. All because someone offered him a social drink of beverage alcohol.

The second step down is dependent drinking, or a habit drinker. The habit drinker mixes a drink when he comes home from the office, or after dinner while he is reading or watching television.

The dependent drinker drinks when things start to build up, when the problems get too great for him. It helps him to forget what has happened. The disappointments and frustrations don't seem to be so great under the temporary glow produced by beverage alcohol.

The third stage is the pre-alcoholic phase. He begins to gulp his drinks, to drink on the sly, to sneak drinks. At a party he is the big-hearted guy who wants to be the bar tender and will always make a drink for himself every time he mixes one for someone else.

In this phase, the individual becomes a chronic liar. Deceit and lying become a way of life to him as he seeks to keep his family and employer from knowing that he is drinking more and more. He is able to look you straight in the eye and speak with the tones of one taking a solemn oath without uttering a single word of truth.

The fourth stage down is problem drinking. Here the individual begins to lose control of his drinking habits. Now, he has reached the stage where he can control the time he starts to drink but he cannot stop when he wants to. He can no longer quench his thirst once it has been aroused by alcoholic beverage. At this point the problem drinker experiences great torment. He goes someplace to do a job and starts to drink and cannot stop. He becomes dead drunk and can only vaguely remember anything that happened.

The fifth step down is the drop into alcoholism itself. He starts to drink because he cannot help it, and he continues to drink in long periods of intoxication because he cannot keep from it. His dependence upon alcohol is so complete that he is terrified at the thought of needing a drink and not being able to get it.

The sixth step down is the subtle descent into chronic alcoholism. While the plunge from problem drinking to alcoholism is sudden and marked, the drift into chronic alcoholism is gradual. He loses one job after another. At this stage, the individual's family and friends have become so disgusted and heartsick they have finally turned against him. He is very much alone. The pattern continues with his going on a long period of intoxication, which finally ends in delirium tremens. He is almost at the bottom.

The seventh step down is organic deterioration. He has reached the place where he no longer cares how he looks. He is dirty and unshaven. His eyes are bleary, and his face is perpetually bloated and flushed. He has undoubtedly had the experience of collapsing and being taken to the charity ward in a hospital, where they have treated him as best they could.

Even more disturbing is the way in which his mind deteriorates under the continual abuse of beverage alcohol. Every mission superintendent sees this effect of alcohol, even in former bankers, lawyers, investment brokers, business executives, and others who come in off the street.

Various surveys have estimated that only 3 to 12 percent of alcohol addicts ever get on skid row. The vast majority are living in their communities, protected by their families and occasionally by their business associates. They hide in their prisons of shame, fearful of facing life. They don't know which way to go. Most do not even want to admit to themselves that they have a problem. They must be jolted by something that shocks them enough to cause them to hit bottom and begin to look up for answers.

Every problem of man has a spiritual solution. God has provided a way of escape. Those who are trying to help alcoholics must believe this. Otherwise, trying to counsel an alcoholic or having a member of one's family ensnared with alcohol addiction can be a frustrating experience. Let me point out five ways you can help your alcoholic.

1. *The first way to help him is to pray for him.* Prayer is so important because the alcoholic is one person who cannot be helped unless he wants to be. He must ask for help before anything can be done for him. All we can do is try to bring him to the place where he wants help and will cooperate with the help he gets. The first step in accomplishing this is prayer.

2. *Present the gospel to him.* "But God commendeth his love toward us, in that, while we were yet sinners, Christ died for us" (Romans 5:8).

We need to be reminded that men are saved from the horrors of alcoholism and are brought to a place of respectability and service by the gospel of Christ. However, I have found that an alcoholic may have to go all the way to the bottom and sometimes onto skid row, because he has not seen the Christian life demonstrated.

"I might not know much about the Bible," Pete told me, "but if I'm going to be free from alcoholism, I've got to have something better than my wife has. As a matter of fact, if what she's got is religion, I know that religion is not the answer to my problem."

We should prayerfully strive to live in such a way that the alcoholic will look at us and say to himself, "I want what that person has."

3. *Give him fellowship.* It is not easy for anyone involved with an alcoholic to give him fellowship. How does a wife who has been beaten in a brutish, drunken rage forget such treatment? How does a wife put aside the ugly fact of her husband's infidelity? Can a mother forget that her children have been neglected and abused?

The answer is found in the reply of the disciples when

Christ told them they should forgive a person who had sinned against them seventy times seven times. "Lord, increase our faith."

We cannot forgive enough to take such an individual back into fellowship without the help and strength that come from God. We must put fear aside and enter into normal activities with him, guiding him into associations with the right kind of friends who will help rather than hinder.

4. *Be longsuffering.* Christ shows his longsuffering to us as a pattern for others to follow in their treatment of sinners. No one needs that pattern more than the one with an alcoholic in the family. We need to have the assurance in our hearts that God is not only interested in the alcoholic but loves him and wants to help him. We must believe that it is his desire to free our alcoholic from the bonds of addiction and to give him a new life.

5. *Be firm.* If an alcoholic is going to be helped, not only must his addiction to beverage alcohol be broken, his very personality is going to have to be redeveloped. If he lies to us, we should quietly but firmly let him know that we know he is lying. The sooner he comes to the place where he has to face the truth, the sooner he is going to be set free from his warped personality and his addiction to beverage alcohol.

It is not wise to threaten the alcoholic. Neither is it a good practice to try to extract promises from him. But if he should voluntarily make a promise when he is sober, he should be held to his agreement.

Rev. Joseph Kellerman, Director of the Charlotte, North Carolina, Council on Alcoholism, gives another warning. "Don't let the alcoholic outsmart you, for this teaches him to avoid responsibility and lose respect for you at the same time. Don't let the alcoholic exploit you or take advantage of you, for in so doing you'll become an accomplice in the evasion of responsibility."

Women often have to go to work to support themselves and their families because of an alcoholic husband. Out of necessity they begin to assume the full responsibility of the home and require nothing of their husbands. This husband has forgotten what it is like to work every day, but he should be willing to assume some responsibility for the support of his home.

In his moments of sobriety share with him the needs of the home, not as a nagging wife but as a loving wife who still believes that the husband is the head of the house. Impress upon him that he should share and give advice in those areas of responsibility.

When he starts working again, don't hold onto your job for reasons of security — because you feel he might have a relapse. If you feel you must keep your job, arrange to live on his salary. Discuss the matter with him and reach an agreement so he will never get the idea that he can fall back on you to take care of things. Work things out so he will always feel his responsibility.

When the individual begins to assume responsibility, it isn't long until he begins to regain his self-respect. His faith in Christ then will enable him to transfer his dependency from an individual or group to God.

•••••••••••••••••••••••••

"The beginning is the most important part of any work, especially in the case of a young and tender thing; for that is the time at which the character is being formed and the desired impression is more readily taken. Shall we just carelessly allow children to hear any casual tales which may be devised by casual persons, and to receive ideas into their minds the very opposite of those which we should wish them to have?"

— PLATO

Wives on the Time Clock

by Martha Nelson
Author, The Christian Woman in the Working World

Ida M. Flemister, in an article in the *American Association of University Women Journal,* stresses the time factor as a major consideration in the solution to the puzzling question which comes to the married woman who has a choice about working: "There is a time for being a wife and a mother and a time for being oneself, for experiencing self-actualization, for finding one's meaning in the context of mankind. It is not a question of 'to be or not to be' but when to be each. These roles may overlap, be sequential, or exist simultaneously."

The happiest women are those who have settled the question as to whether they should or shouldn't be working outside the home, for right now at least.

They have asked themselves such questions as, "How much pressure can I cope with?" "Is my family willing for me to work?" "Has my husband accepted and adjusted to a different routine — is he game for the give and take it requires for me to be a working wife?" And, decision reached, they check and recheck their answers from time to time as family needs and goals change.

Your answer to the second question may come more readily!

Why am I working? In the context of the Christian life, motives are extremely important, for "God looketh on the heart."

Why am I working? For money? Money for what?

———

Copyright 1970 Broadman Press

(There was Harriet who admittedly worked part-time to finance her downtown spending sprees for knickknacks and chocolate-covered strawberries on her days off!) Money to aid an aging parent? To keep the children in college? Is my job just something to occupy my time — busy work? Is it "anything but housework!" — an escape from boredom with husband, to get out of the house, away from the "kids"? Is your work a search for adventure or social contact? Has the desire to be independent, to dominate and exert power over others sent you job-hunting? Or do you work out of a sense of obligation to yourself and to society, to make use of your skills?

Dissatisfactions may stem from motives that do not measure up to one's ideals, and a Christian woman needs to examine her motivations in light of spiritual truth.

Before taking off on a bright autumn morning in search of your next job, be sure you have an answer to the next question:

What do I want out of a job? An army officer's widow whose first love was teaching but who had spent many years out of the working world, on her first job-hunting expedition was offered a spot as a telephone reservationist. It was handy to her home. She took the job and has been there for ten years. Like so many older women reentering the work world, she did not stop to evaluate her interests and abilities before starting out to find the job which was to become the center of her life for years to come.

Judy, an attractive girl fresh out of high school, went to work in a tool manufacturing company steno pool. Her real interest is in interior decorating. Poor Judy, it has never occurred to her that the job she is doing just doesn't fit. No wonder she wanders about the office, visiting, clock watching. The glow she had when she first took the job has given way to a look of patient boredom. Yes, she's doing a fair job in the pool, but at what a price to herself! Why shouldn't she be where she belongs — possibly in a shop where she can see and handle beautiful upholsteries, art objects, handsome furnishings? Though she might have to start as a typist there, too, she could find meaning in the daily tasks to which she is assigned, and she might have a chance to be learning, with possibility for advancement to a creative position in this field of her deepest interest.

"Know thyself" is a good philosophy for anyone, and especially for a woman making a job choice. A thorough self-analysis is a starting point: What are your best talents, skills, and strengths? What job fields would you prefer if you had a choice? A study of want ads; a keen look around at other women who work; a look at your telephone directory's yellow pages to discover the kinds of organizations employing in your area; a check with the public library for books relating to occupations and professions for women; discussions with friends, your pastor, or other trusted advisors; trips to employment agencies (a surprising number of women do not know that the states provide, free of charge, aptitude testing, vocational counseling and job placement) — these preliminary investigations will pay off immeasurably when you find yourself in a job that "fits," and the method is so much more economical than the blind "trial and error" route that may cause dismissals, dissatisfactions, and discontent.

Consider the emotional and spiritual satisfactions to be derived from the job you hold, or think you might like to hold. Do you want work that can be left in your desk drawer with never a thought after hours? There are chapters in a woman's life when this may be extremely desirable, when the children need so much of their mother's time and attention. Or have you the time and energy to apply to a fast-paced, demanding position with the long hours, continuing preparation, social obligations, and numerous after-five meetings which it may require?

Do you want work that involves contact with many people daily? Or do people tire you to the point of sending you into retreat beneath the covers of your bed the minute you arrive home? Maybe work behind the scenes would be more suitable for you. Are you happiest at work with your hands or your mind or with people?

If money is your prime consideration — and it is if you are a waitress picking up tips for a son's college education — you may have the incentive required to keep you happy in the busiest restaurant in town, even though your personal preference might be to serve in a little tearoom nearer home.

Is diversity of tasks important to your sense of well-being, or are you more comfortable in a fixed daily routine? How much does atmosphere matter? Would the noises of machines all about send you home with jagged nerves, and will a quieter spot at less pay be cheaper in the long run?

The serious consideration of advance preparation is advisable for the woman entering the work world for the first time. How much training can you afford and how much time can you give to preparation? Is college or trade school out of the question? What about a high school equivalency test?

What opportunities are available for training? Among government sponsored programs, training for secretaries, clerk-typists, nurses' aides, licensed practical nurses, and other occupational types is offered in many cities. Some philanthropic organizations provide free counsel and retraining for older women and handicapped persons. Adult education courses can mean employment opportunities for the woman who takes advantage of them. One secretary took a course in drapery-making and moved out from her desk in an oil company office to set up her own business as an interior designer, specializing in custom draperies.

Your educational background, your vitality, your family commitments, the circumstances in which you find yourself will affect your job opportunities and choices. The single woman has more freedom to follow her vocational choice than does her married sister who may find herself limited by geographical ties to people, places, and things. But when a woman knows herself and what she would like best to be doing, she may be happy in finding the nearest thing to it and adapting to her situation, determined "in whatsoever state she finds herself, therewith to be content."

To overrate yourself, so far as capabilities are concerned, creates misery and disappointment. The Bible admonishes, "Don't cherish exaggerated ideas of yourself or your importance, but try to have a sane estimate of your capabilities." And to underrate your potential puts you in the category with the man who hid the one talent given him by the Lord, bringing upon himself the displeasure of his master.

The Christian woman maturing in the knowledge of Christ's way may begin to examine her vocation in terms of the service it allows her to render for the good of others. Looking about, she may begin to see through the eyes of God the ever-widening scope of human need in an ever-shrinking world, and a whole new vista of opportunity for service to Christ through work may be revealed. The tasks of alleviating human suffering and meeting human need seem to multiply with every year of man's existence. The desire to serve such needs can be satisfied by service in and through one's daily work.

With current technological changes bringing about extensive automation in which labor-saving machines and decision-making computers are taking over more and more of the tasks heretofore assigned to men and women, the work picture of the future is in for some changes. A noted anthropologist declares that "we can look forward to a day when all the dull, unrewarding, routine, technical tasks can be done by machines, and the human tasks — caring for children, caring for plants and trees and animals, caring for the sick and the aged, the traveler and the stranger — can be done by human beings."

Women have always excelled in the caring professions

and in the helping occupations. It seems that God created woman with a special affinity for people. Could it be that the indefinable discontent of so many women today is a result of their spending their days in positions where their caring touch is not needed?

The demands to staff schools, hospitals, nursing homes, and welfare agencies increase daily, providing opportunities for the Christian woman entering the work world to choose where she might best fit into God's purpose in today's world.

And now the final question that the Christian woman will want to include in her evaluation to determine the "fit" of her job:

Is this God's will for me? When you have sincerely sought your answers to the other questions: Should I be working outside the home right now? Why am I working? and What do I want out of a job? there is yet the still, small voice within that speaks to a woman's heart, if she listens, and helps to confirm her decision.

She need not fear to listen for God's speaking, for he wills for his children only what is best for them.

The still, small voice for which she listens speaks from an infinite comprehension of her interests, abilities, talents, and personality; from an infinite understanding of her past mistakes and her present needs; from an infinite knowledge of the pattern he has planned for her life.

The will of God is not a once-for-all affair, but a daily, continuing revelation. And God stands ready to reveal his will about a woman's vocational choices whenever she seeks it.

Dr. T. B. Maston has said, "The seeking mind, the willing heart, and the obedient spirit cannot help but discern the will of God!"

Seeking . . . willing . . . obedient . . . ask . . . seek . . . find. . . . And when you find the answer, you will know. Maybe not right at first, but you will know.

10

MAKING PROBLEMS PAY

Profit from Your Mistakes

by Douglas Lurton
Author, How to Profit from Your Mistakes

So you have made a mistake, or many mistakes! So have we all. But all do not realize that there are intelligent ways as well as stupid ways of confronting errors. The smart approach is to recognize that it's not so much the mistakes you have made as what you do about those mistakes that really counts — on your job, in a career, in dealing with others at home and elsewhere. You can duck and dodge and alibi and mope and give up trying to eliminate and correct mistakes, or you can use your head and profit from your own errors and those of others.

You profit by facing mistakes squarely. Don't alibi. Man's ego is such that he has an instinctive urge to alibi failure and rationalize what he does, particularly when he makes mistakes. That way he loses. He profits, however, if he intelligently faces up to mistakes, accepts responsibility, and doesn't hide in a fog of alibis.

You can rationalize yourself into a rut of mediocrity or even into an asylum. You can alibi yourself out of a job or out of promotion. There is a study of why thousands were fired from scores of corporations. More were discharged for sheer carelessness, more for simple failure to cooperate, more for plain unadulterated laziness, than for lack of specific skill on the job. And yet it is safe to say that every one of these thousands of failures had a list of perfect alibis and refused to face up to his or her mistakes. *You profit if you don't let mistakes get you down.* The strong men and women bounce back after making mistakes. They have the courage to try to avoid repetition of errors and to improve. The weaklings make mistakes and don't bounce back. They develop fear of trying again and having to make good. They wallow in regrets for past errors. Self-pity is a spoiler. Remorse is a saboteur that can hold you back on any job and in any walk of life.

Babe Ruth whammed out home runs, but also fanned 1,330 times and didn't sulk about it. Thomas Edison made countless mistakes in his laboratories. Abraham Lincoln failed in many ventures. The notable inventor Charles F. Kettering would be the last to claim he never made a mistake. But all of these and countless others in more obscure places had one thing in common — they didn't let their mistakes get them down. They recognized that courage has magic in it, and they bounced back after failure and tried again — and won.

You profit if you learn how to take criticism. The first, almost instinctive reaction to criticism is resentment. Your feelings are hurt! Your ego seems under attack, and an assault on your ego is like a small attack on your life. Many of us resent even our own self-critical thoughts and dismiss them quickly. The multitude resents criticism coming from others and sets up face-saving defenses. But the smart, fully mature man or woman determines to profit from criticism and learns how to take it intelligently.

Adverse criticism may be offered from downright meanness or carelessness; or it may come from a sincere desire to help. Anyone interested in self-advancement should listen to criticism, either mean or honestly offered, with this in mind: the more true the criticism may be, the more it may hurt. Unjust criticism can be rather easily brushed to

one side, but if it really stings, the intelligent approach is
to seek out the elements of truth that may be involved and
take steps to avoid any possible repetition of the criticism.
There is nothing fundamentally new here. It has all been
said before and in fewer words by an ancient and wise
king named Solomon: "Reprove not a scorner, lest he hate
thee; rebuke a wise man and he will love thee."

*You profit most by learning from your own mistakes and
those of others.* Learning from mistakes is a neat trick that
you can acquire if you want to. It is a neat trick because
actually we don't necessarily learn much by so-called experience. That may seem to be a challenging statement —
and it is. But it is a statement that can be proved easily.

A doctor with fifty years of experience is not necessarily
a better doctor than one with ten years of experience. A
half-century as a craftsman does not necessarily mean that
an individual is better than one with a few years of experience. It all depends on how alert the individual is, how
selective he is in piling up his experience.

Unless we learn how to ferret out our mistakes and learn
from them, all too many of us may practice our mistakes as
diligently as we practice our successes.

John D. Rockefeller was a master at analyzing his mistakes as well as his successes. Each night Rockefeller set
aside ten minutes during which he reviewed and analyzed
what he had done during the day. He was critical of all of
his actions and judgments and studied them carefully to
sort out the mistakes when they occurred, to analyze them,
to learn from them.

In this way Rockefeller was using the "scientific" approach to benefit from his mistakes. Here are the steps:

Step one: Determine carefully just what it is you are trying to accomplish and why. What is the job of the moment?
What is its purpose?

Step two: What are the pertinent facts involved? Can
you get additional facts bearing on your problem from

friends, from reading, from associates and leaders or others in a position to know?

Step three: After considering all of the facts available, you should be able to determine various possible courses of action and consider each possible course carefully. Study both its advantages and its disadvantages.

Step four: Narrow down the possible courses of action to the one that comes closest to accomplishing your purpose.

Step five: If you have carefully followed the first four steps and not done a lot of conclusion-jumping, you may be sure that your analysis has given you the one best course of action for you, and the important step is to do something about it, beginning now.

You learn by taking courage from the fact that others, even the famous, make mistakes also. There is a certain measure of comfort for all of us in knowing that there is no man or woman who hasn't made mistakes. No doubt it was this fact that prompted the humorist Mark Twain to point out that man is the only animal who blushes — or needs to!

There is rarely a biography or autobiography that doesn't reveal painful and sometimes costly mistakes. Many mistakes are hidden, but many are broadcast to the world. Not long ago an entire book was filled with the boners and bloopers of scores of the most noted radio and television stars — and when you stumble on the air millions know it!

There can and have been mistakes before the throne and in the seclusion of laboratory or home or factory. Sir Walter Scott, backing away from King George IV of England, sat down hard and smashed a goblet as well as his composure; but his blushes didn't hold him down. Mistakes in full or in part were responsible for certain wallboards, vulcanized rubber, X-rays, aniline colors, photography, dynamite, fiber glass, and many other inventions by people who learned from mistakes.

It is no crime to make mistakes as long as you are trying.

It is, however, almost a crime against yourself, at least, to just be around and do nothing. And the gravest mistake of all is to continue practicing mistakes without learning to minimize or eliminate those errors.

It's not the mistakes you make, but what you do about those mistakes that really counts.

•–•–•––•––•–•––•––•––•––•––•––•–

Read this affirmation out loud: "*I will be a different person when this problem is past. I will be a wiser, stronger, more patient person; or I will be sour, cynical, bitter, disillusioned, and angry. It all depends on what I do with this problem. Each problem can make me a better person or a worse person. It can bring me closer to God, or it can drive me away from God. It can build my faith or it can shatter my faith. It all depends on my attitude. I intend to be a better person when this problem leaves me than I was when it met me.*

— ROBERT H. SCHULLER

Seven Rules for a Good Fight

by Charlie W. Shedd
Author, Letters to Philip *and other books*

Dear Phil,

In one town where I lived two rivers met. There was a bluff high above them where you could sit and watch their coming together. It was a wonderful place for lovers to park and study miscellaneous matters of communication.

I am not thinking right now what you think I am thinking. What I am wishing is that I could take you and Marilyn there and then leave you to watch those two rivers in their meeting.

You would observe that well upstream, before they united, each river flowed gently along. But right at the point of their union, look out!

Those two nice streams came at each other like fury. I have actually seen them on days when it was almost frightening to watch. They clashed in a wild commotion of frenzy and confusion. They hurled themselves head-on as if each was determined that the other should end its existence right there.

Then, as you watched, you could almost see the angry white caps pair off, bow in respect to each other, and join forces as if to say, "Let us get along now. Ahead of us there is something better."

Sure enough, on downstream, at some distance, the river swept steadily on some more. It was broader there, more

Copyright 1968 Charlie W. Shedd and copyright 1968 The Abundance Foundation majestic, and it gave you the feeling that something good had been fashioned out of the conflict.

A good marriage is often like that. When two independent streams of existence come together, there will probably be some dashing of life against life at the juncture. Personalities rush against each other. Preferences clash. Ideas contend for power and habits vie for position. Sometimes, like the waves, they throw up a spray that leaves you breathless and makes you wonder where the loveliness has gone.

No small part of the zest in a good marriage comes from working through differences. Learning to zig and zag with the entanglements; studying each other's reactions under pressure; handling one another's emotions intelligently; all these offer a challenge that simply can't be beat for sheer fun and excitement.

The rule you grew up under at home was, "Never be ashamed of anger. It is a natural part of being a useful person. The only thing you need to regret is when you handle it badly." If I were you, I would pass that bit of philosophy along to Marilyn and make it part of your thinking together. It will be a blessing to your marriage and make you both healthier. Ulcers come from repressing ill-will. So do allergies, headaches, high blood pressure, moods, nagging, infidelity, divorce, and a lot of other things you can do without.

The second thing you should do about hostility is to work up some kind of covenant under which you will agree to settle your differences.

You will remember that in *Letters to Karen* I set down what your mother and I call "Our Seven Official Rules for a Good, Clean Fight." We decided to make these public not because they are the last word, but because they have done so much for us. I am repeating them here with a few comments for your consideration.

1. *Before we begin we must both agree that the time is*

right. The Bible warns that we are foolish to say, "Peace, peace, when there is no peace," but it also offers us this beautiful prayer: "Set a watch before my lips. Keep the door of my mouth." I have found that an excellent petition. There are days when all she wants is tender, loving care. Then there are other times when the light of battle leaps to her eyes and you can sense that she is ready. So, unless you are totally exhausted yourself, push on back to where she ˙has bivouacked her troops and sound the battle cry. Let her know that you love her and if what your love needs right now is war, you're ready too.

2. *We will remember that our only aim is deeper understanding.* One sure test for maturity is the ability to react with sympathy toward hostility sent our way. This obviously is no small accomplishment, but it should be a personal goal toward which you move at a steady pace. When some brickbat hits, our normal reaction is to look for something to throw back. But the great husband disciplines himself to say, "Maybe she's got a problem. How can I help her?" You can do this partially by remembering that most anger is the result of a whole lot which has gone before. Sometimes her rage has such a long history that you actually had very little to do with it. In this sense she's not angry at you as much as she is at those whom you've recalled by whatever it is you've done. Don't ever ask yourself how some innocent little remark, or some insignificant act, could cause such furor. This was only the match that lit the keg where she's been stashing her frustration. What she needs now is ventilation. The big man even learns to postpone his defense until his woman has thoroughly rid herself of whatever it is that's bugging her. Some moments aren't for explanation, but for listening. One of these is when she's only half through.

3. *We will check our weapons often to be sure they're not deadly.* Have you noticed the nuclear-war tacticians using the interesting term "overkill"? What they are talking

about is slaughtering more than necessary to win the war. I think that sounds an important warning for the handling of conflict at home. One thing you sure don't want to destroy is her pride. When a woman's pride is damaged, her sense of values gets warped and that lets loose a cage full of monsters. You will avoid this serious error if you aim to attack the problem, not the person. Any conflict between you should leave you both intact at heart. Keep always before you the thought that you're not fighting to obliterate each other. This isn't Vietnam or some other struggle to death. Then make it your aim to hold the battle fires to just the right intensity. If you do this with skill, the heat you generate may serve to warm your marriage later to a very nice temperature.

4. *We will lower our voices one notch instead of raising them two.* One of the nicest things your mother taught me was that we could get the job done as well by whispering it through rather than shouting it down. Try this just once and I think you'll like it. Obviously, this calls for considerable discipline, but you can bet it's worth the effort. But you better learn some neuter nouns, a few sterile adjectives, and certain phrases that can be interpreted several ways. The tone of your voice, and especially the volume, is something else. The tendency is for the sound to go higher and higher with the mounting ire. So, if you've got what it takes to do this, live by the agreement that you will say it softly as you say it thoroughly.

5. *We will never quarrel or reveal private matters in public.* We've been over this road before, but let's note another thing in passing. It's a good idea when you're quarreling to stay away from your main source of sympathy outside the home. Your best friend, fishing partner, somebody at the office, or your mother may build up your ego and assure you that anyone as fine as you just has to be 100 percent in the clear. But there are two things wrong with running this way when you're wounded: (a) every time

you tell it, you probably make it a little bit worse than it really is; (b) going to them keeps you from going to the one person you'll finally have to settle it with, namely, Marilyn.

6. *We will discuss an armistice whenever either of us calls "halt."* This, too, requires a delicate sense of judgment. If she waves even a drooping olive branch, you'd better open your arms and welcome her there. Because each person is different and every combination of individuals is unique, you must learn by trial and error your own fine line of "enough" and "too much." One couple I know does a clever thing. They have what they call, "the Committee." This is not some outside influence. It is rather their preagreed signal that whenever one of them says, "I think we should refer it now to the Committee," this is their moment for "cease fire."

7. *When we have come to terms, we will put it away till we both agree it needs more discussing.* This is especially important for newly-weds. Many young couples I know operate under the delusion that everything has to be settled this very day. There is one thing wrong with that — it isn't so. Some questions can fall to the floor unanswered and you can still love to the maximum even if there are matters you intend to take up later for further consideration. Point to remember: Don't try to force more unanimity than your marriage is prepared to handle at any given stage of your development. A great husband-wife relationship does not mean that these two have reached the peak of human coalescing. It more likely indicates that they are living up to their capacity for oneness this day with the understanding that tomorrow will give them more capacity for more total togetherness.

There is another all-important consideration in fighting the good fight. This is the offering of apologies, the request for forgiveness, and the assurance that you will do your best to forget.

These things are especially important for husbands because the words, "I'm sorry," and the language of forgiveness seem more difficult for men than women. One poor wife told me recently, "My husband's idea of settling a quarrel is to put me in his sweat box until I say, 'You were all right. It was my fault completely.' The truth is," she went on, "I've just about had it. He thinks that he and God are the only perfect beings and he may even have some questions about God."

Remember then that the measurement of bigness in a man is determined from the spot where he can unbend in true humility to pay his honest debts with these five words: "I was wrong. Forgive me."

But suppose it was all her fault. She really did it this time. Now what will you do? One thing that you can do is to give her an opening. How about saying, "I'm sorry we're having trouble. I don't like it this way. Let's stick together, what do you say?" What she probably will say is, "Well, I was a little bit foolish myself." A woman never forgets things like this. You have opened the gate where she can come through to set the matter straight. She'll love you forever for that.

This movement-to-get-things-settled is always much more important than who started it. Tell yourself that pointing up the origin doesn't matter nearly as much as how to make things right once more. If you keep this goal before you, the day will come when you'll be stumbling over each other as though there were a prize for the person who got there first to restore the relationship.

Another test of how mature you both are is your ability to forget what you've forgiven. You can see that to be a good husband you must work at never forgetting some things while you work at never remembering others. Love, after a quarrel, can be a greater thing than it was before no matter who scored the most points or who brought it on. After the smoke is cleared and the truce is signed, we find that all the time wives are really very much like we are. They dream the same dreams, hope the same hopes, struggle just like we struggle. We learn to admire their abilities, and the things we didn't know when we were fighting actually thrill us now. Always when people get rid of rancor, love comes to take its place. It opens up vast ranges for sympathy and understanding and a genuine desire to know more of what's going on.

It is some goal for any couple to see their marriage as a contribution to that.

Dad

.•--•--•--•--•--•--•--•--•--•--•--•--•--•--•--•--•·

An ideal wife is any woman who has an ideal hus-
band.

— BOOTH TARKINGTON

Should I Confess?

by David Augsburger
Author, 70 x 7, and Radio speaker, The Mennonite Hour

"Let me make it clear," the man said to me, fingering the moisture from his eyebrow, "under no conditions will I tell my wife. She'd never forgive me, and, well, that's just the way it is. She can't even overlook a little thing like, well, you name it. Just let me slip up on any little thing and she'll bring up date and time of day for every other time I did it. No, I can't tell her. She'd lose her temper, slap me once; and then I'd lose my head and — no, I can't."

"Then don't," I suggested.

"You mean, I don't have to tell her all about it to find forgiveness?"

"Well, that all depends on you. If you can accept God's forgiveness and trust him with your guilt feelings, maybe you won't need to open it up with her to get relief."

"That's what I need, relief," he said. "Only if I confess the mess to her, we'll have a fight that'll end everything that's left between us, and tear our kids' hearts out too."

"Couldn't you just leave it right here then — with God? The whole point of confession is to bring healing. To you and to the one you've sinned against. If you're sure that it would only be destructive, then go on without it until you feel — if that time comes — that you must confess."

"All right, I will," he said. "But what if she finds out about it?"

"In that case, I'll stand by you and assure her that you

Copyright 1970 Moody Bible Institute

made an honest break with the affair and were truly repentant."

"One thing you can be sure of; it's good-bye deceit, from now on."

He reached for his hat and was gone, hopefully leaving behind his guilt with the bitter story.

Success had suddenly swept up his wife's business. Regional administration fell into her lap. Money began flowing more freely. Two-day absences grew into four-day conventions.

Fortunately for her, a friend with nothing to do loved to come in, care for the kids, and fix a little food for the husband. But all too soon proximity, availability, mutual loneliness, and the chemistry of evenings under the same roof did their work. The friendly chats turned into intimacy. Duplicity matured into infidelity as weeks multiplied into months of betrayal.

Then the youngest child caught rheumatic fever. The wife, finally feeling motherly concern, dropped her work to nurse the child back toward health.

Then all the tensions between them began to twist beneath the surface. With both women sometimes around the house, he fled it in fear.

So he plunged himself deeper into his work, but nothing silenced the nagging whisper of guilt, the fear that she would find him out and that the scandal would ruin his career, his reputation, his home and life.

So at last he turned to someone to talk it out, insisting, "I've got to get relief but if it can only come by confessing, then I'll forget it." Gradually he opened himself to God. Now, *now* what would he do?

The next day, he was back, and I knew immediately from his face that he had told her and yet somehow everything was all right.

"It was after dinner," he said, "when she asked me point blank, 'What is it about you tonight? You're like you haven't been for years.' What was I to say? I was, well, speechless. And before I knew what I was doing, I blurted it out. I told her. Told her what I'd done to her and to the kids. Told her it'd all happened between me and her best friend.

"She sat, head in hands, until it was all out. Then she asked, 'Is it really true?' 'Yes,' I said. 'And is that all?' 'Yes.' The silence flowed by.

"Then she stood, stepped over behind me and touched my hair. I looked up to see her eyes all tear-shiny.

" 'I forgive you,' she said. 'Let's start over from here; let's go on with life together.'

"It was too much for me to take. Then — then I saw that I was trembling; my teeth clicked for a moment before I caught them; everything blurred.

" 'Why,' she said in surprise, 'why, you're angry.' I nodded my admission. 'You wanted me to hit you, didn't you?' Slowly I admitted the truth.

" 'No,' she said, 'I wouldn't hit you; that would only have justified everything you did. And it might have touched off both our tempers for the last time. No, no, I forgive you. That's our only hope if we're ever going to live again.'

"That's when healing happened," the man told me. "Her forgiving me like that, it, well, it broke my heart, or it broke down my last resistance, my last self-justification. You see, I was still blaming her and her work and busy schedule for my unfaithfulness.

"And her forgiveness was so unexpected, it was like she reached into resources I didn't know she had, and forgave me. She gave me back my life."

Could he have really found forgiveness without confession? Certainly he had to confess it to someone. To a friend who would be understanding and help him face his problem in honesty; to God, the only true Source of forgiveness and release.

But to his wife? That's the crux of a very difficult problem. Yes, the sin of adultery was committed against her. Yes, it needed to be made right. But that's first repentance, secondarily confession.

If a man repents, that is, honestly and completely turns away from his past and its sins, must he confess it all? Certainly confession will bring a tremendous release and relief for his tortured feelings of guilt. But what then? Will she be able to forgive, forget, and accept him again? Will the confession be constructive, bringing healing and health once more to their relationship? Or will it be a block that nothing will be able to remove for her? Will it embed hostilities in her soul that she is not emotionally, spiritually, and mentally able to overcome? Will it be constructive or destructive of love, understanding, and acceptance?

Then when and where should confession be made?

Confession should be as public as the commission of the act. Only those directly involved should be told in your confession. Sin should not be published for general public consumption and speculation.

Confession should be shared where it is a help to another, not a hurt or a hindrance. If confessing your sin would provide another with excuses or tempt him to stumble, don't!

Confession should not be so intimate, so revealing, so painful that it will wound or scar the person to whom it is confessed. Such careless, thoughtless confession to a close friend or lover may bring you release, but it will transfer the painful burden to the other. Do you want to be healed at the expense of another's suffering?

If you should choose not to confess, for the sake of being most redemptive and loving to the other person, be aware that you are choosing the harder, not the easier way. This is true because, essentially, confession is a human necessity.

We discover and experience release from our guilt in direct proportion to our willingness to face our sin, confess our sinfulness, and accept forgiveness.

We must "turn ourselves in." That's true confession.

And true confession has two sides. Confession with only a negative side is a counterfeit. It's the admit-your-failures-and-get-them-off-your-chest variety. But true confession has a positive side, too. It is a confession of dependence and allegiance to God, the great guilt-remover. Let's take a look at both sides of confession.

First, there must be confession of sinfulness.

You must own up. Admit your helplessness, your weakness, your need. Yes, this is the negative side, but it is a necessary side.

Guilt wants to stay hidden. It breeds best in isolation. It loves the dark, unswept corners of our personalities. Like a termite, it eats and destroys when hidden, but when brought to the light, dries up and dies.

Three thousand years ago, David, king of Israel, described the bone rot of guilt like this.

"When I declared not my sin, my body wasted away through my groaning all day long. For day and night thy hand was heavy upon me; my strength was dried up as by the heat of summer. Selah. I acknowledged my sin to thee, and I did not hide my iniquity; I said, I will confess my transgressions to the Lord; then thou didst forgive the guilt of my sin (Psalm 32:3-5).

But that's only the negative side of confession. There must also be a confession of surrender.

This is the positive side. To find real release from guilt, you must also confess your faith — a faith in Jesus Christ who removes guilt of all shapes and sizes.

"You must confess with your own mouth that Jesus Christ is your Lord, and believe in your heart. For it is by believing in his heart that a man becomes right with God, and with his mouth he confesses his faith" (Romans 10:9, 10, paraphrase).

A moment of complete honesty, a moment when a man comes to true confession of who and what he is, is his eternal moment of truth.

A moment of truth before the Master can bring you a motive of truth for all of life. Your whole life with its frustrations, regrets, weaknesses, and strengths can become new as Jesus Christ enters and controls your mind and heart. That's how he makes it all new.

Then you will come to the greatest of all moments of truth — absolute honesty before Jesus Christ. Pledge your whole self to him in a motive of truth and let him be truly the Master of your life. That is the crucial confession that leads to forgiveness.

•-•--•-•--•-•--•-•--•-•--•-•--•-•--•-•--•-•-

"I can forgive, but I cannot forget," is only another way of saying, "I will not forgive." Forgiveness ought to be like a cancelled note — torn in two, and burned up, so that it never can be shown against one.
— HENRY WARD BEECHER

Your Reactions Are Showing

by J. Allan Petersen

Wrong actions are harmful; everyone knows this from painful experience. Actions can adversely affect one's personality and result in serious life damage. But wrong reactions can be as harmful as wrong actions and even more devastating. These reactions can be found in people whose actions on the surface are correct and proper. A person may pride himself on his right actions and truthfully say, "I don't lie, I don't cheat, I don't swear, I don't get drunk, I don't commit adultery." His actions are right and good, yet he may be utterly defeated by his wrong reactions to life's situations and other people's actions. Inner reactions of jealousy, resentment, anger, hatred, fear, self-pity can be unseen but utterly ruinous.

I am only really known by my reactions, not my actions. My actions may be studied, planned, and practiced for your benefit. But it is my spontaneous — unconscious, unscheduled — reactions that reveal what I really am.

What are your driving reactions as you move around in traffic? Some people keep up a steady stream of conversation and advice to every driver on the road. Recently, I saw a man honk his horn, roll down his car window, and yell at another driver. This strong, unplanned reaction revealed what was inside the man.

A young person goes off to college where he is exposed to a little knowledge and education. Then he returns home and looks down on people who have not had this privilege.

———

Copyright 1967 Good News Broadcasting Association

His reaction to his education reveals what he is — how small a person he really is.

My reactions reveal my true self. I cannot react in any manner contrary to what I really am. My nature is exhibited by my reactions. The prophet Jeremiah states what is true of every man's nature: "The heart is deceitful above all things, and desperately wicked" (Jeremiah 17:9). The natural tendency in all of us is to be hypocritical and dishonest.

It is always easy to say: "Well, you know, it is really not like me to act in that way." "Don't judge me by that isolated instance; I am really better than I appear to be." Have you ever felt that way? Of course you have and so have I. The opposite is true, however, for our reactions reveal what we really are inside.

Suppose we take a tea bag and drop it into a cup of hot water. A dark-brown color will flow from that bag until the entire cup of water is dark brown. Did the hot water put the color into the tea bag or only bring out what was already inside?

Squeeze a beautiful lemon, and something sour and bitter comes out. Did the pressure put the bitterness into the lemon or only bring out what was already in? Which is really true?

Have you ever been in "hot water" with your husband? your wife? your children? or your relatives? How did you react? What was your response? Did something "dark brown" come out — a negative reaction of criticism, resentment, retaliation, hatred, or revenge? Have you ever been under pressure — at home, on the job, with responsibilities? And did something sour and bitter come out? Let's be honest; nothing can come out that is not already inside, and the situation only reveals it.

We cannot blame someone else for putting anything into us. A crisis doesn't make the man — it only reveals him. Our real strength comes out when we get into hot water.

The real problem is within, and this is why Jesus said in Mark 7:20-23: "That which cometh out of the man, that defileth the man. For from within, out of the heart of men, proceed evil thoughts, adulteries, fornications, murders, thefts, covetousness, wickedness, deceit, lasciviousness, an evil eye, blasphemy, pride, foolishness; all these evil things come from within, and defile the man."

So my real problem is not external — the difficulty, the pressure, the adversity, the disappointment I encounter. These only trigger a reaction in me that reveals my true nature and my real character. I cannot blame others' actions — my problem is my own inner attitude and reaction. When I honestly recognize these things that come out of me, I can bring them to God and get help. As Amy Carmichael said: "No cup filled with sweet water will ever spill out bitter water, no matter how suddenly it is jarred."

When we react in the same way others act toward us, these people control us. This biblical principle is expressed clearly in 1 Peter 3:9: "Not rendering evil for evil, or railing for railing, but contrarywise blessing."

Suppose I walk down the street and a passing stranger hits me in the face without word or reason. This is a wrong action. He is guilty. But suppose I hit him back. My reaction is the same as his action. I am guilty too — and in that moment he controlled me. He determined what I would do by what he did. Instead of initiating right conduct, regardless of his, I let him decide my response. His ability to provoke a negative reaction in me was stronger than my ability to initiate a positive response. I was completely controlled.

Someone flares at you — do you flare in return? You are criticized; do you return the same kind? Do you feel that the action of another gives you a right to act in the same way? I know people who are controlled by everyone they meet. They never initiate, only react.

First Peter, chapter 3, deals with family relations. It

speaks of a wife and her unsaved husband — how she is supposed to react toward him. The passage also speaks of a husband's attitude toward his wife and how he should honor her as the "weaker vessel."

As a wife, what is your reaction toward your husband? Does his mood determine what your mood will be? If he is upset do you become upset? If he becomes thoughtless and negligent of you, do you in turn neglect him?

One woman said to me not long ago: "My husband absolutely controls me. When he leaves the house in the morning to go to work, he says the one thing that he knows will upset me. He controls me by this one sentence. Whenever he doesn't want to face something himself, he'll just say this to me and it ruins me for all day. What shall I do?"

I told her, "Your husband is wrong for his action; but you are wrong for your reaction. His action makes him guilty; your reaction makes you guilty. You cannot wait for your husband to change. You must draw strength from Christ so that you can change your reaction even though your husband does not change his action. He will then have no more reason to act this way and God will work through you to reach him. You dare not live under the control of anyone else but Jesus Christ."

Husband, does your wife control you? Does her attitude some morning decide what your attitude will be? Does her wrong action determine your equally wrong reaction so that your conduct is determined by what she has done?

I have seen little children control their big parents. If it were not so sad it would be humorous. I remember in one home that a five-year-old boy became angry with one of his parents. He spat out a word of anger. What did the parent do? Exactly what the boy did — spat out an angry word. The child determined by his action what the parent was going to do.

The child became more upset and raised his voice and

said something a little bit stronger. And the parent? He also raised his voice and said something stronger.

Finally the little fellow stamped his foot and declared what he was going to do and what he was not going to do. What was the parent's reaction? He stamped his big foot and said, "No. This is what you are going to do!" The small child controlled his parent like a puppet.

What a tragedy! The parent had no inner command. He did not know how to speak in a kindly, Christian way and mean what he said and get the job done.

The Christian must be controlled by Jesus Christ alone. He alone is our Lord and Master. Through the strength of Christ and the enablement of the Holy Spirit, we can initiate right spiritual reactions regardless of what other people's actions have been.

No problem or difficulty causes us to fail or makes us a cripple; we are defeated from within, not from without. Our reaction to what happens is more important than what happens. Paul said, "And we know that all things work together for good to them that love God, to them who are the called according to his purpose" (Romans 8:28). So to the Christian, it makes no difference what happens. There is a sense in which we have no enemies. Every person and every problem is a friend working together for our good under God's direction.

Was Thomas Edison hurt because he had only three months of schooling? Was George Washingon Carver a failure because he was born in poverty? Was Abraham Lincoln "finished" because he started life deprived, failed twice in business, suffered a nervous breakdown, and was defeated three times for the legislature, twice for Congress, twice for the Senate, and once for vice-president? Right reactions finally brought him to the Presidency. You can't hurt a man like that. Whatever happens to him, the Christian must realize it can be for his maturity and Christlikeness if his reactions are right.

But if we react with resentment, that resentment will waste us. A reaction of bitterness will blight us. Self-pity will lead us to failure and bankruptcy. Our reaction will determine the effect of every temptation and difficulty we face, everything that happens. Only our reactions can ruin us.

Just as we are responsible for our actions, so are we for our reactions. Blaming others for their actions does not relieve us of responsibility for our reactions. Both need to be dealt with.

"See that none render evil for evil" (1 Thessalonians 5:15). In that little word "see" Paul says we are reaction-responsible. He says, "Take it upon yourself to be sure you don't react the way other people act toward you." So often we want help for future situations without taking responsibility for our present conduct.

Secretly we say, "I wish I had not acted that way . . . I'd like to live that situation over . . . I hate myself for doing what I did." But this isn't enough. Everyone feels regret but few take responsibility. Only as I assume personal responsibility can God respond with his ability to help me overcome.

Psychology teaches that anything we "see" we can do. What we can envision we can accomplish. If we can focus on an objective, this very fact means we are able to accomplish it. What your mind can conceive, you can achieve. Spiritually, this is also true.

What you "see" in your reactions can be changed. The fact that you can recognize a need indicates you can do something about it — if you will. Everything depends on honesty in "seeing" it — a strong desire to want something done about it — and initiating action in the right direction.

What action? First, we must admit that we have seen what God is showing us through our reactions. God knows what he has shown us and we can never "unsee" it. Recognition means responsibility.

Second, we must refuse to excuse and defend ourselves. We cannot wait for others to change their actions before we get serious about our reactions. We will wait forever. Husbands cannot wait for wives or wives for husbands. I am still responsible regardless of what others do or do not do.

Third, we must confess our wrong fully. This does not mean in a casual way: "O Lord, you know we are not perfect, and we could be a little better, so help us to act a little better under the circumstances." No! We must personally confess, "Lord, I have sinned in my reactions; I was critical and hateful. Lord, I confess that to you, and ask you to help me with my reactions."

God's wonderful promises are clear. "If we confess our sins" — and wrong reactions are sins — "he is faithful and just to forgive us our sins, and to cleanse us from all unrighteousness." If we confess fully, God forgives us.

The Apostle Paul said, "I am crucified with Christ, nevertheless, I live, yet not I, but Christ liveth in me!" What kind of life did Christ live on earth? What were his reactions? His circumstances were not always pleasant and advantageous, but how did he react to people in every situation? His life can be our life if we really let him invade us. It is not a matter of deciding: "I am going to try and be more like Christ; I am going to try and follow in his steps." It is far more than that, far deeper than that. *It is not our imitation but his habitation.* Christ wants to live in us to control, empower, and enable. We can become Christians — little Christs — channels of his life on earth. His reactions can be our reactions because his life can be ours. This is the secret — Christ liveth in me. No wonder Paul said, "I can do all things through Christ which strengtheneth me." He is able and he is in me.

Ins and Outs of In-Laws

by Gordon and Dorothea Jaeck
Co-authors, I Take Thee

Mother-in-law jokes seem to be one of the most popular forms of entertainment. There is perhaps no other cultural stereotype as powerful. The bad press which mothers-in-law receive caricatures them as selfish, malicious, and interfering. Rarely are they seen as unselfish, thoughtful, and considerate persons.

Recently a group of young couples were given a free association test in which the word "mother-in-law" was unexpectedly inserted. The responses were revealing and included such words as "terrible," "bother," "fight," "ugh," "hatred," and "hell." This reflects rather strikingly the "prevailing climate of pessimism" which often describes this relationship. It also points to the fact that mothers-in-law have two strikes against them at the outset!

Of all the problems faced in marriage, studies uniformly show that with both newly-married couples and those who have been married for long periods of time, in-law problems rank first or second. Our culture's negative conditioning toward mothers-in-law must take some responsibility for this.

Studies reveal other interesting characteristics of the in-law interactional pattern. For one thing, it seems to be predominantly feminine. Seldom do the male members of the two families find themselves at odds. Also, studies show that parents, rather than brothers or sisters, are the focus of fractured relationships.

Many couples are happily surprised to discover that re-

© 1967 Zondervan Publishing House

lationships with each other's families can be one of the most meaningful and enriching experiences they may have. But even these couples have to realize early that these relationships, once established, need to be guarded carefully. And that their own husband-wife relationship may be held in delicate balance in this area. For each partner tends to lose objectivity and perspective with regard to his own parents. It is an irony that the stresses and strains that occur in the larger circle of family relationships often create insecurity in what is normally a stable husband-wife relationship. And unfortunately, this often shows up at times when the whole family is together.

In any situation where strain has developed in the in-law relationship, what is needed most is an honest and direct look at the trouble spots as they first develop. Whether the problems are the result of negative conditioning, divergent backgrounds, or objectionable in-law actions or traits, it is most important that the married couple maintain communication between themselves and work together to form a happy and rewarding relationship with their in-laws.

There are some very simple principles that are important in establishing and sustaining harmonious relationships with each other's families. Some of these are:

1. Establishing a genuine friendship and companionship based upon appreciation, understanding, and acceptance.

2. Recognizing that you may have as many attitudes that are provocative of conflict as your parents-in-law.

3. Keeping tension or strife at a minimum around sensitive areas. Essentially this involves emotional maturity and the capacity for self-control, even under provocation.

4. Accepting parents-in-law as well as parents as people who have an understandable stake in your marriage, and who desire, above all, its success and your happiness.

5. Preserving a healthy independence of your own as a married couple, regardless of proximity. Sometimes this re-

quires a disciplined but loving limiting of time and contacts involving your families.

6. Protecting the privacy of your marriage, in the early years especially. Living with in-laws or having them live with you puts undue strain on any family. When an emergency situation demands it, time limits need to be placed upon the sharing of your home with parents or your living with them.

7. Always remember that in time you, too, will be an in-law. Act accordingly!

The rewards are immeasurable for making the effort to establish a harmonious and loving relationship with parents-in-law. Parents have a wisdom and maturity from which younger couples can well profit. Their continuing interest in and emotional support of their married children can be a valued asset. And their appreciation of your love and concern for them is most gratifying.

Letters . . . telephone calls . . . personal visits, whatever the means used, the message of love should get through to our in-laws. Then they will truly be *in* and not *out* of our lives.

•••••••••••••••••••••••••

Difficulty is a severe instructor, set over us by the supreme Guardian and Legislator, who knows us better than we know ourselves, and loves us better too. He that wrestles with us strengthens our nerves and sharpens our skill. Our Antagonist is our Helper.

— EDMUND BURKE

See the Marriage Doctor

by Clyde M. Narramore

Author, Happiness in Marriage, *and President, Rosemead Graduate School of Psychology*

No sooner had the Bensons returned from their honeymoon than they began to have little disagreements and quarrels. In time, these problems grew into young giants. Each blamed the other. "You're the most stubborn person I've ever met," accused George. "Well, I'm not half as stubborn as you," Betty replied. "You are the most bullheaded person in all the world."

Month after month and year after year their problems nagged them. On several occasions Betty suggested that they go to a marriage counselor. "Why? What can he do?" asked George. "If you weren't so stubborn everything would be all right. Why go and pay someone to tell you something you already know?"

Many couples are like the Bensons. Their marriage is unhappy, yet they fail to seek the help they desperately need. If they were suffering from an illness or injury they would not hesitate to call a physician. They would recognize that the medical profession is trained to treat their physical ills. But, unfortunately, when it comes to an ailing marriage, some couples would rather let their marriage die than seek professional help. With a rugged pretense of self-reliance, they make the unreasonable assertion, "If we can't take care of our own problems, no one else can." The fact is that marriage relationships are often very complex, requiring skilled, unbiased help. In few parts of the world today

---

Copyright 1961 Clyde M. Narramore

will a man try to continue his work without having a trained physician set his fractured arm in a cast. Yet, the same man with a marriage failure may "let it go" for years.

When unsolved marriage difficulties face a couple, it is a comforting fact to realize that professional help is available and of practical benefit. Even as the medical doctor or attorney understands physical or legal problems, there are specially trained people who can give professional help in marriage problems. They can diagnose the difficulties and help to bring about solutions.

To whom shall people turn? Just who are the ones who can give an unhappy couple thorough, lasting help? The following are some who can probably best help in marriage problems:

The *pastor* is probably the nation's number one counselor. He is continually called upon to help many people with various problems. If he is a faithful, Bible-believing minister, he advises according to the authority and power of God's Word. He knows the great promises in the Bible. He knows the only true basis for a wholesome "sound mind." And he has godly wisdom. Since most pastors have varied experiences in counseling, they are also able to help with problems other than spiritual ones. Too, the minister is in a unique position to help many couples because problems often have a basis in or a relationship to spiritual maturity. The Evans, for example, learned this very fact. Plagued by marital problems for years, they finally sought out their pastor for help. "I feel that we should plan on meeting together for several sessions," advised the pastor. "Sometimes such problems have deep roots."

During the next four months the Evans met regularly with the pastor. Sometimes they saw him together, and sometimes separately. In time they began to gain insight into the causes of their maladjustments. Tom, a brilliant young chemist, liked things done on time and in order; Sue, his wife, was very disorganized. These traits affected nearly all they did. As they worked through on their problems, they came to see what caused each other to be the way they were. This insight helped them to understand each other better. In addition, the counseling sessions were stimulating spiritual growth which also enabled them to improve. Tom became more patient, while Sue asked the Lord to help her take more interest in her appearance and her home. Thus, through practical, spiritual counsel, the minister was able to help the Evans have a much happier marriage.

In recent times the *marriage counselor* has emerged as a specialist in helping those with marriage difficulties. A whole horizon of practical and scientific techniques have become his arsenal. In the art of counseling he may have more acute and penetrating access to the client's mind, and quickly recognize the well-classified, recurring problems of marriage.

The marriage counselor brings to his clients a great wealth of experience in dealing with marriage problems. He discusses even the most intimate subjects with poise and ease, causing the counselee to feel at ease. He is unusually skilled in helping couples identify their troubles and in setting up practical ways for achieving a good adjustment.

The *psychologist* includes more of the professional laboratory in his approach. Available to him are the most pointed and helpful of psychometric tests. He will no doubt proceed from the outer "ulcer" to the hidden "abscess" of conjugal trouble. His training has enabled him to find the deeper aspects of the problem, then to counsel.

Skilled in professional counseling, the psychologist is able to lead the counselee into complete discussion of his problem, and thereby uncover the causes of his attitudes. As these are ventilated, they lose their power, enabling the husband (or wife) to feel different and adopt new behavior.

The *medical doctor* holds an important role among professional advisers. He may observe physiological reasons why husband and wife are poorly and unhappily joined. Such failures may be discovered in sexual disability, or a host of general health conditions.

Since many marriage problems have their foundation in health concerns, the medical doctor is often an ideal person to offer professional help. Mrs. Richards, for example, had little idea that her marriage problem actually stemmed from a glandular malfunction. But after she received proper diagnosis and treatment, she felt completely different. Naturally, she was much happier in her marriage.

The *psychiatrist* unites the credentials of a medical doctor with the specialized training of psychology. His role is to detect both the minor and serious difficulties, physical, mental, and emotional.

Because of his training in both physical and mental ailments, the psychiatrist is able to help many married couples. What a person may think is "nervousness" may actually be mental illness for which the psychiatrist can offer professional aid.

Another type of counselor may also be added. He is the well-informed *Christian friend*. When his helpfulness is strictly confidential and spiritual, and when he combines wholesome kindness and cautious good sense, he may have the proved professional worth of the other type of advisors discussed. Many a friend, armed with godly wisdom and unusual insight, has been able to steer a marriage from going on the rocks.

Should the counselor be a Christian? If at all possible, yes! While some marriage failures may primarily be the result of poor physical or emotional health, thus requiring treatment from this approach, it is safe to say that the complex challenge of a marriage problem is such that, whatever else the counselor is prepared to do in the way of assistance, it can be done infinitely better with an undergirding personal Christian experience. And since marriage problems often stem from a spiritual lack, it requires a person with spiritual discernment to offer counsel and guidance in this area.

In most marriage problems the true source of maladjustment comes from the depths of personality. This is true even though the symptoms may appear to be moral, physical, sexual, emotional, or mental in nature. Consequently most marriage problems respond to "non-pill therapy." As a mate is led into discussions of his problems, as he traces the roots and finds the relationship between them and his present attitudes, he will find himself developing new attitudes and reacting in new ways. This is why counseling with a minister, psychologist, psychiatrist, marriage counselor, or another with professional training is so important.

Marriage is too sacred and wonderful to neglect. So when problems and difficulties mar a couple's happiness, it is their obligation to seek assistance. Help is available for those who want it. But even with available counselors, there are those who refuse help. If your husband or wife is one, do not become discouraged. It is not the end of the road. Indeed, roads lead over and around all obstacles. Give your mate time and keep on praying. He or she may be willing later on. For the time being, you have the responsibility to seek help anyway. And when you do, you may be paving the way for him to join you!

·•··•··•··•··•··•··•··•··•··•··•··•··•··•··•·

So you've got a problem? That's good! Do you know of a single instance where any real achievement was made in your life, or in the life of any person in history, that was not due to a problem with which the individual was faced?

— W. CLEMENT STONE

Before the Divorce . . .

by Norman Vincent Peale
Author, minister, and newspaper columnist

Dear Kenneth:

Your letter tells me that you and Nancy are no longer happy together and that you are wondering whether it might be best to end your marriage. You add that since I was the minister who married you, both of you feel you owe it to me to talk the situation over with me before doing anything final. You say you hope that I will understand.

I do understand. I understand that two people who stood before me nine years ago and promised to love and cherish each other forever are about to join the ranks of those Americans who, approximately 800,000 every year, decide to demonstrate publicly that they lack the courage, intelligence, and unselfishness to make a marriage work.

You say that you and Nancy are no longer happy together. Do you really believe that constant happiness is guaranteed in marriage or in any other aspect of life? Aren't you mature enough to know that every marriage has its areas of friction and that the stresses change as you move through the years? You will never solve all your problems; you would be bored if you did.

This belief that each of you is entitled to receive happiness is at the bottom of your trouble. You are not entitled to any such thing! What you do have is the privilege and the problem of giving happiness. When you master that art, you discover that you can't give happiness without getting it back.

———

Copyright 1964 The Reader's Digest

At times I wonder if this obsession with having things just the way we want them, and sulking if they are not, isn't becoming a kind of American disease. Somehow we must get a quality of toughness and endurance back into our concept of marriage. We must stop thinking of marriage as a "maybe" proposition — maybe it will work, maybe it won't, and if it doesn't we can always shuffle the cards and deal again.

Two generations ago, there were plenty of marriages in which the going was rocky. But those people didn't run to divorce courts at the first sign of trouble. They thought of marriage as a contract; it was an affront to God and society to break it. They were like the pioneers who struggled west; there were always more rivers to be forded, more mountains to be crossed. The vast majority kept going until they had reached the goal they sought.

Certainly there are some cases where a marriage has been allowed to die and nothing can revive it. I don't think that you two have reached that point. But you will reach it unless you take some constructive action, and take it quickly.

You say you would like to talk with me. All right. I shall be glad to see you one week from today — if between now and then, you and Nancy will agree to an experiment. If you accept this condition, there may be some point in our meeting. Otherwise, I see little reason to wasting my time — or yours.

Half an hour each day for the next six days is what I ask you to devote to the experiment. I don't guarantee that these will be pleasant half-hours or easy ones. But surely you owe this much to your children, if not to yourselves. Let's face it; the decision on divorce that you are about to make will affect all five of you the rest of your lives.

The experiment I want you to try has been tested and found to work. The equipment you'll need is simple: an alarm clock — preferably one with a loud tick — two chairs, and a quiet room where you will not be disturbed.

Each day, go together into that quiet room, close the door, set the alarm clock to ring in thirty minutes and place it where both of you can watch it. Now, mentally divide the half-hour into five-minute periods.

In the first five minutes, project yourselves into the future. Separately and silently, visualize life as it will be if your marriage breaks up.

Kenneth, ask yourself what happens to a man when he gets a divorce. He loses his home — the comfort, the familiarity, the closeness. He usually loses his children, possibly their respect and affection, certainly most of their companionship. He may also lose his shirt: the costs of divorce are murderous; alimony can cripple his earnings for years. He may find that in his business or profession he has gained the enmity of people who can influence his career. And he will certainly lose some friends; in marital breakups, people tend to side with the wife.

Nancy, in my forty-two years in the ministry I have learned that, emotionally, the wife suffers most from a divorce. Her sense of failure as a person is greater than the man's, her loneliness more complete. A man has his work to fall back on. A woman usually does not.

In the second five minutes, I want each of you to make a supreme effort to stop judging the other and examine yourself. Ask yourself certain uncomfortable questions. Have you magnified this or that grievance out of all proportion? Have you been too rigid in your demands? Have you refused to compromise on key issues? Have you judged your marriage partner guilty while leaving yourself exempt? Doesn't the law of averages whisper that sometimes *you* must be in the wrong?

Do you know why I recommend an alarm clock with a loud tick? Because one man who tried this experiment told me that at the end of five minutes the clock seemed to be repeating over and over again the word at the bottom of the trouble: *self, self, self, self.*

The next five minutes are to be spent thinking about your children. You may believe that an atmosphere of discord and hostility in the home is worse for them than the dislocations of a divorce. But this selfish rationalization is based on an assumption that is not necessarily true — that the hostility and discord are inevitable and will go on forever.

Nancy, I think that you are the one who must refuse to be stampeded into an unwise course of action. My wife is convinced that women hold the solution to the divorce trend — and that they could reduce it sharply if they would study the problems of marriage. Recently at a dinner party I overheard her say, "It is the woman's job to provide stability in marriage, to make the home an 'island of quietness in a noisy world.'" And it is the wife, she said, who has to do most of the adjusting. "That's why marriage is the most demanding and exciting career a woman can choose!"

For the first fifteen minutes you will have been sitting in silence. Now it is time to communicate with each other. I want each of you to read aloud, taking turns on alternate days, these verses from the Bible: St. Paul's First Epistle to the Corinthians, chapter 13, verses 4 through 7. These four verses contain the most profound and inclusive definition of love ever written.

I doubt that you have ever taken time to meditate on just what St. Paul meant: that love suffers long and is kind, that love is not easily provoked, that love endures all things (not *some* things, *all* things). After you have read these four verses aloud, don't try to discuss them. Just close the Bible and think about them for five minutes. Inevitably you will use them as a yardstick to measure your own performance.

Now it's time for that nostalgic game called, "Do you remember?" Let each of you recall from the past and remind the other of some episode that was a moment of harmony and closeness. Perhaps the time you walked together on a beach at sunrise, hand in hand. Perhaps the time you sat up all night with a sick child. Perhaps some tender or ludicrous moment that turned into a family joke. There need be no discussion; just recognition of the fact that once there was love and sharing, and that no possible change of heart can erase those moments — or eliminate the possibility that they might occur again.

In the final five-minute period, I ask each of you, first, to hold one other biblical phrase in mind: "Be still — and know that I am God." I want each of you, speaking aloud, to tell him what you think has gone wrong with your marriage and what your share of the blame may be. Speak from the bottom of your heart.

I can tell you this: I have married hundreds of couples and counseled hundreds of others, and I have never yet known a marriage to fail where the partners had — or had acquired — the habit of praying aloud together. It is an emotional lightning rod that deflects anger and resentment into an area so vast that they are simply swallowed up and forgotten, like pebbles cast into the sea.

This need not be a lengthy process; perhaps one minute will do. And there is no set formula. But I will guarantee if you try, you will find yourself speaking in a different tone of voice, and by the time that alarm clock rings your whole point of view will be subtly changed.

I hope that you will try this experiment. Because, if your marriage breaks up, something in each of you will always regret it. No matter how permissive society has become about divorce, I have never yet known one divorced person who, in total honesty, would not admit to some trace of sadness for the failure of a first marriage.

Not long ago, a colleague of mine preached a sermon in which he said that he had found in one short sentence the answer to many of life's thorniest problems. The sentence was: "The way out is the way through." He meant that when you're faced with a difficult situation, you can't solve it by running away or pretending it isn't there. You have to plow through it until you come out on the other side.

This takes courage, and it takes facing of facts. It takes persistence, determination, control. That's what you two need. If you and Nancy will take courage in both hands and hang on long enough, you will achieve a closeness and a strength that will make your honeymoon years seem like puppy love — which in a way they were. Something in you, some wisdom deeper than your conscious mind, knows this; otherwise, you never would have written to me. The way out is the way through; there *is* a way through. With God's help I think, I hope, I know that we can find it.

Norman

.•--•--•--•--•--•--•--•--•--•--•--•--•--•--•--•.

Everybody believes divorce breaks up families. This is not so. The broken family is not the result of divorce; divorce is the result of the broken family.

— JUDGE PAUL W. ALEXANDER

11

DEEPENING LOVE'S DIALOGUE

Talking with the Heart

by James H. Jauncey

Author, Magic in Marriage, *and Principal, Kenmore Christian College, Australia*

I once married a Norwegian soldier to a Mexican girl. He could speak a little English but no Spanish. She could speak neither English nor Norwegian. How they got together I'll never know. And what might happen in the future as far as communications was concerned, I could not even guess.

But if they were in bad shape language-wise, they were in an infinitely better position than many couples I have known who had complete mastery of the English language. My odd bridal couple had successfully got over their message of love to each other and they seemed in remarkable rapport. Perhaps communication is easy in that stage, language or no language. Later on, the emotions have died down and the hidden needs arise. Learning to talk about the needs is a difficult art, and not many learn it.

Years of counseling in this area have shown me how imperfect language is to communicate the secrets of the soul. Probably people expect too much of language. They use it to express the inner desires and yet to hide them at the

Copyright 1965 Zondervan Publishing House

same time. The real truth is often camouflaged because of pride or anxiety.

The listener, too, doesn't just hear words nor does he interpret them objectively. He colors them with meanings that match his own feelings or wishful thinking. What gets to his heart is often far removed from the truth.

When hatred and bitterness build up on constant personality corrosion, speech becomes almost totally unintelligible. I have often had a warring couple in my office whose language has been so totally misleading that I have had to act as an interpreter.

The wife would make a statement, and I would turn to the husband and interpret: "What she is saying is . . ." When he would answer I would say, "What he means is this . . ."

In many cases when we have cleared away the verbal rubble and revealed what the heart is saying, both have been amazed. Indeed, this is often the secret that can solve an apparently hopelessly deadlocked marital struggle.

Man was not meant to live alone. But marriage does not necessarily bring the togetherness that our Lord referred to when he said, "A man shall leave his father and mother and be joined to his wife and the two shall become one flesh" (Mark 10:7-8).

That kind of union does not come by love alone, least of all by sexual bliss. Neither is it cemented by the coming of children. It only occurs when the personality bares its depths before the sympathetic gaze of a loved one and is accepted for what it is, good or bad. Such baring cannot occur in one session when both let their hair down. It must be a continuing process because needs change with advancing experience.

This communication is a cementing process. After all, isn't this the way a romance often starts? A man and a woman meet casually; they talk and soon they are talking about each other. If there is sympathy and rapport, the personality exploration continues. As it does they become welded together in love. But if this process does not continue in marriage, then the foundations will not grow with the superstructure. But even when you realize that the foundations of a marriage are inadequate, it is seldom too late. You can make a beginning and maybe you can make the structure sound again.

That's what Myra did. She was married to a research chemist. He loved to talk about his work but it was double-Dutch to her. This made her feel inadequate, so to protect her ego she began to shut him up. He was a sensitive man and took the hint. She was relieved and glibly assumed that he could keep his interests in one compartment and her in another.

And so it seemed for some time, until she began to notice a growing aloofness toward her on his part. Normally a cheerful man, he became depressed and sour.

One night she was passing his study when he thought he was alone. His head was cradled in his arms and she heard him whisper. "If only I had someone to talk to."

Myra didn't let on that she had heard, but she got the message. Later on she said: "Tom, if you don't mind explaining to a dunce like me, I sure would like to know what that experiment is you're working on."

His face glowed like a light being switched on. Then he wept a little. "Oh, Myra," he said. "I have so badly wanted to hear you say that."

He not only told her about his experiment but also some office troubles that were eating at him.

From that moment, Myra realized that there is a lot more to listening to a husband than merely interest in the subject matter. Tom's aloofness disappeared and he was a happy man again. Her belated wisdom probably saved the marriage. It certainly made it happy again.

Why is it that we find it so hard to talk even to a loved

one? I mean really talk and not mere small-talk or double-talk.

Pride seems to be the biggest barrier.

This is especially so with professional people: doctors, ministers, and especially psychologists, and for obvious reasons. We are afraid of the "Physician, heal thyself" jibe. In a sense we are as gods among our fellowmen. Our decisions or counsel determine human destiny in many cases. It is hard for us to admit to ourselves, let alone to our wives, that the same ailments which plague the crowd nag at us too.

I believe that it is vitally important for us to realize that under the skin we are all of us just about the same. There isn't a problem that any one of us has, no matter how bad, which is not shared by a million others. No matter how "good" we are, we still have them. Once we admit our frailty to ourselves, it won't be hard to talk about it to our wives.

But we ruin our chances if we are too proud to admit we have such feelings. Actually it is pointless to hide the problem. Most women have the canny capacity to penetrate the bluster and the false facade and to see the frightened man inside.

For many married couples the problem is not so much inability to share; unfortunate experiences have caused a blockage in communication.

John is now as close-mouthed as a clam. His wife complains that he never talks, that he is sullen and morose. I asked him about it.

"I used to talk to her. You know, about my job and all that. I would start to explain a problem I might have. But she would always cut me off. 'That reminds me,' she would interrupt, and be off on some tangent. All that my talking did was to give her a springboard for some topic of her own. She wasn't interested in what I wanted to say."

You couldn't blame him. Yet she didn't mean any harm.

It was just that she was so undisciplined that her mind would be triggered off by any word association and her tongue simply trailed along.

It is easy to slip into this fault. I suggest you check yourself by appraising a recent conversation. What was the subject when it started? Where did it end up? Who started the detours? If it was the other person, fine. This shows that the original discussion had run its course. But if you were the one to start the sidetracking, then maybe you are afflicted with John's wife's complaint.

For sensitive people, ridicule can butcher all desire to communicate the needs of the heart.

When an idea is proposed that we do not like, our first reaction is to kill it. We may do this by reasoned discussion, and this is perfectly in order — there is a good chance that we may come to see the validity of the idea. Or if we are not capable of this, then we may descend to ridicule. In so doing we confess our own inadequacy.

We sometimes use ridicule as a symbol of our own superiority. A statement which we feel is obviously not true to the facts gives one's ego an opportunity to gloat over its supposed superior wisdom.

In this connection, it is wise to realize that problems are relative. A teen-ager's failure to get an invitation to a party may seem like the end of the world to him, whereas to an older person it may be a blessed relief not to have to attend a party. Unless a person realizes that the human emotional response to a problem is often out of all proportion to the intrinsic importance of it, he will never be an understanding listener.

The real measure of the importance of any problem is what it means to the person concerned. An understanding of this will save us from laughing at the "little woman" when she is in tears about a burned cake.

Sometimes an idea or a proposed course of action does have to be discouraged. The person who proposes it may be too emotionally involved in it to see the consequences clearly. But this discouraging should be done very gently, if possible. A little care and thought on our part will enable the person to back down without losing face. Even more important, we should search for the need which is behind the idea, and constructively help the other to an adequate solution.

I cannot emphasize too much this great need for interpersonal communication. It is so vitally important that we should study our partners and make sure that every part of our marriage is adequate. This takes more than a technique. Communication is more than a skill. It requires that kind of love which enables us to see right into the soul. "Bear ye one another's burdens, and so fulfill the law of Christ" (Galatians 6:2).

.•··•··•··•··•··•··•··•··•··•··•··•··•··•·

*The heart of marriage is its communication system.
It can be said that the success and happiness of
any married pair is measurable in terms of the
deepening dialogue which characterizes their union.*
— DWIGHT SMALL

Busy Signal at Home

by Milo L. Arnold

Director, Department of Practical Theology, Nazarene Bible College, Colorado Springs, Colorado

The way to a man's dollars is through his eyes and ears. For that reason, competition for eyes and ears is terrific. Every medium of communication is sharpening its advertising program to a razor's edge in an effort to crowd into our attention. The highest paid people in America are the men and women who can get others to stop long enough to listen. Once people are caught listening, they are bombarded by every market. It isn't that we need more soap or silverware, but industry wants the dollars which might pause even a moment in our pockets.

When you get into your car the radio begins to beg for your ears, the billboards begin to ask for your eyes, and every possible invasion of your attention is in order. The minute you get home, you are lured by your television set, the newspaper, the magazines, the radio, every possible tool of communication. There is color, comedy, action, and appeal. There is suspense, mystery, romance, and even education. Everybody wants to establish communication with you.

A lot of people forget that the communication so cherished by big business is even more valuable within the family.

Your worth to society is canceled out as you cancel yourself as a communicating member of it. Just being present means little if you are unable to make your presence felt

---

Copyright 1967 Union Gospel Press

by relating to others. Communication demands attention and response. A young lady who goes out with two boys at a time will find competition for communication impossible. Both boys will want to talk and hear her talk in response. Her words, her smile, her touch, and every crumb of her attention are worth their weight in gold to them. Sooner or later, she will find that she cannot give enough to satisfy either of them if she tries to satisfy both.

Our families want communication too. They want to hear our voices, to feel our warmth, and to catch our smiles. They want to tell us things, to ask for things, and to share things. When we allow diversions or even work to take up all our attention, we deprive the people who love us of privileges worth a great deal to them and to us. If, when our families try to communicate with us, they always get the busy signal, they'll eventually stop dialing our numbers.

If, when a husband comes home from work, he immediately immerses himself in other things so that his wife cannot get his attention, he will miss something. She has been alone at home all day and wants to chatter. He is communicating on another line, so she gets the busy signal. Gradually he will cancel himself out as a communicating member of the marriage, and loneliness will result.

When a husband comes to the house for lunch, if his wife is giving her attention to the soap opera on TV and he must eat in silence because he gets the busy signal from her inattention, she is robbing both herself and her mate of something very important. The soap company hires trained actors to hold her attention long enough to get in its sales pitch. She should realize that her attention is valuable to the family too.

Many children get the busy signal at the dinner table because the parents are occupied with their own interests. The result is that they may stop dialing the number. The communication between parent and child is diminished to a perilously inadequate trickle of instructions, directions, rebukes, and nagging. What child wants to stay at home if all he ever hears is something he would rather not listen to?

Homes get into trouble when communication is strangled. Sometimes the breakdown is between husband and wife, sometimes between parents and children; but in either case, it creates big problems.

Parents sometimes complain that their children pay no attention to them when they talk about vitally important issues. The parents need to get through to the child with some really big truth but are utterly frustrated. Parents who never talk about trifles with their children will get no audience when they want to talk about serious things. If parents never have time for little people on their laps, for children in their mealtime conversation, or for a child's chatter and stories, there will be a time when they will want to communicate and cannot.

Communication between husband and wife often suffers the same fate. If they do not communicate in daily trifles, they will be unable to communicate in the more deeply emotional experiences. If they do not maintain an open fellowship in peripheral things, they will never preserve the communion essential to the heavier loads of marriage. Communication must begin with trifling things and work toward the important ones. Mountain climbers begin their ascent by surmounting little hills. No artist can paint only masterpieces.

No husband can expect to enjoy sublime communication with his wife if communion is limited to an occasional specific moment. If he has no time for tenderness throughout the routine days, he will be unable to draw from her the fullest companionship in his hours of wistfulness. No wife can expect to nag a husband most of the time and enjoy his tender affection and loving words when she wants them. Communication, like affection, cannot be turned off and on at will. We are persons who communicate, or we are not.

Part of good communication is listening. Our families

can't put on a high-priced dramatic production in order to get our attention. They can't spend millions of dollars courting our ears. If we are looking for that kind of appeal, we will have to settle for the anemic drivel which gushes into our homes through professional entertainment. If we want meaning and warmth, if we want to listen as well as talk, to communicate as well as be entertained, then we must discipline ourselves to be part of the family with a whole-hearted devotion and a sincere interest. He who has little time to listen to his family will come to a time when his family pays him no heed. He who cannot enjoy trifles with his loved ones will stand alone when big issues are being faced. He whose line is always busy when his family tries to communicate will want desperately to establish communion at a time when it is very important but will find the lines down.

Of course, we are not against having newspapers, radios, television, and stereo sets in our homes. They are part of the blessings of God upon our era and can contribute much to family living. The danger comes when we become so attentive to these things that we miss the wistful, timid appeal of a person very dear to us who would like a bit more of our hearts and voices than we have left over to give.

When you really open up for communication, the whole world is waiting — especially the folks who love you and need you very, very much. Your little child wants to borrow you and your lap, your kiss and your Band-Aid. Your growing youngster wants to borrow your heart, your ear, and your help with algebra. Your teen-ager wants to hear the voice of your heart at a time when his or her heart is running quite wildly. A husband wants to borrow an ear, heart, and encouragement. A wife wants a place to cuddle in a strong man's kind affection and tender understanding.

If when your loved ones try to communicate in trifles they get a busy signal, you will soon find the lines are torn down. When this happens, the world becomes lonesome!

Words Can't Say It

by Howard J. Clinebell, Jr. and Charlotte H. Clinebell
Co-authors, The Intimate Marriage. *Mr. Clinebell is Professor of Pastoral Counseling, School of Theology, Claremont, California*

Good communication is the ability to transmit and receive meanings; it is the instrument for achieving that mutual understanding which is at the heart of marital intimacy. Words are not the only communicators. Communication in any close relationship occurs on literally dozens of levels simultaneously.

Suppose a wife greets her returning husband with the words, "I thought you'd never come home." Her husband hears her words, but also receives simultaneously several other messages. There is the tone of her voice and its inflection: is it a whine or a caress? Her facial expression and the movement of her body tell him something; is she smiling or frowning? Does she turn her back or reach out to him? There is also the implied expectation in his wife's remark, sometimes called the "demand quality" of communication. What response is she expecting from him? An apology for being late? A return caress such as, "I missed you too"? An attack: "Can't you let me live my own life?" Or is she asking for a lingering embrace? At the same time, the husband's own experiences since he left his wife that morning help to determine how he will receive his wife's greeting. Thus, it becomes obvious that even the simplest communication is a complicated exchange. The husband's ability to understand his wife's greeting depends on his ability at that moment to sort out and weigh the multilevel messages he receives.

Copyright 1970 Harper & Row

Meantime the wife is also required to translate the many cues she is getting from her husband. Communication is always a two-way street. Both husband and wife are simultaneously sending and receiving messages. Her statement can probably be understood only in the context of what happened between them before he went to work that day. The husband also sends several nonverbal messages as he enters the front door. The time he gets home, the way he walks, the droop or set of his shoulders, his greeting both verbal and nonverbal — all must be interpreted by the wife even as he is interpreting her messages.

In order to strengthen communication in a marriage, a couple needs to learn to use the varied lines through which the messages and meanings are transmitted. There are many ways to say, "I love you!" A fond glance, a tender or playful touch in an appropriate spot, a thoughtful gift, choosing to sit close in a crowded room, listening with genuine interest, a kiss on the back of the neck, a note — perhaps with a private joke — left where it will be found, a word of sympathy or support, a sly wink, preparing a favorite dish, a bowl of flowers carefully arranged, a phone call in the middle of the day, and even remembering to take out the trash are but a few. A part of the joy of marriage is this opportunity to develop an almost endless variety of transmission lines for the meanings that are important to each partner.

Another step in improving communication in marriage is for both partners to learn to listen more fully.

What is needed is deep listening. Such listening is seeing the world through another person's eyes. It is "walking a mile in the other fellow's moccasins."

Gabriel Marcel has said that there is "a way of listening which is a way of refusing — of refusing oneself — and there is a way of listening which is a way of giving — of self giving." To really listen to another means both giving oneself and being willing to receive the other within oneself.

The point at which communication frequently breaks down is not in the speaking or the listening, per se, but in failing to check frequently to see if one really hears and understands what the other means, feels, and intends. Many messages in marriages, as well as elsewhere, are ambiguous. The simple process of checking out meanings by asking questions such as, "Do I hear you correctly?" or "Is this what you are saying?" can break up some of the communication logjams that grow rapidly otherwise. When a person talks, is silent, listens superficially, doesn't listen at all, or listens in depth, he is communicating something.

There is something more basic in marital communication than simply saying and hearing words accurately. What is fundamental is the willingness to consider each other's point of view; this willingness is rooted in a degree of mutual respect.

Another road to productive communication is for both husband and wife to learn the skill of saying it straight. Direct rather than devious, specific rather than generalized statements are required. A wife criticizes her husband as he sits at the breakfast table hidden behind his newspaper, "I wish you wouldn't always slurp your coffee." What she really means is, "I feel hurt when you hide in the newspaper instead of talking to me." Saying it straight involves being honest about negative as well as positive feelings, and being able to state them in a nonattacking way: "I feel . . .", rather than "You are . . ."

Becoming aware of one's own, and learning to translate the other's coded and conflicting messages are steps along the path to good communication. All of us send such contradictory messages occasionally simply because we all have conflicting feelings. It helps to resolve this block if couples can help each other to bring such conflicts out into the open and discuss them.

Of course, not all coded messages are negative. The husband who brings his wife a bottle of perfume "for no reason at all" probably is saying, "I love you! You're an attractive woman! I like being married to you!" Couples whose nonverbal communication is on a positive level most of the time are continually saying to each other, "I care."

"A relationship which spells closeness also spells conflict." Marriage is the most difficult and the most demanding, but also the most potentially rewarding of all human relationships, because it is potentially the most intimate. Because it is the most intimate, it also holds the greatest potential for conflict.

Couples who can learn to value their conflicts can use them to improve the communication skills which make possible the growth of intimacy. Anything alive experiences struggle and conflict. A couple can learn to learn from their fights; they can learn how to keep them from becoming physically or emotionally destructive, how to interrupt them sooner and how to grow closer because of them. Intimacy grows when conflicts are faced and worked through in the painful but fulfilling process of gradual understanding and compromise of differences.

Effective conflict resolution in marriage results from several steps in the communication process. Both partners must first be willing to hear each other's complaints and to accept feelings, however vehement, about them. The couple must then make efforts to narrow down the generalized accusations to the particular issues or differences about which something can be done. They must learn to focus on one issue at a time. Each must state how he himself sees the problem and how he thinks the other sees the problem. When this "checking out" has helped to resolve the negative feelings, the couple can begin to make concessions, compromises, and plans for dealing with their differences. A relatively healthy couple in which both partners have a strong sense of identity can really use their conflicts for growth by following these steps.

No spouse should ever assume that "he (she) knows I love him (her)." A growing sense of intimacy should not require minute-to-minute reinforcement; but even the healthiest husbands and wives have enough doubts about themselves as persons worth loving to need regular affirmation from each other. However, need-satisfying communication becomes interpersonal communion as richer, more multileveled interaction becomes a channel for caring. Couples who have been intimately married for a long time often communicate on deep, subconscious levels. Such communion is something far beyond the mere sending and receiving of messages, as important as these are. It is the result of depth intimacy, the strong marital identity which is the strand of gold thread in a marriage covenant.

Take a look together at your ways of getting through to each other. Discuss the things that block efforts to communicate, particularly during conflict. Think of ways for increasing the opportunities for communication — more face-to-face time together, for example. Do something to increase the number of areas in which you can talk the same language.

A man who had been married for thirty years said: "I still like to hold my wife's hand." He did not get the same electric spark he received when he first held her hand, but holding it gave him a sense of security and strength. At times it gave promise of a more complete physical union. More often the touch of her hand said, "I need you. I'm glad we have each other. I love you now as always." This reaction, he claimed, was more thrilling, more satisfying than the exciting experiences of courtship.

One of the mysteries and marvels of intimacy in marriage is that it offers so many opportunities to find those shared transcendent meanings that ultimately make life worthwhile.

Crossing Barriers and Bridges

by Elof G. Nelson
Author, Your Life Together

In our world of growing impersonality, high mobility, and general affluence, it has become vital to all human life, and most assuredly vital to married living, that spouses communicate in a warm personal dialogue. As Reuel Howe says, "Communication means life or death to persons."

Effective marital dialogue means that both spouses continue to care for each other in spite of differences of opinions. Effective communication also consists of the patience to listen to each other's concerns. As agape love is tempered by understanding, goodwill, humor, and acceptance, communication continues in earnest and the marriage remains secure and meaningful.

But if one or the other fails to love and understanding becomes minimal, barriers develop that often become like prison walls. Marriage then becomes flat, meaningless, and its people seek ways to escape. They are not communicating because they have little or no emotional investment in each other. They share no confidences, have their own private friends, plan separate vacations, often even make their own meals and eat alone. There is no dialogue — no warmth of a meaningful interpersonal relationship. They have a marriage that consists of monologue only. It is brittle and lifeless and soon both know they are in deep trouble.

One of the classical barriers to effective communication in modern marriage lies in the ambiguity and conflict of the roles in marriage. Men and women are not to resemble

———

Copyright 1967 M. E. Bratcher

each other, but are created to complete each other through marriage.

When the husband accepts the role as head of the family and the wife willingly becomes the heart of the home, harmony and freedom for fulfillment and personal development can joyfully materialize. Confusion of these roles causes serious problems in decision-making, breaking down communications and establishing a serious barrier to the need for effective interpersonal dialogue.

Human dialogue takes place on two levels: one below the surface — the contact between persons, and the other on the surface — made up of our gestures and words, and bearing the stamp of our temperament. Effective communication is, therefore, not only verbal, but nonverbal as well. Unless we commit ourselves to our spouses as true persons, there can be no dialogue that satisfies and frees us for consistent life together. Monologue never sees the person of the spouse, for it is only a selfish confinement of an immature person to his own little world. This is why maturity of both man and woman is so important for a good life together.

Mental illness takes up more hospital beds in our nation than any other illness. We should not be surprised, then, to learn that emotional problems are serious barriers to effective harmony in marriages. Man can build machines equipped with warning signals to draw attention to improper functioning, but often ignores his own "tilt" signals — anxiety, guilt, fatigue, emotional frustration, depression, and a serious lack of personal esteem. He continues to let these rule him until serious trouble occurs either in himself or in the sphere of interpersonal relations.

Some marriages may be made in heaven but all marriages must be lived on earth. This is a fact of life. Life's many opportunities should be met by two people who have a living faith in God, a sincere belief in each other, and a satisfactory, workable way of confronting life's problems with courage and confidence.

A happy marriage requires two people settling down and working out normal conflicts, developing daily routine that is meaningful to both. Little "bothersome" things are to be taken seriously, for they mean something to the person who makes an issue of them. Most husbands like to come home to a house in reasonable order and hope to find their wives pleasant and neat. They also do not wish to be burdened with trivial household problems until they have had a few moments to unwind after the day. Wives who know this will wait until their husbands have a brief time to "recover."

Trivialities can become like tyranny when one is in an off-mood and is fatigued or emotionally overwrought. If one knows that something he does greatly disturbs his spouse, agape love should rectify it. Only the selfish and immature mate will deliberately continue to make an issue of it. If trivial things bother you, ask yourself, "Why does this little mannerism of his bother me, and how can I best deal with this thing in myself?" or "How can I help my spouse change if it is a habit that disturbs me?"

Each spouse has a right to be heard — and you can never hear what anyone else is saying unless you are listening. True love is patient and kind; it can wait until my partner has been heard.

The ability to listen well means that we are not only attentive to the words but we are perceptive in our listening to hear the meaning behind those words. Parents who listen to their children from the earliest years and on through adolescence will always have a good relationship with them. Listening conveys the attitude of acceptance and respect. It says to the other person, "You are a worthwhile person — and I read you loud and clear."

I know of nothing as healing to a marriage as the words, "Forgive me, I was wrong," "I'm sorry," and "Pardon me."

Happily married people are never too pride-conscious to use them. These little words have transforming power.

Forgiving someone is a basic ethic of the truly Christian person. The rhythm of a normal family life is alienation and reconciliation — forgiveness, acted out daily, makes possible the climate of comfort and intimacy. As Gibson Winter says, "Forgiveness is the daily bread of married life together." Forgiveness is always cast in the mood of intimacy — it is the product of warm, personal, and realistic encounter. In this there are no minimums.

Marriages that are supportive and intimate must be sustained by the potential each partner has for continued development. Success is never a final thing. There is never a sense of finality to marital adjustments because human personality is never static. As you read, learn, acquire new friends, and assume more responsibilities in life, you keep changing. We are never the same person from day to day, week to week. As people are always developing, so marriages must constantly be in the process of adjustment and change.

You may be able to communicate intimately and in great depth on your honeymoon. How can you plan for intimacy and communication, in even greater depth, five, ten, and twenty years after your wedding day? In a real sense, your happiness in marriage will always be up to you. On your wedding day you vowed to accept very real responsibility to love, honor, and cherish, and in doing this you must also realize that your own continued growth and development do most to sustain that vow throughout all of married life.

Diplomacy at Home

by a staff member, *Royal Bank of Canada Monthly Letter*

Families can live together and prosper and be happy under an extraordinary variety of conditions so long as they observe a few simple virtues, chief of which is the practice of diplomacy.

Whatever the mode of governance, the real heart of family life is to be seen in the behavior of the individual members toward one another. The greatest art known to man is that of living together harmoniously and helpfully. One head of a family, seeking something to decorate the chimney-piece in his library, cast away all other ideas in favor of a plaque bearing two Greek words meaning: "The healing-place of the soul."

The relationship of husband and wife in the family is properly one of equality secured by mutual affection. Marriage is not a mere episode. It is the culmination of two lives, the products of dissimilar circumstances, different upbringing, varying attitudes toward life, and personal ways of doing things. Success under these circumstances is not automatic. It has to be worked for. There are two imperfect personalities to be somehow blended, and there are difficulties from outside to be coped with, such as economic circumstances and changing ways of life.

Effectual communication of thoughts and ideas is vital. The mother's communication with her small baby is simple: smiles, bodily movements, tone of voice, variations in the cry of the baby. Contrast with these the breadth and depth and complication of the intercommunication which goes on between parents and their teen-age children, and between themselves. All the symbols of language are used, plus indirect techniques such as innuendoes, provisos, silence, and manner.

Many of the things that disturb family life are the product of original mistakes compounded by bad manners. Walter Hines Page, distinguished United States ambassador to Great Britain, said: "The more I find out about diplomatic customs, and the more I hear of the little-big troubles of others, the more need I find to be careful about details of courtesy."

If love is the foundation of happy marriage, good manners are the walls and diplomacy is the roof.

The essays written by Addision and Steele have lived through many years. In one of them Steele says: "Two persons who have chosen each other out of all the species, with design to be each other's mutual comfort and entertainment, have in that action bound themselves to be good-humored, affable, discreet, forgiving, patient, and joyful, with respect for each other's frailties and perfections."

Manners for two are fixed by the same rules as are manners for the million, based upon the Golden Rule. They spring from kindness, courtesy, and consideration, with a dash of *savoir faire* — the faculty of knowing just what to do and how to do it.

Members of the family give proof of their high regard for one another by the delicacy with which they frame their requests or instructions. Parents show a happy blend of authority and companionship. They are simple, open, and cordial, void of all arrogance. They are more than kind; they are kindly, and kindliness means a pleasant way of doing a kind thing.

As a minimum, diplomacy in the family asks everyone to be considerate and decent, gracefully remembering the rights of others. At its best, diplomacy is unruffled good breeding, taking care and trouble to see that others are not neglected. It does not take anyone for granted.

The word "tact" covers a great deal that is essential in

diplomacy. It means being completely aware of the feeling involved in certain situations and acting in accordance with what courtesy dictates. It means offering a discomfited member of the family a chance to "save face." It even means the difficult exercise of being generous and gracious while being honest and unyielding — what Ralph Waldo Emerson called "good-natured inflexibility."

The giving of praise and commendation is one of the special privileges and charming graces of family life and one of the most useful tools in diplomacy. Among the Proverbs ascribed to Solomon are these: "A word spoken in due season, how good is it!" and "A word fitly spoken is like apples of gold in pictures of silver."

The commendation need not be confined to achievements, but may show appreciation of effort. It need not be extravagant, but it should not be withheld because it does not seem to be adequate. We are amused by an episode in the life of Napoleon. On a motion to award the great general a pension, the French Assembly decided: "Such glorious deeds could not be rewarded by gold," so gave him nothing.

Jealousy should not be allowed to interfere with the giving of credit and praise. To envy another person his skill or accomplishments or social grace is to grieve over our own lack of these, and is demeaning to us.

Diplomacy is not a cure-all, but it makes room for things to be set right. It helps to solve even the most awesome problems. Simply stated, it finds out what the other person wants and plans how to meet that requirement as far as is reasonable. When both parties do this, agreement is attained.

The factors are: negotiation, conciliation, concession, and compromise, and using these effectively is called "The art of the possible." It is directed toward finding the balance among conflicting desires which will give the greatest all-round satisfaction.

Sometimes the initial efforts fail and different ways have

to be tried. Diplomats do not try to saw sawdust. They get on to a new piece of wood. They bring in a new point or take a new viewpoint. They change some factor so as to give the problem a new surface on which they can get a grip.

One can be a diplomat cheerfully. There are some people who become depressed, and go around as if they were trying to qualify for Shakespeare's description: ". . . like the painting of a sorrow." Being a diplomat in the family can be full of quiet delight and pleasure. Even the simple device of collecting tidbits of information, news, and humor to be trotted out at the diplomatic moment is a satisfaction-giving experience.

Diplomacy in the home is taking care in little ways so as to reduce life's fitful fever. It means making adjustments both of thinking and acting so as to meet and cope with ever-changing situations composedly and with good sense.

Diplomacy does not consist of making promises or holding out prizes. Children are living at the exciting wave front of life. We need to be careful not to offer young people too many hopes, too many choices, too much for too little. At the same time we must not discourage their ambition to be the best in whatever sort of life they choose.

We pay attention to informing and training our minds, but diplomacy requires us to educate our hearts. It means not only keeping the home fire burning but throwing a pinch of incense on it once in a while. It includes some kind deeds done for their own sake without expecting a return.

Even if the bond of family kinship is not so strong as it once was, there is need for the ties of friendship if people are to live happily together, and one of the strong links in friendship is diplomacy. The person who applies diplomacy successfully will not only strew benefits but will reap flowers.

12

MAKING SENSE WITH DOLLARS

Giving Is Living

by A. T. Pierson
Author, George Mueller of Bristol *and other books*

Our Lord's teachings as to money gifts, if obeyed, would forever banish all limitations on church work and all concern about supplies. These teachings are radical and revolutionary. So far are they from practical acceptance that, although perfectly explicit, they seem like a dead language that has passed out of use. Should these sublime and unique teachings be translated into living, the effect not only upon benevolent work, but upon our whole spiritual character, would be incalculable.

Stewardship. The basis of Christ's teaching about money is the fundamental conception of stewardship (Luke 12:42; 16:1-8). Not only money, but every gift of God, is received in trust for his use. Man is not an owner, but a trustee, managing another's goods and estates, God being the one original and inalienable owner of all. The two things required of stewards are that they be "faithful and wise," that they study to employ God's gifts with fidelity and sagacity — fidelity so that God's entrustments be not perverted to self-indulgence; sagacity so that they be converted into as large gains as possible.

Investment. "Thou oughtest therefore to have put my

money to the exchangers" (Matthew 25:27). Money-changing and investing is an old business. The "exchangers," as Luke renders, are the bankers, who received money on deposit and paid interest for its use, like modern savings institutions.

In view of this, the argument of our Lord refutes the unfaithful servant on his own plea, which his course showed to be but a pretext. He dared not risk trading on his own account; why not, without such risk, get a moderate interest for his master by lending to professional traders? It was not fear but laziness that lay behind his unfaithfulness and unprofitableness.

Thus indirectly the valuable lesson is taught that timid souls may link their incapacity to the capacity and sagacity of others who will make their gifts and possessions of use to the Master and his Church.

Idolatry. With all his attractive traits, the rich young ruler of Matthew 19:16-26 was a slave. Money was not his servant, but his master. And because God alone is to be supreme, our Lord had no alternative; he must demolish this man's idol. When he dealt a blow at his money, the idolatry became apparent, and the slave to greed went away sorrowful, clinging to his idol.

It was not this man's having great possessions that was wrong, but that his possessions had the man; they controlled him. His "trust" was in riches; how could it be in God?

How few rich men keep the mastery and hold money as their servant, in absolute subordination to their own manhood, and to the masterhood of the Lord!

Recompense. "Give, and it shall be given unto you" (Luke 6:38). God is an economist. He entrusts larger gifts to those who use the smaller ones well. The future may reveal that God has been withholding from us because we have been withholding from him.

Many servants of God, holding all as God's, spending little or nothing for self, were permitted to receive and use millions for God; and some, like George Mueller, without any appeal to men, looked solely to God. This great saint of Bristol found that it was safe to give to God's purposes the last penny at any moment, with the perfect assurance that more would come in before another need should arise. And there was never one failure for seventy years!

Whatever the blessedness of receiving, that of giving belongs to a higher plane. Whatever I get, and whatever good it brings to me, only I am benefited; but what I give brings good to others — to the many, not the one. But, by a singular decree of God, what I thus surrender for the sake of others comes back to me in larger blessing. It is like the moisture which the spring gives out in streams and evaporation, returning in showers to supply the very channels which filled the spring itself. "It is more blessed to give than to receive" (Acts 20:35).

Real giving. The Lord Jesus watched the offerings cast into the treasury. There were rich givers that gave large amounts. There was one poor woman, a widow, who threw in two mites, and he declared her offering to be more than any or all the rest, because, while they gave out of a superfluity, she gave out of a deficiency — they of their abundance, she of her poverty.

She who cast her two mites into the sacred treasury, by so doing became rich in good works and in the praise of God. Had she kept them, she would have been the same poor widow.

He tells us here how he estimates money gifts — not by what we give, but by what we keep — not by the amount of our contributions, but by their cost in self-denial.

Not all giving, so-called, has rich reward. In many cases the keeping hides the giving, in the sight of God. But when the one possession that is dearest, the last trusted resource, is surrendered to God, then comes the vision of the treasure laid up in heaven.

"Do good and lend, hoping for nothing again" (Luke 6: 35). Much of our giving is not giving at all, but only lending or exchanging. He who gives to another of whom he expects to receive as much again, is trading. What he is after is not another's profit, but his own advantage.

True giving has another's good solely in view, and hence bestows upon those who cannot and will not repay. That is the giving prompted by love. This sort of giving shows God-likeness, and by it we grow into the perfection of benevolence.

Worship. "The altar . . . sanctifieth the gift" (Matthew 23: 19) — association gives dignity to an offering. If the cause to which we contribute is exalted, it ennobles and exalts the offering to its own plane. No two objects can or ought to appeal to us with equal force unless they are equal in moral worth and dignity.

God's altar was to the Jew the central focus of all gifts. The gift laid upon it acquired a new dignity by so being deposited upon it. We are at liberty to set aside some objects which appeal for gifts because they are not sacred. We may give or not as we judge best, for they depend on man's enterprises and schemes, which we may not altogether approve. But some causes have divine sanction and that hallows them; giving then becomes an act of worship.

Eternal purchases. "Make to yourselves friends of the mammon of unrighteousness; that, when ye fail, they may receive you into everlasting habitations" (Luke 16:9). This contains one of the greatest hints on money gifts that our Lord dropped.

Mammon here stands as the equivalent for money, practically worshiped. It reminds us of the golden calf that was made out of the earrings and jewels of the crowd. Now our Lord refers to a second transmutation. The "golden calf" may in turn be melted down and coined into Bibles, churches, books, tracts, and even souls of men. Thus what was material and temporal becomes immaterial and spiritual — and eternal.

Here is a man who has a hundred dollars. He may spend it all on a party, and the next day there is nothing to show for it. On the other hand, he invests in Bibles at ten cents each, and it buys a thousand copies of the Word of God. These he judiciously sows as seed of the Kingdom, and from that seed springs up a harvest, not of Bibles, but of souls. Out of the unrighteous mammon he has made immortal friends, who, when he fails, receive him into everlasting habitations. This is true riches — the treasure laid up in heaven in imperishable goods!

What revelations await us in that day of transmutation! Then, whatever has been given up to God as an offering of the heart, "in righteousness," will be seen as transfigured. Not only the magi's gold, frankincense, and myrrh, and the alabaster box of ointment of spikenard, very precious, and the houses and lands of such as Barnabas, but fishermen's boats and nets, the abandoned "seat of custom," the widow's mites, and the cup of cold water — yes, when we had nothing else to give, the word of counsel, the tear of pity, the prayer of intercession — all will be transfigured.

Never will the work of missions, or any other form of service to God and man, receive the help it ought until there is a new conscience and a new consecration in the matter of money. The worldly spirit blinds us to the fact of obligation, and devises flimsy pretexts for diverting the Lord's money to carnal ends. The few who learn to give on scriptural principles learn also to love to give.

God's unspeakable gift to us should make all giving to him a spontaneous offering of love. Like Mary's, it should bring its precious box of spikenard and lavish its treasures on his feet, and fill the house with the odor of self-sacrifice!

Money, Marriage, and Romance

by W. Clark Ellzey

Author, How to Keep Romance in Your Marriage

Conflict over money ranks high among the top causes of trouble in marriage. The greatest conflict appears in families of the highest income brackets. Considerable trouble over financial problems shows up in marriages on the lowest income levels too. Married people of moderate income apparently have less conflict than those on a high or low level. Research shows that nobody is satisfied with his income, whatever it is, and everybody seems to think all his troubles would be over if he could only make more money.

A careful study of money troubles in marriage shows many causes. Bad management is chief among them. Traditional attitudes and expectations regarding who should earn and spend money contribute their share. In addition, what may appear on the surface to be financial trouble may actually be personality conflict, with the bills at the end of the month merely the battleground. Emotional instability can also express itself financially. Whatever the cause, when money and conflict are tangled up in marriage, romance is seriously threatened.

Today more than half the homes and farms in the United States are in the names of women. According to a recent national survey, it is estimated that about 80 percent of all inheritance comes to women, and about the same percentage of life insurance beneficiaries are women. Conservative estimates suggest that women control about 40 percent of the entire national income.

Copyright 1965 Association Press

Today nearly 50 percent of all women employed in full- or part-time jobs are married. The man is no longer the sole breadwinner. In many marriages the wife is making as much money as her husband and in some marriages she makes more than her husband. In many instances the masculine ego is tied up with the role of breadwinning, and romance may be dulled if the wife works.

Some women need to secure a paying job for reassurance of their feelings of worth when nearly all values are declared in terms of money. Some just do not like housework and prefer to employ someone else to do it. A wife may feel that she must work, in spite of parental responsibilities, in order that the family may have what it needs. Experience in some job compatible with marriage may prove invaluable if the husband is temporarily or permanently incapacitated, or if his death throws total financial responsibility suddenly upon the wife.

In marital conflict over who earns the money, discussion may lead to understanding, and understanding may contribute toward adjustment as surely as with conflict for any cause. A wife may need to understand that her husband cannot change overnight even when he thinks he should and tries to do so. Emotional attitudes are not so easily reconditioned as intellectual concepts, especially when they are tied up with the ego. A husband needs to understand that his wife may not fit the traditional picture of "the woman's place is in the home," at least to perfection, and that she may have needs as a person which require consideration if he loves her for herself, and not just as an instrument for his own satisfaction. A reexamination of expectations on the part of both husband and wife to see if they are only traditional or if they fit the circumstances of today's world, grounded in practical considerations, may enable a couple to work out financial problems arising in the emotions.

Today, in approximately one-third of all families in the United States, women manage all the money, whether they contribute toward the family income or the husband is the sole provider.

If both husband and wife are contributing to the family income it may be easy for each to think of his earnings as his own money and spend accordingly. They are in a "we" relationship, but each may operate as if it were "my" money. They are married, except financially.

Men and women do not always see things alike nor do they value things alike. There have been frequent fireworks in marriage because a wife bought something which she prized highly and her husband could see no value whatever in it. A man can cause volcanic eruptions by purchasing some long-desired "thing," which looks to his wife like an inexcusable waste of money. Projecting our own evaluations upon others, especially in marriage, can cause trouble over finances. Accepting the fact of individual differences and of the right to act accordingly is not easy, but such an attitude contributes toward harmony in marriage and smooth sailing on financial seas.

More than one couple have fallen in love and landed in marriage only to discover that they were in a monetary trap. Some have survived by facing the situation realistically, battled to make a go of it on a very meager income, and dug their way out by both partners working.

It is a bitter pill for a married man to have to admit that he cannot handle his financial affairs, but the person who, admitting it, seeks the help of some capable financial adviser is likely to come out on top much sooner, and with less pain than the person who tries to cover it up.

Our credit system has permitted us to achieve beyond what is likely under any other system. But installment buying can become a money trap to those who follow impulse and have never learned to control desire. All our psychology of salesmanship is calculated to induce buying, whether we can afford to buy or not. Business and industry have employed some of the best psychologists in the world to persuade the public to buy. Consumers in general are not organized as business is, and none of the world's great psychologists are being paid to help the public develop sales resistance.

The personal immaturity which reveals itself in the compulsive need to "keep up with the Joneses" can lead marriage into the proverbial financial hole. The solution is not in acquiring more money — because there are always more and better Joneses. This trap can be avoided only through revising one's outlook on life, reorganizing one's sense of values, or just plain growing up. A person may need to discover why it seems so important to keep up with the Joneses. That discovery involves self-examination, and almost any good book on the development of personality will help with the understanding that children depend upon others for their self-regard. Those who reach adulthood and still depend upon others for their feelings about themselves have never grown up. Marriage is for people who have matured, if they want romance.

Those who find themselves in a marriage without having developed the skills of managing money would gain much in taking whatever course of training might be indicated.

Long-term planning enables some married people to appear to have no financial problems. Some marriages are under strain because there was no planning for children even after they were discovered to be on the way. Unforeseen emergencies can throw a marriage off the track unless there is some plan to enable the couple to meet them. Too many couples are living in resentful misery during the retirement years because there was no planning for the time of less economic productivity.

Most of us could have some of the things now beyond our reach if we knew how to make our money go further. Unnecessary conflict exists in some marriages where there is money enough if the couple only knew how to use it. Love may be the most important thing in marriage, but it grows stronger when it rests on a balanced budget. Romance may be a firm reality when it stands on the solid foundation of a businesslike management of financial affairs.

In all the research thus far, there is no correlation between the amount of money people have and their happiness in marriage. Apparently money cannot buy romance, nor can a limited income keep it out.

Money is necessary but its powers are limited. It is no substitute for tender affection freely given. It cannot buy trustworthiness. Those who depend upon money and the things which money can buy are helpless and hopeless when money is gone. The seers of the ages have understood this truth only too well. Observation from scientific research today verifies the insight phrased centuries ago, "Better a dinner of herbs where love is, than a stalled ox and hate therewith" (Proverbs 1:17).

.·•··•··•··•··•··•··•··•··•··•··•··•··•··•·

More than 15 million American homes now live on two paychecks, with husband and wife each working at an outside job, so the success of the marriage often depends on their ability to handle wisely not merely the paychecks but the demands of the jobs themselves. If either partner puts the job ahead of the home, there will naturally be trouble; but, beyond this, each should be mature and wise enough to see the other's need for security and affection as well as for self-expression and advancement. Intelligent teamwork in attaining these goals without mutual neglect is imperative. Indeed, the problems that can arise from two paychecks ought to be talked out fully before marriage, and plans made to avoid them. The two-paycheck home, which will probably become commoner each year, is a real test of adult personality.

— Paul Popenoe

Keep Your Money Alive

by D. G. Kehl
Professor of English, Arizona State University

The lowly groundhog, having seen the shadow of death, will leave his spouse and offspring in a relatively more desirable financial condition than will one out of two Christians. No court-appointed woodchuck administrator will apportion his store of clover and alfalfa, with a windfall going to profligate prairie dog relatives. Nor will it be necessary for Mrs. Groundhog to apply for legal guardianship of her brood and post a bond to administer their affairs. The cozy, tri-level burrow will pass to her free of any entangling legal claims. And not even the down of a single dandelion will be blown away in costly legal fees.

Have you, through the provision of a bona fide will, prepared an answer if God should say to you: "This night thy soul shall be required of thee: then whose shall those things be which thou hast provided?" (Luke 12:20). Whether you are twenty-one or seventy-one, whether you last another fifty years or get run over tomorrow, you should face the prospect of your death and consider God's will — and yours.

Both the state of man on earth and his earthly estate are gifts from God. "Every man," wrote Solomon, "to whom God hath given riches and wealth, and hath given him power to eat thereof, and to take his portion, and to rejoice in his labor, this is the gift of God" (Ecclesiastes 5:19). "Every good gift and every perfect gift is from above, and cometh down from the Father of lights," James reminds us (1:17).

These gifts from above, good and perfect in themselves,

are bestowed in trust. But if the trust is broken, if the recipient misuses or — almost as serious — disuses it, even a good gift can cause a harmful influence which will survive its recipient.

"The evil that men do lives after them," says Antony in Shakespeare's *Julius Caesar;* "the good is oft interred with their bones." Money is potentially good or evil, depending upon its use. By failing to specify in a legal will the disposition of their estates, many otherwise conscientious Christians allow their money's potential for good to be interred with them and unwittingly cause evil to live after them.

"Money is powerful for good if divinely used," wrote George MacDonald. A will enables the Christian to assure that his money will be divinely used. God's behest for man's bequest is clear: "Set thine house in order (or give charge concerning thy house): for thou shalt die, and not live" (Isaiah 38:1).

William Shakespeare's will, undoubtedly one of the most famous in history, indicates both his spiritual and material preparation for death. "I commend my soul into the hands of God my Creator," Shakespeare wrote, "hoping and assuredly believing, through the merits of Jesus Christ my Savior, to be made partaker of life everlasting; and my body to the earth whereof that is made. Item: I give and bequeath unto my daughter Judith one hundred and fifty pounds of English money, to be paid unto her in manner and form following . . ."

The rich farmer who failed to make spiritual preparation for death God called a fool; certainly the Christian is foolhardy who fails to stamp the image of God upon his estate by specifying its disposition in a way that will glorify God.

In most states where an individual dies intestate (without a will) and leaves children, the surviving spouse may receive only one-third of the estate. The law may tie up half or more of the estate until the children are grown. Money needed for your children's education could be frozen

during the very time they need it. Further, it is unlikely
that the administrator appointed by the court to settle your
affairs would share your Christian principles and philosophy.
And if guardianship is required for minor-age children, the
court also makes the decision.

A will permits you actually to "make" the laws by which
your estate is distributed and managed after your death.
It enables you to name a godly Christian to serve as guardian for minor children. It lets you name an executor to
settle your affairs and allows you to designate bequests to
Christian institutions and churches.

A Christian need not be obsessively morbid about death
as John Donne, the great seventeenth-century English poet,
seems to have been. Donne reportedly had on his writing
table a portrait of himself in his shroud so that he would
avoid frivolous thoughts and think only sober ones. Mor-
bidity about death should not be a part of the Christian's
attitude, but wise and realistic preparation should be. The
intent to leave part of one's estate for Christian work cannot
be enforced unless it is specified in a legally drawn will.
Therefore, to have no will is to defeat the Christian cause
by default.

The words of Paul are straightforward: "If any provide
not for his own, and specially for those of his own house, he
hath denied the faith, and is worse than an infidel" (1 Timothy 5:8). Failure to make a will is a serious sin of omis-
sion, but it is more — it is a sin of disobedience to God's
behest, disobedience involving lack of devotion to one's
family and to the cause of Christ.

You can — and should — have the last word concerning
the disposition of your estate — for the glory of God. It is
paradoxical that Christians who during their lifetimes would
never once consider giving their money to the cause of evil,
allow it by default to fall, after their death, into the hands
of evil men.

Inscribed on a tombstone in a Pennsylvania cemetery are

these words: "If a man not make a will before he is dead, his wife should hit him with a neck yoke on the head." Stated somewhat less whimsically, intestacy often results in confusion, injustice, and deprivation to families and the cause of Christ.

Paul's admonition that all things be done "decently and in order" applies to the matter of wills. The only thing worse than having no will at all is having a defective one, a potentially cruel booby trap. Consequently, preparing a will is not a do-it-yourself proposition. Lawyers charge as little as $20 for drawing up a will, and even a detailed one rarely costs more than $50. E. N. Harrison disposed of an 80 million dollar railroad empire with a will of ninety-nine words, possibly costing as little as $10.

Consider these precautions: Don't change a will by writing over or scratching out. Don't sign more than one copy. Mention percentages rather than specific sums. Choose an executor both for his business sense and his Christian philosophy. Don't let your will become invalidated by being out of date.

Above all, don't postpone making your will; tomorrow may be too late. The following entry appears in John Wesley's diary: "In the evening one sat behind me in the pulpit at Bristol who was one of our masters at Kingswood. A little after he left the school he likewise left the society. Riches flowed in upon him, with which, having no relations, Mr. Spencer designed to do much good — after his death. 'But God said unto him, Thou fool!' Two hours after, he died intestate and left all his money to — be scrambled for! Reader, if you have not done it already, make your will before you sleep!"

Do it indeed. It is a matter of love and death.

The "10-70-20" Formula for Wealth

by George M. Bowman

Author, Here's How to Succeed with Your Money

Before you get into this, call your spouse so that you can read it aloud.

It is a simple formula for dividing your income that can change a slave into a prince.

No, it is not a get-well-quick drug designed to give you a momentary lift. It is a tried and proven remedy that will make you financially healthy.

For a formula to be successful at making you a success with your money, it must enable you to do three things:

1. It should reveal to you a plan to provide for future prosperity.

2. It should enable you to comfortably support yourself and your family.

3. It should provide a way by which you can pay off your debts.

If you will adopt the "10-70-20" formula — no sides missing, it makes provision for: savings and investment; living expenses; debts. All at the same time! Now look at the diagram on the next page.

Never lay aside less than 10 percent for your future estate. That is, 10 percent of your net income after taxes and tithe have been paid. Put this 10 percent to work at building an estate for you and your family.

Always remember, there is more pleasure in running up a surplus than there is in spending it. Let me illustrate my point with hard, sound facts.

Copyright 1960 Moody Bible Institute

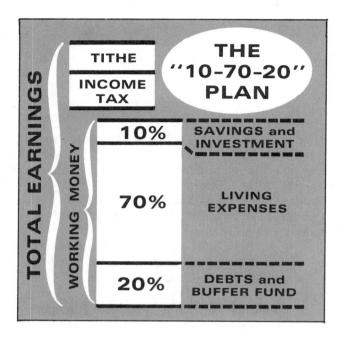

Suppose your net income is $350 a month. The formula calls for a saving and investment of $35 a month. Under guidance, you put this to work in a cross-section of select securities and earn an average of 6 percent compounded yearly. Suppose you have thirty-five years left during which you will draw an income. Do you know how much your $35-a-month investment would amount to at the end of that time? Your total deposits would amount to $12,600 but you would be worth $33,205.20 in cold, hard cash!

That is an extra $20,605.20 that your monthly investment of $35 earned for you. That's about four years' extra earnings that you received. But you didn't have to work for that money. You were wise. You learned that one does not have a large amount of money by working for it; to have such an amount one must have money working for him.

For those of you who earn larger incomes, the returns would be larger proportionately. For example, $50 a month at 6 percent would amount to $47,436 in thirty years. Your total investment would be only $18,000.

Now, here is an unusual thing. Every person I know who has tried this for any length of time, claims that the investment of 10 percent of their net income did not interfere with their standard of living at all. The secret of it is this: you must accept this as an absolute law in your life — a law you will not disobey.

Once you have assumed that you must get along without that 10 percent, it will never be a burden to you to pay that small amount from your income to buy financial peace of mind for yourself and your family.

Some have learned to do it easily by assuming that they have received a cut in pay equal to 10 percent of their net income, and they just have to live on what's left. After a short while they discover that the 10 percent isn't missed at all.

Never allow your living expenses to exceed 70 percent. Here is where you really put the controller to work. The controller is you. You must determine to control your living expenditures so that they never rise above seven-tenths of your net income. For some, this might mean two or three evening dinners a week with only macaroni and cheese or hamburger steak, but don't worry. You'll soon be eating porterhouse steaks — smothered in mushrooms!

Your living expenses will include some or all of the following: home payments, medical and insurance costs, utilities, home maintenance costs, miscellaneous. You must keep your living expenses within 70 percent if this formula is going to work for you.

Use 20 percent to pay debts. To pay debts without pain

has been a universal problem since man decided to lend money to his neighbor. It is easier to pay debts than to avoid them. But you must have a plan. And that plan must provide that you pay not more than 20 percent of your net income to rid yourself of back bills. Here's how to handle your debts:

Make a list of all your creditors and how much you owe them. Then determine what percentage of the entire amount you owe each one of them.

Then, figure that percentage of the total amount you have allowed for paying debts (20 percent of net income), and place it alongside each creditor's name. For example, let's say that your list of debts looks like this:

Bank loan	$ 500
Car	800
Television	200
Personal loan	500
Total	$2,000

Let's assume that you are earning a net income of $400 a month. You have, according to our formula, 20 percent of $400 or $80 a month with which to pay off your debts. The amount you pay each of your creditors will be as follows:

Bank loan	$20	(25% of total)
Car	32	(40% of total)
Television	8	(10% of total)
Personal loan	20	(25% of total)

Do you see how simple it is to calculate how much you should pay each of your creditors? "But," you argue, "my payments are far more than 20 percent of my income!" All right, you must visit all your creditors and sell them on the idea of lowering your payments to comply with the formula. If you do not do this, you will upset the entire plan by dipping into your allowance for living costs; or worse still, by tapping your savings — just to pay debts. Remember, you are your number one creditor! Don't make the mistake of thinking this formula cannot work for you. It will work for anyone who is willing to put it to work in his own life. The wealth of any nation that has a democratic government usually finds its way into the hands of a few of its citizens — comparatively speaking. Do you know why? Because the few know how to obey the rules that lead to success with money. That's why. There is no reason under the sun that you and I cannot be among the few who obey the rules.

"To possess money is very well; it may be a most valuable servant; to be possessed by it, is to be possessed by a devil, and one of the meanest and worst kind of devils."

— Tryon Edwards

·•··•··•··•··•··•··•··•··•··•··•··•··•··•·

Money management is not so much a technique as it is attitude. And when we talk about attitudes, we are dealing with emotions. Thus, money management is basically self-management or control of one's emotions. Unless one learns to control himself, he is no more likely to control his money than he is to discipline his habits, his time, or his temper. Undisciplined money usually spells undisciplined persons.

— Robert J. Hastings

Teach Your Kids to Manage Money

by William Bard
Free-lance writer

Your daughter's record player blares dozens of records all day long. Your son makes constant requests for more "date" money. These "minor" annoyances can indicate serious financial irresponsibility on the part of your children! By placing them on a budget based on a weekly allowance (rather than haphazard handouts), you will be helping yourself in the short run — and teaching the youngsters a valuable long-term lesson.

The first step, say experts at the National Consumer Finance Association, is to establish the allowance. Explain to your child why he needs a budget, and let him get into the act. Ask him to draw up a list of his weekly expenditures. A youngster likes being treated as an adult, and if you handle the budgeting as a lesson in life, rather than punishment, he won't resent it.

It might be a good idea to discuss each item with him to see if all his expenses are necessary. By limiting his "incidental expenses" — and holding the line firmly — you will be forcing him to keep a careful watch on his cash while allowing him some latitude and choice. But be sure to allow adequate money for lunches, carfare, school supplies, and church donations.

A firm policy on allowances benefits your youngster and saves wear-and-tear on your wallet. When your child has a "crisis" — he'll need more money than you give him. Try not to succumb to his touching pleas for more than he's due — but suggest in advance several ways for him to build up emergency funds.

Make sure he knows some surefire methods of earning "extra income." Babysitting, lawnmowing, or dishwashing, for you or a neighbor, are some examples of work he can easily do.

Encourage him to save. Give him a short-winded but farsighted lesson in banks and interest, and open a savings account in his name. Eventually, the account can be used for college or as a "nest egg." Parents can deduct certain deposits made in a child's savings account from their taxes under the Uniform Gifts to Minors Act. Don't insist that your child save all his money; financial experts say he should have practice in spending as well!

A third way in which your child can conquer a "crisis" will teach him about credit. Give him a small loan — and as he pays it back, deduct a token interest from his allowance. This will teach him that to establish credit he must also establish his reliability. Fatherly credit given to a child will show him he can have what he wants now by paying for it as he uses it.

Loans, savings accounts, and "moonlighting" won't teach your child much if he doesn't learn how to use his money. The limits you place on his allowance may help, but you should provide him with additional guidelines on shopping. Warn him against making foolish expenditures just because he's earned or saved some extra money. Be tactful in what you tell him. Limiting his financial freedom will eliminate the important lesson mistakes can give him. If the house fills up with feathers, fragrances, goldfish, and posters — and your child chronically complains of "insufficient funds" even after you've budgeted him — you'll know it's time for a little talk about excess.

Remember that part of teaching him how to use money depends upon how *you* use it! Repay all your debts on time. Don't be excessive — but don't be afraid to show your youngster the benefits of good money management, such as a baseball game, a family outing, or some other expenditure made for leisure's sake. You'll be letting him know that financial responsibility has its rewards. The point that can't be stressed enough is: don't give in! The only time you should "break" the budget is when you quietly add to his savings account as college rolls around. There is no "financial crisis" a child has that can't be met in an adult way. This doesn't mean you should take all the fun out of childhood by setting unreasonable limits — but if some degree of discipline isn't provided, the youngster won't be able to "cash in" later on the fun of being a grownup!

•••••••••••••••••••••••••••••••••••••••

Premarital counseling should pay a great deal more attention to the economic difficulties which a young couple will face, says Robert O. Hermann, of the University of California in Davis. Discussing the increase in teen-age weddings, Dr. Hermann points out that, in addition to meager financial resources, they usually have problems because of their unrealistic expectations and adolescent values. Their "impulsive spending behavior," and the "almost obsessive need" for an automobile, and, of course, their lack of any economic guidance or education all spell trouble, increased by the commonly rapid arrival of the first child. "Because of their low incomes, teen-age couples must depend to some extent on consumer credit and parents' assistance," with all the problems inherent in each. In short, "the financial problems facing teen-age marriages are so numerous and so complex that even well-prepared and well-informed teen-age couples may find them almost overwhelming."

— Journal of Home Economics

William's Partner

by Philip Jerome Cleveland

It was a bright, promising day when a boy just sixteen years of age said farewell to his people and turned into the wide world to seek his fortune. As he trudged along, an aged gentleman, captain of a canal boat, recognized the boy and stepped to his side.

"Well, William, where are you going?"

"I don't know," answered the honest lad. "I must make a living for myself."

"There is no trouble about that. Just be sure you start right and you'll get along nicely."

"But there is only one trade I know."

"And what is that, my boy?"

"Making soap and candles."

The old salt grasped the boy's shoulder as he said: "Well, let me pray with you once more and give you an old man's advice. Then I will let you go."

The two knelt and prayed. Then the captain spoke seriously.

"Someone will soon be the leading soapmaker in New York. It might as well be you as the next fellow. I sincerely hope it will be you. Be a good man, William; give your heart to the Carpenter of Nazareth."

The old man paused a moment and then looked deeply into the youth's solemn eyes. "Listen, William. Give the Lord all that truly belongs to him, a portion of every dollar you ever earn. Make an honest soap, give a full pound and I am certain that the Lord will bless you. Make him your partner, William."

The lad thanked the earnest captain and turned his face

toward the great city. Lonesome and far from home, he nevertheless remembered words his mother had spoken to him and the advice of the aged Christian man. He decided to seek first the kingdom of heaven and become a Christian.

The first dollar earned brought up the matter of the tenth — the Lord's share. "If the Lord will take one-tenth, I will give that."

Ten cents on every dollar was set aside for the work of the Master. He engaged in the soap business, made an honest soap, and gave a full pound. He said to his bookkeeper one day: "Enter an open account with the Lord in our business book."

"Wh-wh-at?" stammered the bookkeeper.

"An open account with the Lord and carry one-tenth of all our income in the ledger. It shall be his!"

William prospered and his business doubled, tripled; he found himself growing rich. "Give the Lord two-tenths," he ordered a few months later.

Business increased amazingly. "Give the Lord three-tenths." Soon the message was changed to four-tenths and five-tenths.

Never did a soap manufacturer have a more surprising and stunning rise to fame and popularity and fortune.

And what was the name of the boy who followed an old canal-boat captain's advice? It is known all over the world even today for fine soap: William Colgate.

•-•-•-•-•-•-•-•-•-•-•-•-•-•-•-•-•-•-

Don't think that friendship authorizes you to say disagreeable things to your intimates. The nearer you come into relation with a person, the more necessary do tact and courtesy become.

— OLIVER WENDELL HOLMES

13

DISCOVERING SEXUAL INTIMACY

What the Bible Says about Sex

by Billy Graham
Evangelist and author

A man prominent in public life plans the seduction of a beautiful young woman; repulsed, he rapes her, then casts her off, with tragedy resulting for both.

The wife of a government figure tries in vain to seduce her husband's young associate — then charges him with attempted rape, causing his imprisonment.

The people of a great city, boasting of their sexual "freedom," turn to perversion, with both male and female homosexuals flagrantly practicing their deviations and demanding the right to do so openly.

Are these accounts taken from today's newspaper? Not at all. Though they all have the ring of today, they are taken right from the Bible. A book that has never gone out-of-date, the Bible could properly be called the world's most reliable textbook on sex. No book deals more forthrightly with the subject. As history, it records without distortion the sexual aberrations of its times. As biography, it refuses to gloss over the sex sins of its heroes, but details them and their consequences with straightforward explicit-

---

Copyright 1970 The Reader's Digest Association, Inc.

ness. As philosophy, it sets forth the changeless standards of God.

In this day of the "permissive society," we hear many voices on the important subject of sex — most of them confusing. I think it is time we listened once again to the biblical admonitions upon which Judeo-Christian moral standards were built. Sex education is a burning issue in many American communities. I am convinced that sex education without moral guidelines could be disastrous.

One thing the Bible does not teach is that sex in itself is sin. Far from being prudish, the Bible celebrates sex and its proper use, presenting it as God-created, God-ordained, God-blessed. It makes plain that God himself implanted the physical magnetism between the sexes for two reasons: for the propagation of the human race, and for the expression of that kind of love between man and wife that makes for true oneness. His command to the first man and woman to be "one flesh" was as important as his command to "be fruitful and multiply."

The Bible makes plain that evil, when related to sex, means not the use of something inherently corrupt but the misuse of something pure and good. It teaches clearly that sex can be a wonderful servant but a terrible master; that it can be a creative force more powerful than any other in the fostering of love, companionship, happiness — or can be the most destructive of all of life's forces.

The "thou shalt nots" of Scripture are not pious prohibitions aimed at taking all the joy out of life; they are signposts set by God himself to protect our happiness and to help make our life's journey as tragedy-free as possible. Every command that God gives is for our good.

This truth gets too little emphasis in these days when a "sexual revolution" is being proclaimed, when enticements to illicit sex leer from every side. The flood of "sexploitation" grows daily worse — in novels, magazines, movies,

TV, advertising. Meanwhile, the church as a whole remains mute.

In many churches, one can attend services for a full year without once hearing the word "sin" mentioned. Not a few ministers and teachers of religion have fallen prey to this permissive thinking, which holds that there are no absolutes, that the right or wrong of an act depends upon the circumstances of time and place. As for such acts as premarital or extramarital sex, these are said to be justified "if the relationship is meaningful" and "if it hurts nobody else." With even religious leaders talking this way, it is small wonder that youth is bewildered, and that the church's moral authority is eroding almost to the vanishing point.

To counter the disastrous effects of this new permissiveness, which is, as has been said, nothing more than "the old immorality brought up-to-date," we need a bracing dose of biblical morality. Amid our shifting moral standards, the commandment "Thou shalt not commit adultery" stands as firm today as when God wrote it on tablets of stone. That commandment has never been revoked or watered down. No man ever really "breaks" it — though many have broken themselves upon it. And so have nations.

We of the Western world, on a sex binge never before equaled in modern times, should be wise enough to heed history's lessons. For history conclusively teaches that the decay of a nation inevitably follows the decay of its sex standards. Theologian Paul Tillich, in his book *Morality and Beyond,* stated flatly: "Without the immanence of the moral imperative, both culture and religion disintegrate." And sociologist Pitirim Sorokin has warned that "the group that tolerates sexual anarchy is endangering its very survival."

To God's people, living in societies given to the worship of obscene fertility gods and goddesses, ancient Israel's prophets thundered this commandment repeatedly. And to Israel's young, her teachers constantly recounted the stories of biblical characters caught up in what might be called "sex situations," driving home the lesson that sexual sin can only make the strong weak, the wise foolish, the great ordinary.

Illustrating the nobility of chastity was Joseph, handsome young servant of the Egyptian ruler Potiphar, who resisted the allurements of Potiphar's wanton wife and who went to jail rather than betray his ideals. And Daniel, who in Babylon dared to decry the immoralities of Belshazzar's court and predict to the ruler's face his kingdom's finish; and who lived to become prime minister under three kings and two empires — one of the greatest statesmen of all time.

Stories of the otherwise great who allowed moral weakness to stain their images included Samson, the strongest of men, whose undoing began with his unbridled lust and ended in the infamy of Delilah's lap and his own tragic suicide. And Solomon, who, given wisdom above all others, nevertheless besmirched his life through lecherous dalliance with innumerable concubines. Most tragic of all, perhaps, was David, Israel's greatest king, whose guilty anguish over his adultery with Bathsheba was expressed in the saddest prayer in all literature: "Have mercy upon me, O God. Wash me thoroughly from mine iniquity, and cleanse me from my sin. For I acknowledge my transgressions; and my sin is ever before me."

Tristram Coffin says in his book *The Sex Kick*: "Modern lovers have learned to fornicate but not to love. Contraception and antibiotics have put sex within the 'safe' area, lessening the fears of pregnancy and venereal disease." But, as others have said, no one has invented a diaphragm for the soul and conscience. And so thousands have learned, as David did, that nothing can etch such indelible scars of guilt as sexual sin.

The New Testament backs up in every way the sex ideals found in the Old Testament. Jesus endorsed the prophets' strictures on illicit sex — and went beyond them. He warned: "Ye have heard that it was said by them of old time, Thou shalt not commit adultery. But I say unto you that whosoever looketh upon a woman to lust after her hath committed adultery with her already in his heart."

Writing to Christians in vice-ridden Corinth, the sex capital of the ancient world, where temple prostitutes accommodated both men and women, St. Paul said: "Know ye not that your body is the temple of the Holy Spirit? He that committeth fornication sinneth against his own body." There is almost no aspect of human sexuality that the Bible does not deal with. Even the "unnatural" acts of sex are portrayed — and condemned with blunt candor in both the Old and New Testaments. Speaking through Moses, God commanded: "Thou shalt not lie with mankind, as with womankind. It is abomination." The Apostle Paul said, "Neither the impure . . . the adulterer . . . the pervert . . . or the foul-mouthed shall have any share in the kingdom of God."

Nowhere does the Bible suggest that the battle between the flesh and the spirit is easy. Neither does it suggest that to be tempted is sin, or that it is abnormal to experience sex hunger. But it does teach, by precept and example, that there are spiritual resources we can use to overcome our illicit urges.

Shining through the Bible is God's readiness to forgive sin, sexual or otherwise, and his eagerness to bring peace of mind and heart to the repentant. But the natural consequences of our sins will have to be suffered. The ugly memories cannot be forgotten; the illegitimate baby cannot be unborn. David was forgiven his adultery, but he had to take his punishment.

Concerning sex sin, Jesus always dealt tenderly. There is no more wonderful illustration of Christ's compassion than his defense of the woman taken in adultery. Ringed by the self-righteous about to stone her, he said, "Let him who is without sin among you cast the first stone." As he spoke, his finger wrote some words in the dust. What the words were we are not told. But, seeing them, the mob of accusers quickly dispersed. Whereupon Jesus said to her, "Neither do I condemn thee; go, and sin no more."

For all those caught in a web of sexual confusion and guilt, that is still the divine Word.

•●··●··●··●··●··●··●··●··●··●··●··●··●··●·

The man and woman who share a wholesome concept of sex, and who, through love and companionship, find themselves impelled toward complete identification through physical oneness, can reach heights of communion with each other that overflow into gratitude to God for the wonders of his creation. This attitude is achieved through realizing the truth about sex, seeing it as the source of life and fellowship, knowing that sex is of God — thus it is good.

When sex is understood in this light, the married sexual relationship is altogether right and lovely. Since the sex function for humans is an act of choice, not limited to the initiation of life, but capable of being lifted into lofty experiences of fellowship, there is given to mankind the potential also of exercising choice as to offspring. Therefore whatever contributes, without physical or emotional damage, to aiding human choices as to the number and timing of their young, as well as enhancing their sexual responsiveness, becomes desirable as a procedure for husband and wife.

— JOSEPH B. HENRY

The Art of Married Love

by David Mace
Author, marriage counselor, and Professor of Family Sociology, Wake Forest University

There are many causes of unhappiness in marriage. Some are complex and difficult to deal with. But one is simple and comparatively easy to remove. Yet it probably causes thousands of marriages to drift on the rocks every year — quite unnecessarily.

I can best describe it as a fundamental misunderstanding between men and women about love and its sexual expression. As a marriage counselor, I have recognized the problem again and again as the real — although unrecognized — difficulty between husbands and wives who come to me for help.

Let's begin with the man. What impels him into marriage? Many considerations, of course — the need for companionship, for a home of his own, for children. Yet most urgent is his need for sexual fulfillment. This urge is strong and persistent — as it ought to be, in view of the end it serves. When a man dreams of marriage to the woman he loves all his feelings toward her are grouped around this central and significant desire.

In order to achieve it, however, the man knows that he must make himself pleasing to the woman. The trouble is that once the man has won the woman in the sense of having made her his wife he may think that the billing and cooing are unnecessary. He tends to dispense with the "frills" of lovemaking.

Many a man just doesn't see that there is anything wrong with this. If you ask him whether he still loves his wife he replies at once that of course he does. If you ask for evidence, he points out that he chooses to go on living with her despite all the other charming women he might have, that he works hard to provide her with a good home and that in this particular way or that he has modified his habits to agree with hers. What more could any woman want?

Perhaps it's time now to consider what the woman does want. Her orientation toward marriage is subtly different. Like everything else about her it's more complex. Consequently it isn't so easy to assess.

I would venture the statement, however, that the basic drive which impels a woman into marriage is the need for a secure and sustained love relationship. Of course this includes the sexual expression of love, but for a woman that is never so important in itself as for the normal man. For a woman, physical intimacy is essentially part of something wider and deeper. Her evaluation of sexual experience is almost entirely conditioned by the atmosphere which surrounds it, the overtones of emotion which vibrate through it. Unless the setting is right, it may be meaningless or positively distasteful.

This again is what nature intended. The female doesn't have to concern herself unduly about seeing that the sexual encounter takes place. The male does that. Her function is to exercise discrimination and to encourage or discourage the male according to how he behaves. All he is immediately concerned about is to win her. But she is concerned with the implications — parenthood and homemaking. She wants a man whose love will last, who will not abandon her when as a mother she becomes vulnerable and dependent.

That is why she needs to be repeatedly assured of love. It isn't that she is vain and wants to be flattered. (The probability is that men are vainer than women.) It is that instinctively she withdraws from giving herself sexually except in an atmosphere of continuing love and protection.

So a woman is supremely happy when she knows that her man deeply loves her. She knows that her physical charms represent not only a reward which she gives him for his devotion, but also a means of making him love her more than ever. In short, she knows that she can exchange sexual satisfaction for love if she manages skillfully. Not that the average woman doesn't enjoy the physical expression of love as much as her husband. But all the time, she approaches it in a different way.

Now we see why a wife can be deeply hurt and offended when her husband seems to take their sex life for granted. Yet many may fail completely to comprehend this. To him what is important is his constancy. Repeated assurances of his love may seem not only unnecessary but theatrical.

Yet the wise husband knows that his wife's happiness will be incomplete so long as he neglects the small tokens of love which, after all, cost so little in relation to what they achieve. It is curious how some men will praise their wives to their friends yet seldom praise them to their faces.

If a husband persistently starves his wife of love he may find her becoming sexually unresponsive. I have known such men who complained that their wives were frigid. They were themselves entirely to blame. What every man should plainly understand is that in lovemaking his wife's function is response, and there must therefore be something to respond to. By failing to create the atmosphere of love, a man may render his wife so incapable of response that he finds himself deprived of the sexual fulfillment which is so important to his happiness.

I have said enough about how the husband may fail his wife. Now let's see the pattern the other way round. For the wife may just as easily fail her husband.

Because a man's need of sexual fulfillment in marriage is so strong, he will be bewildered and deeply hurt if he is denied it. If his wife then assures him that she still loves him he will be yet more bewildered. How can she say that, when she doesn't prove it in the most obvious way? He will inevitably feel that she is hypocritical. In time the love he once had for her may even turn to hate.

Remember that for a man the emotion of love culminates in sexual union. If that climax is denied him the whole process is brought to a standstill. The word love, the caress, the act of endearment — how can he offer these lesser expressions when the greater expression which they symbolize and to which they lead is spurned? Surely the wife who accepts one but rejects the other is a hypocrite; so he thinks.

The wife who doesn't understand this can easily wreck her marriage. And she will not find understanding of it in her own instinct (because here she is different than her husband.) That is why some wonderful women make a complete muddle of things and then are at a loss to know what went wrong.

Once two people really grasp the truth and understand what has gone wrong, they can usually, with a little help and encouragement, put it right. It's essentially a question of getting the couple to strike a bargain: he will try to meet her need for affection and attention because in giving her happiness he will find her more responsive to his needs. Once the deadlock is broken, warm feeling flows again. As their own individual needs are increasingly met, they become more able and willing to give themselves to each other.

I know that a great many married people could be happier together if they were more fully aware of this difference between men and women. Mishandled, it can certainly wreck marriages. Rightly managed, it enriches rather than estranges. The husband is able to draw from his wife a sexual response which enables her to value their physical intimacy as much as he does. At the same time the wife, through her own outgoing love, is able to kindle in her husband an affection and gratitude which make him eager to please her at every possible opportunity. And that is a description of a happy marriage.

The Superlatives of Sex

by S. I. McMillen, M.D.

Author, None of These Diseases, *and College physician, Houghton College, Houghton, New York*

"Doctor, I can't sleep, and I can't enjoy anything any more. I know when my trouble began — when Gil started to play cards with a bunch of fellows. They don't gamble, but they go out one night every single week to an expensive hotel for a big steak dinner. Then they play cards until one or two in the morning. Everything is on the up and up, but . . ."

Pretty Mrs. Steiner choked a bit and then continued. "Oh, I know I'm foolish. But still, here is the way I look at it. With our five children, we have to watch every penny to make ends meet. I've told Gil that I get tired and nervous staying home month in and month out. I've asked him to take me out to the movies or to dinner once in a while, but he always says there is no money for that and a babysitter, too. But he takes the little money we could use for recreation and spends it on himself. As a result there is considerable tension between us, and we aren't enjoying each other at all."

Here was a marriage falling apart because an important cohesive had been lost. The password to a happy marriage is "together" — live together, play together, work together, think together, and plan together. Two people cannot be held together long unless there is some sort of binding force, and sexuality is a short-lived binder, as the sex marriages of Hollywood have long demonstrated. Because sex is the only cohesive that many couples know anything about, it is

Copyright 1963 Fleming H. Revell Company

not strange that about one out of every three marriages falls apart.

There is one binder that has never failed to hold two people together — love; "Love never fails." This love is not the "puppy love" played up in novels and on TV. What is love, the element so essential to every happy marriage?

Although most people understand the meaning of sexuality, few have a clear conception of what love is. The vagueness concerning love is evidenced by the fact that the dictionary gives eight different definitions. Here I wish to discuss only the meaning of love as an outward reach of the mind to help and please others. Love in this meaning of the word is not sexual, yet this kind of love must be present if the superlatives are to be obtained from sex. The superlatives in sex — the best, the most, and for the longest time — are only possible when thoughtfulness, consideration, and love for others exist.

Man is continents away from the superlatives when he blatantly asserts that he is going "to look after No. 1," both in his business and his sex life. He perpetually berates his wife for her faults, yet he can't understand why she doesn't exhibit enthusiasm for him and his approaches. Although he has had several liaisons with his secretaries, he fails to realize why none of them satisfied him. Variety and frequency is a mocking substitute for quality.

This highly-sexed, egocentric individual gets practically nothing out of sex for the simple reason that he is sadly lacking in love. As a result, he is always disappointed and frustrated sexually.

Dr. Carl Jung recognized the underlying reason why many a man has such an unhappy existence: "It arises from his having no love, but only sexuality . . . and no understanding, because he has failed to read the meaning of his own existence."

Yvonne had this kind of a problem. She put her head

on my desk and sobbed. After awhile she blurted out, "I was only kidding when I said something about Mike's mother. But he got mean and said something awful about my mother. Then I slapped him good and hard across his face. Just what he deserved! But the big brute up and punched me in the face. Look at my eye! I'm moving out! I'm taking my two kids and going back to Mom's. I love Mike, but I can't take this!"

Then, as Yvonne held an ice bag over her left eye and looked at me with the other, I gave her a little marriage counseling, somewhat belated, to be sure. I ended my lecture with words something like these: "Yvonne, in every marriage, situations are bound to arise in which one of the partners must give in, out of consideration and love for the other partner. Don't feel sorry for yourself if you discover that you are the one who has to give in most of the time. I have strange but good news for you: when you give in to Mike, you are losing your life in the one and only way to find life and worthwhile happiness. The secret of happiness in married life depends on each partner making small sacrifices, readily and cheerfully.

"You say you have love for Mike. Is it the kind of love that suffers long and is kind? The only love that will stand the acid test of everyday living is that which God describes and gives to those who walk in the light of his commandments: 'Love is patient; love is kind and envies no one. Love is never boastful, nor conceited, nor rude; never selfish, not quick to take offense. Love keeps no scores of wrongs. . . . There is nothing love cannot face; there is no limit to its faith, its hope, and its endurance. Love will never come to an end.' "

Love is a basic necessity, not only for obtaining the superlatives of sex but also for living. Dr. Smiley Blanton, in his book *Love or Perish,* says: "For more than forty years I have sat in my office and listened while people of all ages and classes told me of their hopes and fears. . . . As I look back over the long, full years, one truth emerges clearly in my mind — the universal need for love. . . . They cannot survive without love: they must have it or they will perish."

Many couples are not happy. They go through the motions of sex but have no sexual fulfillment. If they have other affairs, their frustrations only increase. They hardly ever sense that the feelings they long for can only be obtained where love for one another exists. There can be no real ecstasy unless the sex act expresses a love and intense awareness of the needs and desires of the other. Wrangling during the day will make sex lifeless and mechanical, if not repulsive.

Love is as essential to happiness and mental health as is food to our physical well-being. Men particularly fail to comprehend that sex alone is inadequate nourishment for a happy marriage. Orgasm in men is almost a purely mechanical act, while in women it is much more complex. A woman must be fully aware of the man's thoughtfulness for her, of his fidelity to her, and of his love that puts her pleasure ahead of his own.

Psychiatrist Max Levin recognized that unselfish love is necessary for obtaining the superlatives in sex: "It is obvious, then, that maturity is a prerequisite for a happy marriage. In the immature state of infancy there is no obligation to give. The infant receives; he is not expected to do anything else. The success of a marriage will depend in great degree on the extent to which the partners have outgrown their infantile dependency and achieved the capacity to assume responsibility, to wish more to give than to receive."

The love that is thoughtful and unselfish makes life's greatest dream come to pass, but sex without love can make of life a horrible nightmare. One of many who discovered this truth the hard way was the prodigal son. His was the voice of immaturity; removed from his father's precepts and wasting the endowments of money and body "with riotous living," his soul became an empty void inhabited only by haunting echoes. He hit bottom in one of life's pigpens where he yearned to eat the empty husks that the hogs were crunching. He discovered that sex in a country removed from God's will is empty, disappointing, and ugly. Self-gratification is ever a one-way street — with a hogpen at the end.

As the young man remembered that his father's house always had "bread enough and to spare," he discovered that "the horrible religious inhibitions" were not as bad as he had been led to believe. He began to sense that there is a close relationship between proper inhibitions and abundant blessings.

When he had left home, his immaturity was evidenced by his attitude of "Give me." When he returned, repenting, the spirit of "Give me" was absent. In its place was thoughtfulness for others — "Make me a servant."

How important is the matter of sex in the marriage relationship? Dr. Emil Novak, of Johns Hopkins Medical School, states convincingly that "there are many women who are physically and emotionally normal, who love their husbands devotedly, who have borne children, yet have never throughout their married lives experienced any great degree of physical satisfaction from the sex act. Nor do they feel frustrated or cheated."

In fact, some authorities state that less than half of married women have ever experienced sexual orgasm. However, the emotions they derive from the sexual act are beautiful and completely gratifying without any need for physical climax. Their emotions are diffused throughout their bodies. To them the glowing embers of hardwood are just as satisfying as the quick, bright flash of a little gunpowder.

Because of their ignorance of these facts, many young women develop frustrations and resentments that tragically worsen the marital situation. If thoughtfulness for one another predominates, then these same women will experience increasingly greater satisfaction from the marital relationship. Possession of God-given love will prevent frustrations, unhappiness, and divorce, with their long trains of mental and physical diseases.

Someone has said: "The cure for all the ills and wrongs, the cares, the sorrows and the crimes of humanity, all lie in one word: 'love.' It is the divine vitality that everywhere produces and restores life. To each and every one of us, it gives the power of working miracles if we will."

•--•--•--•--•--•--•--•--•--•--•--•--•--•--•--•--•

"Have ye not read, that he which made them at the beginning made them male and female . . . and they twain shall be one flesh?" (Matthew 19:4, 5). It is important to realize that the sexual passion is not just tolerated in marriage, condoned as rather unworthy yet all the same necessary. Sex intercourse enjoyed rightly and in a human way is an act of the virtue of purity. It is none the colder for that. Purity is not the absence or denial of passion, but is passion justly ordered. In this matter a married couple will help one another. Their bodies are granted, their passions satisfied, not by indulgence, for that defeats its own end, but by a human act full of grace that does not diminish but rather increases the ardor, even the passion, of love.

— T. G. WAYNE

Understanding Sex in Marriage

by Herbert J. Miles

Author, Sexual Happiness in Marriage, *and Professor of Sociology, Carson-Newman College.*

The Bible is not basically a book on science, agriculture, art, music, architecture, or sociology. Yet the Bible contains many ideas concerning these and many other topics. In a similar manner, the Bible is not a book on sex. However, it does contain many specific ideas concerning sex and how sex fits into the total plan of creation. It should be helpful to any couple to study carefully some of the Bible passages definitely related to the place of sexuality in marriage and family life. Let us examine seven such passages.

1. "So God created man in his own image, in the image of God created he him, male and female created he them. And God blessed them, and said unto them, Be fruitful, and multiply, and replenish the earth and subdue it" (Genesis 1:27-28).

God created both man and woman as complete individuals. On the nonphysical side of their nature, they are persons, made in the image of God. They are personalities that are intelligent, rational, free, and accountable. On the physical side, they possess physical bodies including sexuality and the capacity to reproduce. In the command to "be fruitful, and multiply," we have sex in the creation of man and woman for the purpose of procreation (reproduction). This is basic in the plan of God in creation.

2. "And therefore shall a man leave his father and his

Copyright 1967 Zondervan Publishing House

mother, and shall cleave unto his wife; and they shall be one flesh. And they were both naked, the man and his wife, and were not ashamed" (Genesis 2:24-25).

The central part of this passage is the phrase: "shall be one flesh." This phrase refers to the bodily and spiritual union of husband and wife in sexual intercourse. It includes a definite sexual experience (orgasms) for both husband and wife. This "one-flesh" relationship does not refer specifically to reproduction, but rather to sex as a profound personal experience of spiritual and physical pleasure between husband and wife. Many other Bible passages clearly emphasize this same concept (Genesis 24:67; Ecclesiastes 9:9; Song of Solomon). The nature of this pleasure is at the same time both physical and spiritual. It involves the total physical body and the total mental, emotional, and spiritual nature of both husband and wife. It involves the action of the total personality. God created this one-flesh experience to be the most intense height of physical intimacy and the most profound depth of spiritual oneness between husband and wife. It is well to note that Jesus quoted this passage as a basis for his ideas about marriage (Matthew 19:4-5; Mark 10:9).

3. "And God saw everything that he had made, and behold it was very good" (Genesis 1:31).

When animals were created, the Genesis record states, "God saw that it was good" (Genesis 1:25). However, when God created man and woman, male and female, in his image, "Behold, it was very good."

The meaning of this passage is that the Creator-God formed in his mind a plan to create male and female persons in his image. After the creative act, he viewed his finished product, man and woman, and they appeared to be an accurate duplicate, a perfect reproduction of his original purpose and design. What is it that is good? The "maleness" of man is very good. The "femaleness" of woman is very good. Both man and woman were created with physical, reproductive bodies. At the same time, they were created spiritually in the image of God. That is, they were persons characterized by self-consciousness, self-knowledge, self-control, the ability to think, to choose, to will, etc. This total, complete unit of mind and body is "very good."

4. "My son, attend unto my wisdom, and bow thine ear to my understanding; that thou mayest regard discretion, and that thy lips may keep knowledge.

For the lips of a strange woman drop as an honeycomb, and her mouth is smoother than oil: but her end is bitter as wormwood, sharp as a two-edged sword. Her feet go down to death; her steps take hold on hell. Lest thou shouldest ponder the path of life, her ways are movable, that thou canst not know them. Hear me now therefore, O ye children, and depart not from the words of my mouth. Remove thy way far from her, and come not nigh the door of her house . . ." (Proverbs 5:1-8).

"And why wilt thou, my son, be ravished with a strange woman, and embrace the bosom of a stranger?" (Proverbs 5:20)

This passage gives strong and stern warnings to young men about the misuse of their sexual life. They are instructed not to express their sexual nature in promiscuous intercourse with loose women. Then, these exacting negative warnings are followed by beautiful positive instructions indicating how young men should meet their sexual needs. These instructions are as follows:

"Drink waters out of thine own cistern, and running waters out of thine own well. Let thy fountain be blessed: and rejoice with the wife of thy youth. Let her be as the loving hind and pleasant roe; let her breasts satisfy thee at all times; and be thou ravished always with her love" (Proverbs 5:15, 18-19).

This passage in clear and distinct tones states that a young man is to meet his sexual needs in sexual intercourse with his wife. To do so will fill him with happiness, joy, and rejoicing. His wife is described as tender, gentle, beautiful, graceful, charming, and satisfying. She is referred to as his "cistern" (verse 15), his "stream of running water" (verse 15), and his "fountain" (verse 18). These three figures are symbolic of his wife as his sexual partner. Just as a person's thirst may be continually satisfied by drinking cool, fresh water from a cistern, a clear running stream, or a fountain, so a man's sexual thirst should be regularly met in sexual experiences with his wife. The last part of verse 19 may be translated, "Let your wife's love and your sexual embrace with your wife intoxicate you continually with delight. Always enjoy the ecstasy of her love." Not only is a man's behavior, when he is meeting his sexual needs in marriage with his wife, represented as wisdom and intelligence (verse 1), but God is represented as always knowing, watching, and approving this relationship (verse 21). It is obvious that this entire chapter is discussing sex in marriage as a unitive pleasure between husband and wife. Procreation and children are not mentioned.

5. The clearest passage in the New Testament setting forth the basic truths of the Christian point of view on sexual adjustment in marriage is 1 Corinthians 7:2-5. For our purposes it is helpful to give this passage the following free translation:

"Because of the strong nature of the sexual drive, each man should have his own wife, and each woman should have her own husband. The husband should regularly meet his wife's sexual needs, and the wife should regularly meet her husband's sexual needs. In marriage, just as the wife's body belongs to her husband and he rules over it, so in marriage, the husband's body belongs to his wife and she rules over it. Do not refuse to meet each other's sexual needs, unless you both agree to abstain from intercourse for a short time in order to devote yourselves to prayer. But because of your strong sexual drive, when this short period is past, continue to meet each other's sexual needs by coming together again in sexual intercourse."

There are three ideas concerning sexuality that stand skyscraper-tall out of this passage, commanding our attention.

A. Both husband and wife have definite and equal sexual needs that should be met in marriage. The primitive idea that sex is man's prerogative and that his wife should submit to him, remaining passive and silent, is not only in violation of known scientific facts about woman's sexual nature, but is also in violation of the clear teaching of this Bible passage which states in precise language (1 Corinthians 7:3), "The husband should regularly meet his wife's sexual needs." The passage is saying that women have a definite need for regular sexual experiences in marriage and it assumes that regular sexual orgasms in a sexual experience with her husband are due her, and are necessary to complete the unitive nature of marriage.

B. It is not the responsibility of the husband to meet his own sexual needs, nor is it the responsibility of the wife to meet her own sexual needs. It is a cooperative experience. In this manner, the total needs of both are continually met.

C. The fact that husband and wife enjoy meeting each other's sexual needs as life moves on in this unitive relationship does not conflict with the Hebrew-Christian concept of a devout spiritual life. Rather, this Scripture implies that an efficient Christian life and an efficient sexual adjustment in marriage really go together. Note that Paul intersperses the husband and wife's sex life with their prayer life (1 Corinthians 7:5).

6. "Finally, brethren, we beseech and exhort you in the Lord Jesus Christ that . . . you ought to live and to please God. . . . For this is the will of God . . . that you abstain from immorality; that each one of you know how to take a wife for himself in holiness and in honor, not in the passion

of lust like heathen who do not know God. . . . For God has not called us for uncleanness but in holiness" (1 Thessalonians 4:1-7, selected sentences from the R.S.V.).

By entering marriage the right way one performs the will of God.

These instructions are given "by the authority of the Lord Jesus" (verse 2, Williams).

7. It is necessary to consider the Song of Solomon in order to give an adequate summary to the teaching of the Scriptures on sex life in marriage. It exalts fidelity between married lovers. The Song of Solomon describes pre-New Testament Jewish ideas about love and sexuality in marriage. The Song of Solomon describes in vivid poetic language the physical bodies of married lovers, and does not offend (6:1-10; 7:1-9). Techniques in sexual arousal between husband and wife are implied (2:3; 8:3). The feelings, the attitudes, the imaginations, the dreams, the spiritual joys, the sexual joys, and the romantic happinesses of married lovers are beautifully described.

There are many other passages in the Scriptures that give similar ideas about sex in marriage. In Hebrews 13:4 we are exhorted to "let marriage be held in honor among all, and let the marriage bed be undefiled. . . ." In Exodus 20:14 the command, "Thou shalt not commit adultery," assumes a positive command, "Thou shalt meet thy sexual needs in marriage."

Many young couples entering marriage do not possess clear ideas about the relationship of sex life to basic Christian teachings. Sometimes they entertain vague ideas that sex is necessary, but somewhat "worldly." They have these ideas simply because no one has ever given them a true picture of Bible teaching on this subject. Couples need these basic principles and guidelines to assist them in focusing and crystallizing their own ideas and attitudes on sexual matters into a mature and consistent whole.

Birth Control in Christian Marriage

by J. Allan Petersen

A generation ago parents would no more discuss birth control openly than they would have thought of flying to the moon. Now both have happened. Man has been on the moon and the terms "population explosion" and "birth control" are some of the most common in today's vocabulary. And what was not generally considered a serious concern in that past generation has become a pressing, worldwide problem today. It has broad social, political, spiritual, and moral implications, and is related to famine, pollution, even survival. Congress has established a Commission on Population Growth and the American Future. There has been the sudden emergence of the Zero Population Growth Movement. A proposal has been introduced in Congress that would provide tax incentives to those with only two children, while others advocate some sort of bonus for having no more than a specific number. One government leader considering the environmental pollution in the United States says we are confronted with a "populution problem."

But there is another pertinent consideration: what does the Bible say about birth control? Reasons can be compelling and arguments logical, but these do not establish their morality. We must have a clear understanding of God's divine will for ethical decisions in the realm of marriage and birth control, as in all other areas of life. Let us put simply and within the reach of all, the basic biblical principles that relate to this intimate and yet social problem.

First, birth control is not a basic moral issue. The Bible gives no clear or definite word for or against it. There is a surprising silence on this subject. Scripture speaks strongly and unmistakably about stealing, lying, adultery, and drunkenness, but not a word against birth control. Some refer to the sin of Onan (Genesis 38:9-10) but actually his sin was the refusal to obey the law which required him to beget a son to bear his brother's name. Planned parenthood was not involved at all. Even Genesis 1:28, where God said unto our first parents, "Be fruitful and multiply and replenish the earth," was not an obligation to beget children as much as it was a promise of offspring.

God has no problem in enunciating what he considers of primary importance. There are instructions and principles relating to every marriage and family responsibility. The Bible says much about sex, the role of partners, parental responsibilities, and morality, but nothing on this matter. God could have given a universal law for every family if he desired, but he did not. Since there are so many other factors to be considered, such as age, fertility, and ability, all families cannot be poured into the same mold. Nowhere does the Bible indicate that every man and woman must be married and assume the responsibility of parenthood, nor does it teach that sex in marriage is only for procreation and every interference with this is sinful.

When the Scriptures do not speak clearly and positively on a definite subject, it must then be decided on the basis of scriptural principles. These must be honestly applied by each one with a desire to discover and fulfill God's will for the individual family.

Second, the Bible does teach that one of the results of marriage is procreation, and that children are a blessing. Psalm 127:4-5 states this graphically: "Children are a gift from God; they are his reward. Children born to a young man are like sharp arrows to defend him. Happy is the man who has his quiver full of them."

Over and over again the Bible tells of couples who desired children, prayed for them, and greatly rejoiced over them. What parent has not learned that children satisfy a normal desire, bring deep joy, and help the parents themselves to grow and mature. The presence of children opens up an entire new world to a couple and can be a means of bringing them closer together and discovering a fulfillment found in no other way. The matter of a family should be frankly discussed before marriage, and every married couple should desire to have children.

For the sake of clarity, it should be noted that the birth control movement has never advocated childless marriages, but only the proper spacing of children and limiting offspring when to do so was in the best interest of parent and child. They have taught that children should be planned for and that they should bless every married couple's union. They have not advocated a selfish escape, but a wise and practical planning for children.

Let us not forget that babies are important to God's plan. Whenever he wants to accomplish something great on the earth, he causes a baby to be born. Christ himself was welcomed into a family as a special gift from God, as were all the prophets and apostles.

Third, the Bible does not say how many children a family is to have. This would be impossible. About one in five American women never bear even one child because they are relatively sterile. Others sustain injuries or surgery that limit their child-bearing capacity. The number of children must be determined by the parents themselves.

The families in the Bible were not all the same size. Author and psychologist Dr. Clyde Narramore reminds us: "God does not have the same blueprint for every family. It is interesting to note of the Old Testament saints that while some, like Jacob, had large families, many others had small families. Jacob had twelve sons, Joseph only two. The parents of Moses had but three, and Aaron had four sons. In some instances, men and women of the Bible had no children at all. The number of children in each family followed no set pattern." Each family situation is different, and each has its own resources and problems. The consideration of one family may not apply to another, and each must find God's desire and will in their personal situation.

This point is well summed up by Dr. Merville Vincent, assistant medical superintendent of Homewood Sanitarium, Guelph, Ontario. "No person or law can tell a couple how many children they should have or how they should be spaced. This decision is in the area of Christian liberty. Christians know their entire lives, including their sex lives, belong to God; therefore they must act with love rather than selfishness. They must observe the times and circumstances in which they are living, and through reason and the guidance of the Holy Spirit they can make responsible decisions."

Fourth, God holds parents responsible for each child they have. Parenthood is a total responsibility, not just a biological process. We are responsible for a child's well-being and development, his spiritual growth and nurture, and his mental and social maturity. Having children is more than just giving birth to them. It is possible to sin against children already born by having others, and the preservation and maturing of life already in existence take precedence over a life that does not exist.

Dr. Julius A. Fritze, author and professional marriage counselor, reminds us: "Too many children may destroy a marriage. In such instances, the whole family suffers. The children are underclothed, undernourished, underloved, undereducated, and become underdeveloped emotionally; and many are thrown on society to be supported by tax money. It is most essential that a husband and wife know themselves and the amount of care they can give to an offspring. Remember, there is a big difference between being a biological reproducer and a parent."

God encourages a couple to have children and also to understand the obligations they assume when they do. The greatest tragedy today is not families that are too large, but parents who do not take their God-commanded responsibility for the children they do have, regardless of the family's size. I know one couple who desired twelve children, but had given no serious thought at all to the proper care and training of any of them. Dr. Narramore notes: "Thoughout the Scriptures, parents are taught to give time and attention to each child. Parents are exhorted, 'Train up a child in the way he should go' (Proverbs 22:6). They are not only instructed to teach their children but to do it diligently (Deuteronomy 6:6-7). Teaching a child diligently requires not only time but understanding and patience. Parents who leave the instruction of their children entirely to the schools are neither wise nor obedient."

The parents who are shirking these responsibilities are adding to the "moral pollution" problem, which is more serious than pollution of the environment alone. Dr. Vincent also emphasizes parental responsibility. "Nothing is more detrimental to a child than to feel that his parents wish he had not been born. Scripture emphasizes the concept of responsible parenthood in 1 Timothy 5:8. It is irresponsible for a couple to bring more children into the world than they can nurture spiritually, financially, emotionally, and educatonally."

Fifth, everyone believes in some form of birth control. No one believes a woman should bear all the children she can possibly have from marriage to menopause. No one suggests that a woman should always be pregnant. All major religious groups, Protestant, Catholic, and Jewish, agree on the need for responsible parenthood, but disagree on permissible methods of attaining this objective. They all believe in planned parenthood, though they vary in technique. Some individuals and groups believe only in the so-called rhythm method, a relatively safe period, and feel that any use of other means is questionable. But rhythm is also a method of family limitation. Even those who interrupt or refrain from sex relations for fear of conception are also practicing birth control. On the principle of birth control, everyone agrees that some kind is necessary — the question concerns only the method.

Sixth, the method of birth control must be honestly faced. Some speak with alarm regarding a method which is "contrary to nature," "interfering with nature" or "natural law." In some circles, it is common to assert that the rhythm method is natural, and any scientific or mechanical method is against nature and therefore sinful. Dr. John Rock, an eminent Catholic medical scientist of Harvard University Medical School, has this to say: "The rhythm system is to be considered an unnatural method, for it is during the fertile period that the whole psychosomatic physiology of the healthy female is preparing and intended by her primate nature for coitus."

Scientific contraceptives are an interference with nature. No one denies this. Dr. Dwight Small, in *Design for Christian Marriage,* comments: "Is not civilization replete with means of interfering with nature, most of which we depend upon and take for granted in our day-by-day living? Pasteurization is an interference with nature; the 'natural' thing would be for babies to drink milk that contains germs, and for a certain percentage of those babies to die of milk-borne disease. Vaccination is an interference with nature. So is a haircut! So is the use of soap. Man is constantly intervening in the course of nature and in environment. His very dignity is his God-given ability to govern nature and make it serve higher purposes in the human enterprise."

The physician uses an anesthetic for child birth and surgery, the farmer dehorns or emasculates his cattle, the gardener prunes his grapes, the home owner cuts his grass, a man shaves his beard, everyone trims his toenails — all of these contrary to nature! Dr. Vincent asks, "If the use of scientific means for preventing the conception of life is morally wrong, why is it not also unethical to prolong life by interfering with nature in the use of scientific medicine, sanitation, hospitalization, and all kinds of public health measures?"

We must not confuse natural law with moral law. God has placed man under moral law, but he is over natural law. This is inherent in what God said to our first parents when he told them they were to "have dominion" (Genesis 1:28). In his book *Planned Parenthood,* Dr. Alfred M. Rehwinkel elaborates: "Man is free, is able to choose, to judge, to apply past experience, to weigh the consequences, and himself determine the course of his own action — all, of course, within the moral law. To deny man this freedom is a denial of the essential elements of human personality, and is placing man under the law of necessity and degrading him to the level of an animal."

So man has been given great liberty to use his God-given abilities and capacities for the glory of God and his own highest good. This is the history of human civilization. Granted, some will abuse these privileges and use them for selfish ends, but this does not vitiate their proper use. We don't determine the right and wrong of a thing by what people might do with it. And the Bible certainly makes it clear that man will be held accountable to God for all of his choices, in every area of life.

Seventh, how does a couple decide what to do regarding birth control and what God's will is for them? Attitude and honesty are the guidelines. Since the Bible does not speak expressly regarding birth control, the matter must be considered on the basis of related circumstances and the "spirit of the law." A selfish and willful refusal to have any children clearly violates the spirit of God's Word. God promises wisdom to those seeking it (James 1:5). God assures us of his guidance if we acknowledge him in all our ways (Proverbs 3:6). And this certainly includes such important areas as sex and family planning.

From a very practical standpoint, a couple should ask themselves important questions:

1. Can the spiritual, economic, and educational needs of the children be met if another child is added?

2. Are we emotionally able to personally care for more children?

3. Will another child affect the physical well-being of either parent, especially the mother?

4. Is there the possibility of some genetically transmitted illness?

5. Does our manner of living provide enough space for children to play (e.g., in a cramped apartment)?

6. Is our vocation such that a larger family will not limit our effectiveness? (e.g., pioneer missionary work.)

7. What is the population picture in our area? Do we live on a jungle mission station? in India? Canada or the United States? The answer could vary.

8. Do we consider having a child a sacred trust, and are we prepared to assume total spiritual responsibility, and will we make our decision prayerfully, soberly, and in the fear of God?

On the basis of these considerations, this becomes a very personal matter for each family. They cannot blindly follow someone else's example, neither judge another couple for their differing conviction or decision.

To summarize, Dr. Rehwinkel states: "The question of birth control and planned parenthood belongs to the realm of Christian liberty. But Christian liberty is never absolute and never means irresponsible license. The conscientious Christian will always exercise that liberty in the fear of God, and within the whole plan of God concerning man's purpose in life. The Christian has dedicated his whole life, his sex life, and his procreative functions to the will and glory of God. A Christian applies to all phases of his life the words of the apostle, 'Therefore whether ye eat or drink or what-soever ye do, do all to the glory of God' (1 Corinthians 10:31)."

Eighth, what method of birth control should be employed? This too is a matter to be decided by a couple with their own consciences and on the basis of competent medical advice. Dr. Abraham Stone, in February 1958 *Reader's Digest,* states: "The ideal contraceptive must meet three requirements. It must be entirely harmless, without possible injury to wife, husband, or future children. It must provide a high degree of protection. And it must be acceptable, that is, simple to use, low in price, and aesthetically satisfactory." Whether the now well-known "pill" meets these requirements, you must decide with your physician. Even though nine million American women are using it, medical research men still disagree on its safety and the possibility of harmful side effects. Each couple must find agreement of attitude and purpose, resulting in a shared conclusion, and employ a method satisfactory to both parties.

•●··●··●··●··●··●··●··●··●··●··●··●··●··●·

Sex life in marriage is not automatic any more than it is only animal. It is an experimental, explorative adventure which two persons may undertake together over a long period of time. There are degrees of achievement in sex adjustment just as there are in all other aspects of marriage.
— W. CLARK ELLZEY

14

WARMING THE EMPTY NEST

The Best Is Yet to Be

by Wayne Dehoney
Author, Homemade Happiness

Marriage is like driving a car; you must keep your hands
on the wheel throughout the journey, not just at the outset.
This is what psychologists mean when they talk about
the "progressive menaces" of life. "Menace" may not be a
happy way to describe the experiences of matrimony, but it
does convey the idea that marriage is never a static relationship. And in the progress of a normal relationship, a
couple is continually encountering changing situations that
demand a new orientation, a new pattern of reaction, a new
way of facing life.

Dr. Lofton Hudson has divided the progressive cycle of
marriage into five stages: (1) family founding, from the wedding until the first child is born; (2) childbearing, from
the birth of the first child until the first child enters school;
(3) child rearing, when the first child enters school until
the first child enters college or leaves home; (4) child
launching, from the time the first child leaves until the last
child leaves; (5) the empty nest, when the parents are
alone until the death of one of the mates.

A marriage can get into trouble at any time in this cycle

Copyright 1963 Broadman Press

whenever the couple fails to mature. However, it is a significant and tragic fact that many couples successfully navigate the difficulties of the first four stages only to find their marriage "on the rocks" after twenty years of married life when they come into the last stage — the "empty nest."

When two parents wave good-bye to the last child, they are entering into one of their most critical periods of marital adjustment. Two roads are open to them. They may accept the situation as life's good gift to explore new heights of marital happiness and achieve a richer "togetherness." Or they may travel a road of increasing loneliness, bitterness, and neurotic behavior. The latter route may ultimately end in the divorce court when the husband-wife relationship is so inadequate and insecure. They are unprepared for the test of the "empty nest."

What causes middle-aged husbands and wives to fail the test of marriage in the mature years and bring upon each other, their children, and society the grief and waste of divorce after twenty years of married life? Obviously, a marriage that is held together by external circumstances of superficial bonds — the pressure of public opinion (divorce is wrong and what would people think?); responsibility to the children (we must stay together for the sake of the children); or sex — is a prime prospect for the divorce court when these single factors begin to lose their significance.

However, there are many more other subtle hazards that now threaten the marriage. One common problem is the decline of sexual vigor and the imbalance of the sexes. In the middle years it can throw the marriage into a tailspin. This fact alone accounts for many of those baffling marriage crack-ups and moral failures when a respected and sensible man seems to lose all reason in an infatuation for a younger woman who is inferior to his wife in every way except age. The simple fact is that the panic-stricken husband is afraid of becoming impotent and the younger woman makes him feel "young again."

A wife often interprets the decline in her husband's erotic activity as a sign of declining love and loss of interest in her because she is no longer "fully a woman" and capable of childbearing.

Thus, the fear of decreasing physical attractiveness, as well as decreasing physical ability, often plays psychological havoc with a marriage in these years. An abundance of love, tender understanding, and keen insight on the part of both is the only adequate solution.

Another hazard is that physical goals have been attained and the couple often lacks new goals to command a common devotion. In an enduring marriage, a couple is bound by a continuing "oneness" of purpose in the pursuit of new goals that issue out of a reservoir of shared interests and spiritual values built up through the years.

Often there are many indications that a marriage in the empty-nest stage is in trouble long before the union may be disrupted by divorce. Dr. Clifford R. Adams has suggested the following danger signals which indicate trouble ahead.

Poor communication: too preoccupied, too tired, too harassed at the end of the day to make an effort to communicate or to respond to each other.

Declining compatibility: compatibility is measured not necessarily by the number of hours spent together but by the "oneness" of purpose shared when together and apart.

Increasing inability to compromise: evident when a couple consistently fails to solve their problems through a process of "give-and-take."

Lack of cooperation: in standing by decisions, sharing in responsibilities, accepting the unpleasant or inconvenient circumstances necessitated by employment, and so on.

Increasing selfishness.

Chronic criticism or nagging.

Neglect or indifference.

Escapist behavior: such as preoccupation with "loner" hobbies; excessive viewing of movies or television; addiction to drinking or gambling.

We can rightly conclude that of the 40,000 marriages of twenty years' duration or longer which are dissolved in the divorce court each year, many could have been saved if one or both partners had recognized the warnings and acted in a way to correct the basic problems.

Thus we have seen that the stage of the empty nest is one of the progressive menaces of marriage. It is a time of crisis for some and they fail. Yet, on the other hand, it is a time of new opportunity for many others and they succeed gloriously!

Entering into this companionship stage of marriage can be as a "second honeymoon" for a couple. At last, they have time for each other. They find that the greatest expression of married love comes, not in the parental tasks, but in the marital tasks of needing each other and being needed, of a shared destiny together.

The inhibitions of early marriage are gone and the husband and wife are at ease with each other. The love, the confidence, the understanding, and the trust they share is sealed, not created, by their sexual union.

This is the time for exploring new depths of love: the security in giving security, the pleasure of giving pleasure. The wife realizes how needed she is and how marvelously successful she can be in augmenting her husband's self-esteem and self-assurance as he begins to experience the physical limitations and psychological hazards of aging. The husband discovers anew his wife's need for companionship and shared activities as he fills the void left by the children's departure. As the garden of matrimony is cultivated in these years, each discovers a new sense of significance and meaning to the other, a new security in each other, and a new dimension and richness in their love. In this stage, as they share the sunshine of joy and happiness together, they also probably will share sorrow, as parents and other loved ones die. There may be sickness and anxiety — for their own health and the health of the other. But in sunshine as well as shadow, the bond of togetherness grows stronger with the passing of the years.

As we grow and mature, our love grows and matures. The ecstatically happy, romantic, erotic love of youth soon fades. But the passing years bring a deepening bond of a different kind of love. Looking back, we say, "We thought we were in love. But we really never knew true love and happiness until now!" For out of the struggles and conflicts and adjustments of marriage comes the mature emotion of true marital love, the richest and most rewarding of human relationships.

Yet, life and marriage demand of us one more major adjustment — the mental and psychological idea of "growing old." For many people this is the greatest single adjustment they face in life and in marriage.

In facing the challenge of growing old, there are some simple rules that will help.

First, accept the fact of the passing years. Don't cling to youth! The mature man who is "still one of the boys" and flirts with silly young women is a ridiculous tragedy. And the mature woman who tries to act and dress like a schoolgirl is an unhappy absurdity. One woman confessed, "The happiest day in my life was when I stopped trying to look twenty years younger than I am and decided to be myself."

Second, stay young in heart. Refusing to grow old in heart is not an illusion of wishful thinking. It is a process of successful personal adjustment. It is the consequence of keeping one's face forward in faith and optimism. It is expressing practical Christian faith which says, "Forgetting those things which are behind, and reaching forth unto those things which are before, I press toward the mark for the prize of the high calling of God in Christ Jesus" (Philippians 3:13-14). The great apostle wrote these bright words of hope and optimism when he was an old man in prison, facing the certainty of execution!

Third, keep being useful and active with the passing of the years. Don't give up at fifty and sag.

Wayne Dennis of Brooklyn College studied the lives of 156 well-known scientists who lived to age seventy or beyond. He found that the decades of the forties and fifties were the most productive. In the sixties and seventies their output was still 80 percent and 65 percent of their peak. But in their twenties they were the least productive. Four major poets who lived to be over eighty did more work in their last decade than they did between twenty and thirty.

Bismarck, who died at eighty-three, did his greatest work after he was seventy. Gladstone took up a new language when he was seventy, and at eighty-three he became the prime minister of Great Britain for his fourth time. At eighty, Tennyson composed "Crossing the Bar," the tenderest poem in our language. At eighty-eight John Wesley, with undiminishing eloquence and power, was preaching daily. Michelangelo painted his world-famous *The Last Judgment* at sixty-six.

Fourth, as the milestones of the years roll by, spend more time anticipating the glory and the wonder of death and eternity. For a Christian, death is not a benediction that ends life but a prologue that introduces eternity. That is why the Apostle Paul could say, "I am in a strait betwixt two, having a desire to depart, and to be with Christ, which is far better; nevertheless to abide in the flesh is more needful for you" (Philippians 1:23-24).

Today as never before, two people possessing a personal faith in each other and God, with a Christian perspective of marriage, join hands and hearts and promise with more assurance than ever before.

Grow old along with me!
The best is yet to be:
The last of life, for which the first was made;
Our times are in his hand
Who saith, "A whole I planned;
Youth shows but half; trust God: see all, nor be afraid!"

— Robert Browning

•··•··•··•··•··•··•··•··•··•··•··•··•··•·

While Thomas Moore was absent for a prolonged period in a foreign land, his lovely wife contracted a serious disease which left her scarred and disfigured. It greatly troubled this once-beautiful woman that she would appear so different when her husband returned. She feared that her disfigurement would alter her husband's love and their happiness, so she delayed writing him the sad news because of this fear. A friend who knew this fact felt that her husband should be apprised of what had happened, so he wrote to Moore. When he heard the sad story he sat down and wrote his wife the following letter in poetry:

> *Believe me, if all those endearing young charms*
> *Which I gaze on so fondly today,*
> *Were to change by tomorrow and flee in my arms*
> *Like fairy gifts fading away;*
> *Thou wouldst still be adored, as this moment thou art,*
> *Let thy loveliness fade as it will;*
> *And around the dear ruin, each wish of my heart*
> *Would entwine itself verdantly still.*

You've heard the song — you have sung it — but you may never have heard the story, so there it is. That is true love.

Prepare Your Wife for Widowhood

by Donald I. Rogers
Author, Teach Your Wife to Be a Widow

Too many husbands fail to comprehend one significant and binding pledge in the marriage vow: "With all my worldly goods I thee endow." In a worldly sense that's the backbone of the contract, and the "until death do us part" is no escape clause. Even after death a man should guard the welfare of the girl he married.

The American husband, in seven cases out of ten, passes to his reward before his wife does, frequently leaving only an insurance policy and a mortgaged home. Seldom is this enough to provide the skimpiest existence for his survivors. It's the rare wife, moreover, who knows all she should about her husband's business, income, investments, debts, and budget. Yet she may have the whole problem dumped in her lap without an hour's notice.

Not until their joints begin to creak do most men think in earnest about what will happen to their wives after they are gone. But any man of thirty should be more concerned than a man of sixty. If he dies, his wife may face up to forty years of widowhood. She has to make the insurance money stretch further, and is more likely to have a home to pay for and a family to raise. A husband should start teaching his wife to be a widow as soon as he can. It's not morbid; rather, it's sensible and kind. And if the problem is approached sensibly it may in the end contribute substantially to a longer life for the husband, since few things are more destructive of health than worry.

Copyright 1964 Donald I. Rogers

The first step in the wife's education can be taken right after the honeymoon. The groom should then put the management of household finance in her hands. After all, he will be busy enough working to earn the family's income. The wife might undertake to pay all the bills, manage the budget, figure out how much insurance can be carried, work out the income taxes. She should keep track of deductible expenses, charting the entire tax program.

In this way she'll have to be acutely aware of her husband's business expenses and investments. She will, through the years, acquire some knowledge of the business world. She may soon be asking why hubby allows $200 to lie idle in the checking account when it could be earning interest at a savings bank. Women have a penchant for details that men seldom possess. Once she's inoculated with the business bug, a wife will be the best business partner a man ever had. And he'll know that if she comes into a sum of money — say, from his insurance — she'll not be stampeded into squandering it.

The next step is insurance. Any man's a fool to be without all the insurance he can afford. It's a good investment, sound planning, and the easiest way to build an estate. If a man has a mortgage he should eke out enough insurance to cover it, so that the survivors will have their home free and clear.

How should the benefits be paid? It depends on the wife's business sense. If you're an average earner your insurance money will be more than she is accustomed to handle. Will she get the illusion that she is rich, buy that good coat and other things she's always wanted, forgetting that there'll be no further income? Insurance companies have long been aware that an overwhelming majority of widows spend their lump-sum insurance within a year after receiving it. To meet this situation they have worked out scores of different programs which call for staggered monthly or annual payments to beneficiaries. In other words, instead of getting $15,000 cash, you can arrange for your wife to get, say, $200 a month for a specified period.

If you can teach your wife to be a sound business manager, however, it's sensible to leave the money in a lump sum and let it work for her. Insurance companies pay some interest for the use of money left in their possession, but it doesn't approach the earnings a widow could realize by investing in stocks and bonds through a good broker. Furthermore, money invested in most common stocks will keep pace with inflation.

I'm teaching my wife to handle her investments herself. The "education" costs a few pennies a day — the daily newspapers. We study the financial pages and pretend to buy some selected stocks. We've learned something by trial and error without risking a cent. All wives should acquire some elementary knowledge of stocks and the stock market in case they want to — or have to — invest their husbands' insurance money or manage their estates.

Another step in teaching your wife to be a widow is to prepare her for some gainful occupation so that she could, if necessary, be self-supporting. A friend of mine told me that his wife could get along if anything happened to him — she was a secretary before their marriage and she could earn her living again if necessary.

I felt it my duty to point out that they have been married fifteen years and during that entire time the wife has never so much as typed a letter. She's rusty at her trade and a great many younger and more proficient gals have come along since. Perhaps she could become secretary to a church committee and take down the minutes of the meetings in shorthand, just for the practice. Maybe she could help her husband with some of his correspondence. The same kind of career planning might be a wise safeguard for other wives.

It's a good idea for the wife to meet her husband's banker and lawyer, so that when she has to consult these men she will not be dealing with total strangers. She ought, indeed, to learn the basic facts about banking. There is a startling ignorance of the bank laws as they affect widows. A man's bank account is frozen when he dies. In some states the death of one of the joint-checking-account depositors results in the immediate freezing of half the account until taxes are settled. It is well, therefore, for a wife to keep some emergency money in her own savings account to tide her over the expensive days after her husband's departure.

Some states where there is an inheritance tax (as in New York) insist that banks seal a safe-deposit box upon the death of its renter. The box may not be opened until a state tax appraiser is present. This applies even if the box is jointly owned by husband and wife. For all this, a safe-deposit box is an ideally safe place for policies, deeds, and other important papers. However, it is advisable to have records of the insurance policy at home: name of company, amount of the policy, its number, date of execution, and beneficiary.

A sensible precaution is to prepare a letter of final instructions and leave it in a handy place for your wife. The letter should cover the many things a widow ought to know about her husband's insurance, investments, debts, and what others owe him. It should give her the essential practical details about his estate and other taxes, what to do about every item of his property, and his ideas of a budget tailored to her new income.

The most important thing for a husband and wife to realize is that there will be less money for a woman as a widow than she had as a wife, despite insurance. This simple and logical fact is seldom faced squarely. Having faced it, a man will recognize the urgency of preparing his wife to be a widow.

How I Conquered Grief

by Catherine Marshall
Author, Beyond Ourselves *and other books*

When Peter Marshall was pastor of the Westminster Presbyterian Church in Atlanta, we had a close friend who had known much sorrow. She used to look quizzically at Peter and me — young as we were, very much in love, fresh in the enthusiasm of our faith in the goodness of God.

"Neither of you has ever had any real trouble," she would say. "You're bound to have some sooner or later. I wonder if you will feel then as you do now?"

In the years which followed, we had our share of trouble — much illness, and finally my husband's premature death at forty-seven. But today I still feel as we did then. In fact, I believe in God's love more firmly than ever, because now my faith has stood trial.

Trouble of some kind, especially bereavement, is the common experience of mankind. Since my husband's death, many people have written me to ask: How does one endure it? How does one keep one's faith and deal with sorrow constructively? Let me quote one typical letter which reveals a number of quite human reactions to grief:

"My wife, Marie, died three years ago. I just don't know how I've gotten through the agony of separation since then. People are always saying, 'Time heals,' but in my case each day is worse than the last.

"I've tried plunging into work sixteen hours a day. But everything seems futile without Marie. I try to pray, but my prayers just hit the ceiling and bounce back. What good

Copyright 1953 Atlanta Newspapers, Inc.

purpose could God have had in taking Marie and leaving me here alone?"

First, let me say that I deeply sympathize with all who have suffered thus. Sorrow is a wound in the personality, as real as any physical mutilation. After a time, during busy hours, one can forget the pain. Then tiny things bring it back: opening a drawer and coming across a Christmas card written in a well-known hand; the sight of a distant figure reminiscent of a well-beloved form, wearing the same kind of slouch hat. And suddenly, the old pain is back with stabbing force.

But though I sympathize, I have learned that the first really helpful step to take is to face up to the fact that your grief is essentially selfish. Most of us grieve not for the interrupted happiness of the one who died but because of our own loneliness and need. Sorrow is usually interlaced with self-pity. Facing up to this squarely for the sin it is, is like opening a window to let a breath of fresh air into a fetid room. We must deal with this selfishness as we deal with all other sins: by confessing it to God and asking his forgiveness and release. Such a confession requires stern action at a time when the heart is sore, but it is more healing than all the expressions of sympathy from others.

Everyone bereaved goes through a period of sharp questioning and self-reproach: "I wasn't sympathetic and understanding enough. Why didn't I show more love and gratitude while he was alive?" There is one healthy road out of this self-reproach. If your conscience bothers you about any past mistakes or failures, deal with them as you dealt with self-pity. Confess them one by one to God, have them freely forgiven, and forget them even as God has promised to do.

Few people avoid this merciless self-reproach. The only healthy road out of it is to face up to life as it is, not as we wish it might have been. For the God I know is a realist, and he expects us to be realists too.

I often wonder how those who during sunny days can't be bothered with God manage to survive sorrow. I have found, in time of trouble, that there is no substitute for him, for grief is sickness of the spirit, and God alone is physician to the spirit.

But, my typical correspondent asked, "What good purpose could God have had in taking Marie and leaving me here alone?"

The problem of evil — why a good God lets good people suffer — is forever with us. I have no pat answer. But we must remember that this old earth is enemy-occupied territory. Disease and death are of the enemy — not of a loving Father. Yet I do believe that when Marie was stricken God had some plan by which he could bring good out of it.

Admittedly, it takes courage and no little faith to take the next constructive step: hunt for the open door, the new creative purpose, rather than stand weeping before the closed door of grief. But God is the Creator. It isn't possible for him to be negative. If we are to cooperate with his purposes (the only way of getting our prayers answered), we too must be creative and positive. God's way of binding up our broken hearts will be to give us worthwhile work to do in the world.

At one time I did not think life worth living without my husband. Yet I can testify that today I am truly happy. That happiness by no means dishonors Peter; it is exactly as he would have it.

How did that come about? I took the steps of confession I have mentioned. Then I prayed that this tragedy which I did not understand would nonetheless "work together for good." God has answered that prayer in an astonishing way.

Once during a long illness I wrote in my journal, "One of my deepest dreams is to be a writer. Through my writing I would like to make a contribution to my time and generation." Less than a month after Peter's death, it was as if God put a pencil in my hand and said, "Go ahead and write. Make your contribution. I promise to bless what you write." And he has blessed every attempt, beyond all imagining.

Something else even more wonderful came of this new-found career. Peter and I were drawn closer together than ever before. And through a divine alchemy my writing has become the vehicle for continuing Peter's earthly ministry. Many people who have read what I have written about my husband say that they have been profoundly helped by his words and the example of his deeds. In so-called "death," his ministry has been widened, deepened, "multiplied by infinity."

And, as a final benediction, slowly, imperceptibly there has come into my life the definite feeling of still being loved, cherished, and cared for. It has become the most comforting and sustaining force of my life.

I would not have you think that there is anything unique about my case. The help for which I prayed awaits your prayer. God's answer for you will not be the answer he had for me. It will be made to fit your needs, your own dreams, by a God who loves you personally.

•٠٠٠•٠•٠٠٠•٠٠٠•٠•٠٠٠•٠•٠٠٠•٠٠٠•٠•٠٠٠•

If a thing is old, it is a sign that it was fit to live. The guarantee of continuity is quality. Old-fashioned hospitality, old-fashioned politeness, old-fashioned honor in business had qualities of survival.
— EDDIE RICKENBACKER

The Later Years

by A. Donald Bell

Author, Family in Dialogue, *and Professor of Psychology, South-western Baptist Theological Seminary*

Many of us are in the category of two older gentlemen who were discussing their coming retirement. The younger of the two asked his friend, who was beginning retirement, what he planned to do the first year. The older man answered that he was going to get a rocking chair and put it on the front porch. Then the younger continued to question and asked, "What are your plans for the second year?" The older man answered with a wry grin, "Then I'll start rocking!" This attitude is typical of many of us and is seen in the poem that says:

> I get up each morning, dust off my wits,
> Pick up the paper and read the obits.
> If my name is missing, I know I'm not dead,
> So I eat a good breakfast and go back to bed.

In the past we have thought of the active life span as going up to the later years, with the senile period projected as some "extra life" not too related to previous living. Such a concept of old age is artificial and harmful. Thinking in terms of passive, inactive living is unhealthy at any age.

The average person must prepare for retirement in several ways.

First, he must create interests for retirement. One ought to begin in young adulthood to develop interests which he will gradually increase toward his maturity and retirement.

Copyright 1968 Zondervan Publishing House

A retirement activity must be creative and productive.
Retirement activities must be personally satisfying. This means that they must not be radically different from the previous routine, yet give variation.

Retirement activities must be active and functional. Even heaven will not be a completely passive state of being. Life must grow, unfold, and create to be satisfying. Therefore, one should increase these interests as his vocational work decreases.

Enjoyable activities ought to be planned with eagerness, which will make retirement preparation an active experience.

A second area of readiness is, of course, financial. A good retirement plan should include some revenue of a current nature where the dollar value will change with the times and complement a fixed pension or annuity income.

Now, consider the time of retirement. One's retirement program ought not begin with a calendar date — the reaching of a sixtieth or sixty-fifth birthday. It should really begin as early as possible so that one's life may go through successive changes toward that end. There are two types of retirement situations.

1. The person employed by someone other than himself is in one position. He must cultivate an avocational activity which will become his full-time activity in retirement. As the individual matures, he increases interest in this activity and decreases the tension involved in his full-time vocational work. Therefore, when the retirement date comes, the transition to this avocational activity as a full-time function is easier. A person in mature years who changes his way of life overnight usually brings on an early grave.

2. The second group includes those who are self-employed. They must develop the will power to actually reduce their life's work as they increase this avocational activity. It may cost them money, but this long-range, graded program is essential.

Eventually, they should be working three-quarter time on their job, then one-half time, then one-quarter time, and thus reduce gradually to retirement. All the time the retirement function has been increased at the same ratio. Only as we gear our working lives to such a program can we enter into retirement interests successfully.

While many people plan ahead about the place of retirement, they should have been thinking more about attitudes, emotional, social, and spiritual preparation. These are more significant. What value is it to be in a beautiful place if one is unhappy, friendless, or insecure? The place is not that important. The person and his fulfillment is more important.

Some test questions relative to location might be:

1. Do I "feel good" in the place?

2. Am I familiar with the locale — have I tested it previously on vacations and visits?

3. Are there friends whom I already know and do I have assurance that they are "my kind of folks" with my convictions and interests?

4. Is the climate and the geography good for my health and habits now? Will it still be when I am older, and perhaps feeble?

5. Are there constructive work opportunities available for me? Are there facilities and companions for the continuance of avocations, interests, and hobbies?

6. What about spiritual provisions: churches, friends, and religious activities for my continued spiritual growth? Real, basic security comes from these resources. Also, one's faith will enable him to make new friends with common concerns.

7. What is the cost of living — as I shall be living? Is my information based on rumor or is it factual? Am I really familiar with insurance costs and taxes there? What are the local predictions, economically, for the future?

8. If I were limited in strength and activity, could I be happy and contented there?

9. Is it the locale for the expression of activities and habits to which I am accustomed or just for those I think I might like?

10. Are there cultural and social groups and activities which will be satisfying and stimulating to me?

11. Is good medical service available?

12. Is the place accessible? Can I easily get around when I can no longer drive? Can friends and family visit me with facility?

13. Is the locale near, too near, or too removed from loved ones?

14. Have I some assurance that these conditions and friends will wear well — can I live with them permanently?

Many times the older person is wise to "retire" right where he has been living.

Life in retirement must have a focal point of love and interest. Friends with common interests are needed. But the older person must continue to feed friendships.

Often, the key to the social contacts of older people lies in a good recreational schedule. Recreational and hobby activities which involve other people are best, of course, as means of social contact.

There are unlimited opportunities for activities which will be personally satisfying and also create friendships. Here are some examples:

1. Serve on church committees;
2. Work in a church library;
3. Keep the church guest register;
4. Entertain special groups such as soldiers and students;
5. Baby-sit;
6. Visit shut-ins;

7. Read to blind or shut-in persons;
8. Make things for children;
9. Teach knitting or crocheting in institutions;
10. Fix things for friends and neighbors;
11. Make choir robes for the church;
12. Help with church or school mailings.

Someone offered a prayer with which we would like to conclude:

"Lord, thou knowest better than I know that I am growing older, will some day be old,

Keep me from getting talkative, and particularly from the fatal habit of thinking I must say something on every subject and every occasion.

Release me from craving to try to straighten out everybody's affairs.

Make me thoughtful, but not moody, helpful but not bossy. With my vast store of wisdom it seems a pity not to use it all, but thou knowest, Lord, that I want a few friends at the end of life.

Keep my mind free from the recital of endless details, give me wings to get to the point.

Seal my lips on my aches and pains. They are increasing and my love of rehearsing them is becoming sweeter as the years go by.

I ask for grace enough to listen to the tales of others' pains. Help me endure them patiently.

Teach me the glorious lesson that occasionally it is possible that I may be mistaken.

Keep me reasonably sweet; I do not want to be a saint; some are hard to live with, but a sour old person is one of the crowning works of the devil.

Help me to exact all possible fun out of life. There are so many funny things around us and I don't want to miss any of them."

— Anonymous

INDEX

HQ 10 .P47
J. Allan Petersen, ed.
The Marriage Affair

DATE DUE
